Racial Discrimination in
Economic Life

Racial Discrimination in Economic Life

Anthony H. Pascal
Editor

Lexington Books
D.C. Heath and Company
Lexington, Massachusetts
Toronto   London

Contents

List of Tables   vii

List of Figures   ix

Introduction, *Anthony H. Pascal*   xiii

Part I   **Theory and Measurement of Racial Discrimination and Its Effects**   1

Chapter 1   Race Differences in Income   3
Albert Wohlstetter and Sinclair Coleman

Chapter 2   Models of Job Discrimination   83
Kenneth J. Arrow

Chapter 3   The Effects of Minimum Wages by Race, Age, and Sex   103
Marvin Kosters and Finis Welch

Chapter 4   The Economics of Racial Discrimination in Organized Baseball   119
Anthony H. Pascal and Leonard A. Rapping

Chapter 5   The Process of Residential Segregation: Neighborhood Tipping   157
Thomas C. Schelling

Part II   **Mathematical Analyses of Racial Discrimination**   185

Chapter 6   Some Mathematical Models of Race in the Labor Market   187
Kenneth J. Arrow

Chapter 7   The Simple Mathematics of Information, Job Search, and Prejudice   205
John J. McCall

Index   225

List of Tables

Table

1-1   Earnings for Males Who Had Earnings, by
Occupation Group of Longest Job, by
Color, 1967   49

1-2   Earnings for Females Who Had Earnings, by
Occupation Group of Longest Job, by
Color, 1967   51

1-3   Income for Males 25 and Over by Years of
Schooling and Color, 1967   57

1-4   Income for Females 25 and Over by Years
of Schooling and Color, 1967   61

3-1   Average Shares of Normal and Transitional
Employment and Average Coefficients of
Marginality: Quarterly Average of U.S.
Civilian Employment, 1954-68   108

3-2   Estimated Elasticities of Employment Shares
and of Marginality Coefficients with
Respect to the Effective Minimum Wage   112

3-3   Least Squares Estimates of Distributional
Parameters and Elasticities with Respect
to the Minimum Wage for Employment by
Age-Color-Sex Classes   116

3-4   Estimated Percentage of Aggregate Employment
Covered by Federal Minimum Wage Legislation,
1954-1968   116

3-5   Federal Legal Minimum Wage, 1954-1968   117

4-1   Distribution of 784 Major League Baseball
Players by Age, Race and Origin, 1968   123

4-2   Educational Attainment of 784 Major League
Baseball Players, 1968 (Percent)   123

4-3   Statistical Explanation of Major League
Baseball Players' Salaries: Regression
Results, 1968-69   130

4-4   Players Who Received Bonuses in Excess of
$20,000 by Year of Entry into Organized
Baseball, by Color   136

4-5   Black and White Individual Cumulated Lifetime
Batting Averages, Nonpitcher Veterans,
Through 1967   138

4-6   Black and White Individual Batting Averages,
Nonpitcher Nonveterans, Various Years   139

4-7   Latin Black North American Black and White
Individual Cumulated Lifetime Batting
Averages, Nonpitcher Veterans, Through 1967   140

4-8   Season Batting Averages of American Blacks
and Whites, 1953-67 and 1967, and Percent
American Black Players   144

4-9   Latin and North American Blacks by Baseball
Club and League, 784 Players, 1968 (Percent)   146

4-10   Latin and North American Black Baseball
Players by Position, 784 Players, 1968
(Percent)   147

7-1   Probability of Remaining in Poverty for the
Period 1962-65 ($3,000 poverty line) by
Sex, Age, and Color   208

7-2   Probability of Remaining in Nonpoverty for
the Period 1962-65 ($3,000 poverty line),
Males by Age and Color   208

7-3   Differences in Annual Income between Whites
and Nonwhites by Education and Experience,
1960   208

List of Figures

Figure

(Figures 1-1 through 1-25 all indicate
white/non-white differentials)

1-1   Distribution of Total Money Income to
        Families, 1967   11

1-2   Distribution of Total Money Income to
        Persons, 1967   12

1-3   Ratio-at-Quantiles of the Income Distribution
        for Familes (95% confidence limits), 1967   13

1-4   Ratio-at-Quantiles of the Income Distribution
        for Persons (95% confidence limits), 1967   14

1-5   Distributions of Total Money Income to
        Persons (male), 1966   16

1-6   Distribution of Total Money Income of Men
        and Women, 1967   17

1-7   Distribution of Family Income, South and
        Non-South, 1967   20

1-8   Annual Growth Rates in Median Family Income
        (1966 prices), 1947-1967   21

1-9   Total and Subperiod Growth Rates in Median
        Income (1966 prices)   22

1-10   Annual Growth Rates for Median Income of
        Persons, 1948-1967   23

1-11   Income Distribution of Total Money Income
        to Persons, 1967 and 1949   26

1-12   Ratio-at-Quantiles Comparison for Persons,
        1949 and 1967   27

1-13	Total Money Income to Persons, Differences in Ratios of Nonwhite to White Incomes at Selected Percentiles, 1949-67	28
1-14	Ratio-at-Quantiles Comparison for Families, 1947 and 1967	29
1-15	Ratios of Income to Persons at Selected Percentiles of the Income Distribution, 1949, 1959, and 1966	30
1-16	Ratios of Wage and Salary Income of all Wage and Salary Workers and of Year-Round Full-Time Workers, 1939 and 1967	31
1-17	Ratios of Income at Selected Percentiles of the Income Distribution for Males, 1949, 1959, and 1966	33
1-18	Ratio-at-Quantiles Comparison for Families, 1945 and 1952	34
1-19	Illustrations for Case Where the White minus Nonwhite Income Differences (or for Log Scale the Nonwhite to White Income Ratios) are the Same for all Quantiles	37
1-20	Relative Male Income Adjusted for Age, 1967	42
1-21	Changes over Time in Age Adjusted Relative Income for Men, 1949 and 1967	43
1-22	Ratio-at-Quantiles of the Income Distribution for Males, with Adjustment for (10-class) Occupational Categories, 1967	50
1-23	Ratio-at-Quantiles of the Income Distribution for Females, with Adjustment for (7-class) Occupational Categories, 1967	52
1-24	Ratio-at-Quantiles of the Income Distribution for Males 25 and Over, with Adjustment for Years of Schooling Completed, 1967	59

1-25   Ratio-at-Quantiles of the Income Distribution
              for Females 25 and Over, with Adjustment
              for Years of Schooling Completed, 1967   62

3-1   Hypothetical Relative Employment Patterns of
              Marginal and Intramarginal Classes Over
              a Cycle   107

3-2   Joint Effects on Employment of a Change in
              Labor Demand and Minimum Wage for Two
              Hypothetical Skill Distributions   111

4-1   Hypothetical Distributions of Baseball
              Playing Ability   141

4-2   Hypothetical Relationships between Ability
              and Expected Income   142

5-1   Frequency Distributions of Neighborhood
              Racial Tipping Points: Four Hypothetical
              White Populations, A,B,C, and D   162

5-2   Cumulative Frequency Distributions of
              Neighborhood Racial Tipping Points for
              White Populations A and B   163

5-3   Cumulative Frequency Distribution of
              Neighborhood Racial Tipping Points for
              White Population C   164

5-4   Cumulative Frequency Distribution of
              Neighborhood Racial Tipping Points for
              White Population D   165

5-5   Frequency Distributions of Neighborhood
              Racial Tipping Points: Four Hypothetical
              Black Populations, E,F, and G   170

5-6   Superimposed Cumulative Distributions of
              Neighborhood Racial Tipping Points for
              White Population C and Black Population G   171

7-1   Edgeworth Box Diagram Illustrating the Gains
              from Trade Between Two Economic Entities

and the Impact of Discrimination on the
Final Outcome   210

Isoquant-Isocost Diagram Illustrating the
Determination of Factor Inputs and the
Effect of Discrimination on Factor
Purchases and Production Costs   212

Introduction

The essays collected in this book present findings of research projects that were part of The Rand Corporation's program of studies on the connection between racial discrimination and economic opportunity. Three of the studies—those by Wohlstetter and Coleman, Kosters and Welch, and McCall—were supported by the Office of Economic Opportunity. The remaining articles, by Arrow, Schelling, and Pascal and Rapping, were sponsored by Rand itself, with the help of the Ford Foundation in Rapping's case. They grew out of interests in both the theory and the actuality of race relations, which were stimulated by ongoing Rand research in such fields as urban affairs, welfare, education, housing, and crime.

In the first essay, Wohlstetter and Coleman break fertile new ground with the presentation of a broad statistical review of race differences in income over the past three decades in the United States. The authors estimate the extent and some of the components of race differences in income along the entire income distribution, and also investigate changes in these differences since 1939. They explore relative changes in the situations of families and of individual workers by sex and age as well as race. The influence of occupational structure and educational attainment on racial disparities is explored as is the impact of the business cycle. In examining theories proposed to account for racial disparities in economic welfare, they are concerned with comparisons of policies designed to reduce income differences and other policies that have related but distinguishable objectives.

Some aspects of the larger study, of which this monograph forms a part, are reported on more fully in "Racial Economic Equality and Other Good but Different Things," a paper read at the American Economic Association Annual Meeting, December, 1971, in New Orleans, to be published elsewhere at a later date.

Chapter 2 is intended to demonstrate the advantages and disadvantages of neoclassical analysis as a tool for studying racial discrimination in the economic sphere and to suggest possible areas of fruitful research. Arrow concentrates on racial discrimination effected through wage differentials. Wages for black workers will fall short of their marginal product by the marginal rate of substitution between black workers and profits, the rate being computed at the black/white ratio in the labor force. Tastes of employees may also enter the picture; in addition, the costs of hiring white labor may be relatively high where whites are expected to work for black supervisors. Neoclassical theory, then, can offer a coherent and not implausible explanation of the impact of racial discrimination, accounting in a gross way for the known facts.

A simple model is presented whereby an employer can purchase black labor at a fixed price, but for which labor he must choose some point on an indifference curve between wages and the proportion of whites in the firm. The implications—no wage differentials on one hand, and segregation on the other—are respectively contrary to, and harmonious with, observation. In short, we experience a failure of convexity—extreme alternatives are preferred to compromises.

If the nonconvexities are small on the scale of the entire economy, then something like a competitive equilibrium is still possible. We must look at the long-run adjustment processes. If we start from a position where black workers enter an essentially all-white world, the racist feelings of employers and of employees will lead to a difference in wages by race. The forces of competition and the tendency to maximize profits operate to mitigate these differences. The basic fact of a personnel investment on the part of the employers, however, prevents these counteracting tendencies from working with full force. In the end, we remain with wage differences coupled with tendencies to segregate.

The research for Chapter 2 was done as part of a Rand study on the measurement of racial discrimination. The text presented here is slightly altered from that of the Marshall lectures delivered by Professor Arrow at the invitation of the Faculty of Economics and Political Science of the University of Cambridge, April 14 and 15, 1970.

Chapter 3 traces the pattern of employment fluctuation within certain classes of workers—defined by race, age group, and sex—in the U.S. economy, and it also estimates the influence of minimum wage legislation on the pattern of employment changes. Understanding this pattern should improve our ability to predict the distribution of the costs that result from economic instability in an economy in which racial feeling is endemic.

Using employment data for the period 1954-68 from the Bureau of Labor Statistics and data on the level of the minimum wage and the extent of coverage of the legislation, Kosters and Welch have analyzed the distribution of fluctuations in aggregate employment in the U.S. economy between whites and nonwhites, between males and females, and between teenagers and adults. The analysis indicates that a slackening in the pace of economic growth will adversely affect nonwhites, particularly teenagers.

The relative income position of nonwhites has shown marked improvement over the past decade. Part of this improvement, however, may be attributable to the sustained economic expansion of the early 1960s and thus may be subject to rapid erosion as the expansion slows or is reversed. Nonwhites (except for adult females) are disproportionately affected by employment fluctuations.

The impact of short-term employment changes falls most heavily on teenagers. Teenage males are more sharply affected than females, and nonwhites more than whites. Increases in the effective minimum wage have heightened the vulnerability of teenagers to short term changes, and have decreased their share of normal employment. These effects, moreover, are disproportionately concentrated on nonwhite teenagers.

Chapter 4 explores the impact of race on salary, assignment, and promotion in major league baseball, which is utilized as a "laboratory" industry in which the effects of racial attitudes may be more clearly observed than is possible in other industries. Baseball is a calling in which the quality of formal schooling and the general cultural background of an aspirant make relatively little difference in his ability to succeed, in which ability is clearly apparent to interested observers, and in which the link between ability and reward can be observed. Differences in earnings for individuals of equal ability but different color should then be relatively unambiguous measures of discrimination in this labor market. Pascal and Rapping conclude that big league teams seem to reward players commensurate with their ability but that substantial evidence exists consistent with policies of racial segregation and entry barriers in baseball.

They feel that the findings derived for baseball may be characteristic also of the situation in other parts of the economy. Baseball, after all, is an industry composed of wealth-maximizing firms. It differs merely in being highly public and, since 1948, in being highly prone to praise its own "enlightened" racial attitudes. In fact, taking at face value the public relations rhetoric of baseball spokesmen, if racism is as subtly pervasive as it appears to be on the diamond, it is likely to be exceedingly powerful in the plants, offices, and stores where discriminatory treatment can still be masked by complaints about the absence of qualified applicants.

The ethical tenets of official American culture, as well as the difficulties of sustaining patently unjust salary treatment, mean that in baseball and in other fields racism will be expressed through less obvious forms of discrimination. The article shows that basing entry, promotion, and assignment on race rather than merit is one important form.

Chapter 5 examines the process of residential segregation by concentrating on the phenomenon known as tipping. The author demonstrates the ways in which the distribution of individual tolerance for neighborhood racial mixing, perceptions of what constitutes the neighborhood, expectations about the future, costs of moving, the general state of the housing market, and the size and character of a city's minority population can all interact to generate an outflow by the majority even in a situation where each member of that majority had been willing to live in an integrated neighborhood.

An understanding of tipping is important, not only for what it tells us about the likely prospects for residential integration, but because it also has implications for the operations of labor markets, which the other chapters of this book explore. The more tipping is endemic to neighborhoods and to schools, the more likely will be the continuation of racial inequality in preparation for jobs, at least according to some researchers. Finally, as Schelling points out, tipping may occur in firms, occupations, and industries directly, and thereby defeat attempts to achieve integration on the job and equality in labor markets.

Chapter 6 is supporting analysis originally prepared as the Technical Notes for Chapter 2. This chapter was also part of the research for the Rand study on the measurement of racial discrimination. The various models that underlie the arguments presented in Chapter 2 are formalized and manipulated. The central model, presented in Chapter 2, is supplemented by the consideration of additional factors; for example: (1) the notion of hierarchy on the job, that is, the fact that supervisors and subordinates, the skilled and the unskilled exist; (2) the longer-run implications for segregation and on-the-job discrimination as firms adapt themselves to opportunities generated by the existence of race prejudice; (3) the effects of positive costs associated with hiring and personnel turnover; (4) the fact that skin color may represent a cheap source of information and may therefore be used by an employer in discriminating against what he believes to be an inferior worker; and (5) the possibility that the qualities of an individual worker may not be known to the employer beforehand. These themes are elaborated in the various sections of Chapter 6.

Chapter 7, drawn from Rand's research project for the Office of Economic Opportunity, is an analysis of racial discrimination in job markets where the presence of uncertainty is explicitly considered. Employee as well as employer discrimination is addressed in the analysis. McCall demonstrates how the presence of uncertainty and the fact that information is costly may lead employers toward the use of stereotypes and may make them appear prejudiced when they merely lack information and seek profits. Employees may engage in similar processes when they search for jobs.

Although the value of discrimination is positive, the theory presented in Chapter 7 assumes that value is a function of the business cycle. A changing economic environment is assumed to induce employers to engage in experiments, for example, hire nonwhites in periods of tight labor markets. The outcomes of these experiments may alter his attitude toward nonwhites, and in this way discrimination could decline in a very natural way. Similarly, with nonwhite employees, their beliefs regarding the intensity of discrimination in certain industries would never be altered unless they or someone in their information network were employed by these industries. Again in periods of tight labor markets, employees are also assumed to be experimenting with new industries and revising their beliefs concerning discrimination intensities. The main point in both of these illustrations is that discrimination by both employers and employees is explicable on purely economic grounds when uncertainty is explicitly considered and, furthermore, changes in the economic environment may cause both employers and employees to alter the beliefs that give rise to discriminatory practices.

This series of interrelated essays illuminates several aspects of racial dynamics as they operate in America's economy and society. Together they demonstrate that the application of social science theory and the techniques of statistical measurement can help to identify some of the causes of a complicated and anguishing social problem and point the way toward remedies.

Anthony H. Pascal

**Part One
Theory and Measurement
of Racial Discrimination
and Its Effects**

Race Differences in Income

ALBERT WOHLSTETTER
SINCLAIR COLEMAN

I. Introduction

This chapter summarizes findings from an analysis of income disparities between whites and nonwhites[1] in the United States. It deals with present and past relative money income of whites and nonwhites at various points in the distribution of each. The empirical results are themselves of interest. They contradict many of the most familiar statements of the last few years on these subjects, in particular statements about the low and high ends of the nonwhite and white income distributions and their changes. Furthermore, they provide a concrete context for clarifying and illustrating the meanings of some related but distinct goals in an area of urgent policy concern. These goals are frequently confused. Yet programs directed to one of these ends may do little or nothing to achieve another. Clarification here, then, can have a pragmatic value.

Section II treats current income disparities; Section III, changes over time. Section IV deals with three major components of the income disparities: differences in age structure, years of schooling, and job distribution.

Recent Views

Some useful empirical studies have been done of relations between white and nonwhite income, and some suggestive theoretical models of discrimination have been proposed. We have benefited from them. Nonetheless, not only the popular, but also the professional literature abounds in statements about the relations of nonwhite and white income distributions and their changes over time that do not seem to square with our own results (as summarized in Section V). Sometimes the contradiction is only apparent but more frequently it is genuine. It is sometimes said, for example, that the income gap between the races is greatest at the lowest levels of income distribution. And there has been, up until very recently, a rather widespread impression of decline or stagnation, especially at the bottom. Such impressions have been common not only among militants but among moderate civil rights advocates, and not only among polemicists and politicians in ephemeral pamphlets; they occur rather often in the writings of able economists and sociologists in the course of serious (and generally illuminating) studies. The following quotations are more or less typical:[2]

4

Current Race Differences Smallest
at Top of the Distribution

The degree of inequality of incomes of whites and nonwhites is related to position in the relative income distribution. Inequality is less at higher levels of the income distribution than at lower levels.

Harold Guthrie, 1969

Inequality Among Nonwhites Increasing
More than Inequality Among Whites

The reality seems to be that some Negroes, especially those in the middle and upper income brackets, are gaining rapidly on whites, while others, particularly those in the slums, are losing ground in relative terms . . .

Edmund K. Faltermayer, 1968

. . . in terms of employment and income and occupational status it is quite possible the Negro community is moving in two directions, or rather that two Negro communities are moving in opposite ones. Obviously such a development would be concealed—cancelled out—in aggregate statistics that list all "nonwhites" together.

Daniel P. Moynihan, 1967

Absolute Decline

the economic position of the Northern Negro deteriorates rapidly . . .

Bayard Rustin, 1966

It is a stark reality that the black communities are becoming more and more economically depressed.

Stokely Carmichael and Charles V. Hamilton, 1967

. . . there has been almost no change or change for the worse in the daily lives of most blacks.

Martin Duberman, 1968

Although it is true that the income of middle-class Negroes has risen somewhat, the income of the great mass of Negroes is declining.

Whitney Young, Jr., 1968

Absolute Stagnation of Lowest Fifth

[In the period 1947-66,] about two-thirds of the lowest income group—or 20 percent of all Negroes—are making no significant economic gains despite continued general prosperity.

National Advisory Commission on Civil Disorders, 1968

*Widening Gap Getween White and Nonwhite
or Lower Nonwhite to White Ratios*

Title of an article comparing 1949 and 1959 incomes, "Decline in the Relative Income of Negro Men."

Alan Batchelder, 1964

The income gap between this country's whites and nonwhites is wide and getting wider.

McGraw-Hill Special Report No. 2005, 1968

[The National Advisory (Kerner) Commission, in its main comprehensive comparison between Negro (actually nonwhite) family income and white, states that] . . . although it is growing, Negro family income is not keeping pace with white family income growth. In constant 1965 dollars, median nonwhite income in 1947 was $2,174 lower than median white income. By 1966, the gap had grown to $3,036.

National Advisory Commission on Civil Disorders, 1968
Not Closing, Stable Ratio

[It is] startling . . . that there has been very little change in the ratio of nonwhite family income to white family income over the last decade and a half.

Rashi Fein, 1967

Nor has discrimination declined. The average Negro family income has consistently remained near 55 percent of the white income. For a given average income level the white and black distributions have similar shapes, but the Negro distribution lags approximately thirty years behind the white. On the basis of relative measures such as these, discrimination has neither declined nor increased. In absolute terms, however, between 1947 and 1967 the average income gap between white and Negro families widened from $2,300 to $3,100 (in 1967 dollars). Relative measures indicate a stable pattern of discrimination, absolute measures a more intense pattern.

Lester Thurow, 1969

Negro incomes are growing as fast as white, but while Negroes are increasingly well-off absolutely, the gap remains nearly constant in relative terms.

Edward C. Banfield, 1970

. . . while the absolute condition of the Negro has improved markedly in the last decade, his relative position has improved barely perceptibly. . . .

John F. Kain, 1969

*Increase or No Decline After World War II,
then Decline After Korea*

[There was a] . . . "failure of the economy in the second postwar decade to match its performance in the first."

James Tobin, 1967

... [the Negroes] maintained their wartime gains in the immediate postwar period. ... The Korean War prosperity ... represented the apex of Negro prosperity, at least relative to white prosperity.

Arthur M. Ross, 1967

Not all of these views are based on studies and some of the studies have been
affected by rather severe limitations. For the most part:

1. Even where these writers talk of income distributions or make inferences that
   depend on the distributions, they have actually compared only medians or
   means; or where they have used distributions they have selected only a few
   points or used summary statistics (such as the Gini coefficient) that essentially enable comparisons only of inequality among nonwhites with inequality among whites, which is not the same as comparing inequalities in income
   between nonwhites and whites.
2. They have focused on one or a few income series—for example, family income or male income—and have sometimes drawn invalid inferences from
   these magnitudes to others—for example, total money income to persons.
3. They have sometimes drawn conclusions about personal income that really
   apply only to places or to job categories—conclusions that do not apply to
   net figures covering both the starting and end points of migrations from one
   place or occupational category to another.
4. In estimating changes over time, they have sometimes used rather short time
   spans or pairs of years sharply affected by the cyclical variability of nonwhite
   absolute and relative income.
5. Some inferences that depend implicitly on assumptions about trends have
   been based on cross-sectional analysis at an arbitrary point of a cycle—a point
   poorly located to sustain such inferences.
6. For very early periods before income data by color are available, changes in
   nonwhite to white income ratios have been estimated by very coarse occupational indices that neglect nonwhite to white real income changes within
   occupations. This is sometimes done by analogy with production indices
   where prices are held constant; but in the present case changes in real income
   are a product of changes in occupational distribution and in real income
   within occupations. This second factor in the product has been ignored in
   these studies.
7. They have sometimes used absolute dollar differences to draw welfare conclusions more appropriately based on percentages or logarithms.
8. They have ignored sampling errors, even though these can be estimated from
   much of the data and are relevant for inference.

What This Part of Our Study Does

The part of our study summarized here has:

1. Compared white and nonwhite income along the entire distribution of each and developed several statistical measures and graphic devices for this purpose.
2. Used data, including unpublished data from the Current Population Surveys, to construct distributions of wage and salary income, of total money income to families, and total money income to persons 14 years old and over, with several socioeconomic breakdowns of each; extended the personal earnings and family income series of distributions back to 1945 and the wage and salary distributions to 1939; extended the continuous series of income to persons 14 years and over from 1953 back to 1948.
3. Systematically used data on sampling errors, varying for different points on a given distribution and at different calendar dates, to estimate errors in our income ratios and in various functions of them. These error estimates permit inference about the probable longitudinal and cross-sectional relations of various distributions.
4. Estimated the effects on nonwhite relative income of differences in the distribution of whites and nonwhites by age, years of schooling, and major occupational categories.
5. Explored briefly, in the course of this work, the relations to the data of various economic theories of discrimination in the marketplace; genetic explanations of income differences between whites and nonwhites; queuing models of the relative instability of nonwhite and white income during the business cycle; human capital theories of formal schooling and on-the-job training as an investment process; and a model of the dynamics of relative improvement in terms of migrations from one place, job category, or industry to a higher income place, job category, or industry (in which the movers come from the top half of the distribution at the point of origin but, to begin with, are in the lower half of the distribution at the point of destination).

Other parts of this study completed or in process but not summarized here:

6. Use unpublished Current Population Survey or Survey of Economic Opportunity data tapes to estimate the joint effects of various components of the disparity.
7. Analyze the effects of redistributing nonwhites among detailed occupations.
8. Use a new, generally useful, and powerful statistical measure of the relative internal inequality of two distributions to compare inequalities among nonwhites with inequalities among whites and to estimate changes over time in such internal inequalities. (The measure used to compare inequalities within groups is a parameter of the same ratio-at-quantiles function useful for comparing inequalities between the groups.)
9. Analyze and illustrate, on the one hand, the relations and differences among programs to reduce unemployment, to eliminate poverty, or to reduce internal inequalities in society as a whole and, on the other, programs

addressed to the problem of eliminating inequalities of opportunity and income disparities between whites and the nonwhite races.

10. Explore various political and sociological theories of relative deprivation and discontent.

Qualifications

Several disclaimers are in order. Although our study has been almost entirely concerned with income, this does not imply that we believe income disparities are the only important problem of race discrimination, or that the only such problems of importance are economic, or even that they are all quantifiable. But clearly a broad range of social, political, and economic problems is reflected in income disparities, and income data are among the most complete and tractable of the available quantitative measures. Moreover, income *is* important. Among other things, nonwhites do want more income and more income relative to whites.

Our primary data source has been the Current Population Survey (CPS), a monthly survey conducted by the Bureau of the Census. The CPS tabulations, currently based on a stratified sample of about 50,000 households, contain the most complete figures currently available. However, some qualifications regarding these data are still in order. First, there is the problem of underreporting; whites have more of a principal kind of income that is underreported—self-employment income. On the other hand, some hold that nonwhite income is underreported because more nonwhites, especially men, are missed by census interviewers. Then there is the problem of price differences in and out of the ghetto: these seem to favor whites, but there are no reliable estimates of the magnitudes of these differences. The partial exclusion of members of the armed forces introduces another unknown bias. We have considered, at least in a gross way, a variety of other possible sources of error (variation in access to public services, differences in imputed income from property, differing family structure and dependency ratios, differing age distributions of nonwhites and whites, the relative instability of nonwhite income, and, since the data used are money income before taxes, possible differences in effective taxes). On the whole, a rough evaluation suggests that the data understate the current nonwhite relative disadvantage and also appear to understate the relative improvements over time. Nevertheless, substantial uncertainties are inevitable. These are problems that are introduced by the income data, and inferences about income inequality have to be so qualified.

There are three main income concepts used in the CPS tabulations: (1) wage and salary income; (2) earnings; and (3) total money income. Wage and salary income includes the income of employees, that is, regular pay, bonuses, tips, commissions, and so on. Earnings include wage and salary income plus self-employment income. Finally, total money income includes earnings plus rental income, interest, dividends, and transfer payments of all sorts such as welfare, social security, alimony, and others. We have dealt primarily with total money income in our study, since this is probably the best readily measurable income indicator of one's command over goods and services. Other types of income are important for certain classes of questions regarding racial income differences but, except where otherwise indicated, all of the references to income in this report mean total money income.

II. Current Income: 1966 and 1967

When we speak of current incomes, we mean mainly 1966 and 1967, sometimes 1968 and 1969, and never 1970. There is an inevitable long lag between the receipt of income in a given year, a report on it in the sample survey the following March, and the processing of the survey data and further analysis and publication. Similar data and publication lags in the past partly explain the disparity between what a good many authors have been saying about "current" nonwhite and white income and the greatly changed actual income at the time of saying. It is a hazard of the profession that should inspire a prudent check with more recent indirect measures as well as cycles and trends.

The upshot of an analysis of the 1966, 1967, and 1968 data is that very large disparities exist between nonwhite and white family income and between the incomes of nonwhite and white persons 14 years old and over who have income. These disparities appear on the whole to be understated by the data, though they are the most complete figures currently available. Moreover, the disparities affect not only the middle and the lower end but the entire income distribution. Drastic reduction in such differences requires work not only on the nonwhite poor, or on reducing "inequalities" in general, or on the "hard core" unemployed, but also requires large changes in the occupational distribution of nonwhites and in the ratio of nonwhite to white earnings within occupations. It will take time, energy, resources, and intelligence.

Averages

In looking at current differences in income between whites and nonwhites, we will look first at averages. Median family income for nonwhites in 1966 was $4,628 and for white families $7,722, giving a nonwhite to white median income ratio of 59.9 percent. Median total money income to nonwhite persons (including all persons 14 years old and over who received income) in 1966 was $2,099 and for white persons $3,499, giving a nonwhite to white ratio of 60.0 percent.

We shall refer mainly to two sorts of income receiving units: families and persons. Income to families[3] is of substantial interest in considerations of welfare and consumer behavior. It has, however, a good many limitations, especially for comparing race differences. Family units at any given time vary greatly in the number of persons that compose them, in number of earners, and in the amount of doubling up (the combination of young married couples or of the elderly with family heads in the prime of life). Moreover, family structures vary as between nonwhites and whites. Family structures also vary over time for both nonwhites and whites. These changes over time have differed as between nonwhites and whites. For example, although white women participate less in the labor force, since World War II they have increased their participation more than nonwhites. For such reasons it is important to deal not only with families as receiving units but also with persons.[4]

The ratios improve slightly for both persons and families in 1967. For families, median nonwhite income was $5,141 and median white income was $8,274, for a ratio of 62.1 percent. For persons, median nonwhite income was $2,322 and for whites $3,725, giving a ratio of 62.3 percent. Data for 1968 indicate that the ratios at the median for both families and persons were about the same as in 1967.

Distributions

We are interested, however, not only in comparing white and nonwhite incomes in the center of the distributions but at all other parts of the income distribution as well. The statements cited earlier, for example, include some that say that at any given time the ratio of nonwhite to white income is lower in the low-income quantiles than it is at the high end—that nonwhite relative income increases with increasing quantiles of income; that inequality among nonwhites is greater than among whites and, moreover, is increasing; that ghetto rioters are particularly sensitive to where they stand in relation to other Negroes, not to whites, and believe that inequality among nonwhites is increasing (Caplan and Paige, 1968); and that better-educated Negroes compare themselves with whites of equal schooling and therefore feel *more* deprived than uneducated Negroes. (On this assumption, and contrary to the preceding case, the latter are supposed to compare themselves with whites who are not much better off than they.)

Such statements manifest a variety of interests and beliefs about the distributions of nonwhite income. To compare the distribution of income to whites with the distribution of income to nonwhites, we use several methods. One is illustrated in Figure 1-1. Here we have white and nonwhite incomes for families in 1967 plotted against proportions of the population. The vertical scale on the right gives us the proportion of families with income greater than the amount shown, and the leftmost vertical scale gives us the quantiles—the proportion of families with income equal to or less than the amount shown. Incomes are plotted on the horizontal scale. For example, in Figure 1-1 the incomes at the 33rd percentile are about $3,500 and $6,500 for nonwhites and whites, respectively. Since the income scale is logarithmic, equal distances on the graph between white and nonwhite incomes indicate incomes in equal ratios.[5]

From Figure 1-1, it is clear that income differences between whites and nonwhites involve differences not only in median incomes or in the proportions in

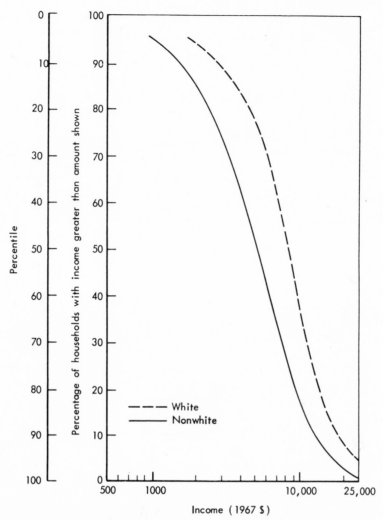

Figure 1-1. Distribution of Total Money Income to Families, 1967. Source: For this Figure and for all Subsequent Figures and Tables where not otherwise specified, the source is the *Current Population Survey*, United States Bureau of the Census.

poverty but in the entire distribution. This illustrates the need to distinguish objectives. Reducing the number of poor—as defined by an arbitrary poverty line—does not help nonwhites above that line, but of course most nonwhites above the line are closer to it than whites and they receive smaller incomes than whites in corresponding positions of the income distribution. Figure 1-2 gives us a similar picture of income to persons in 1967. Again, as in the case of families, income differences exist at all points of the income distribution.

For a considerable part of the distribution of family income in the modal

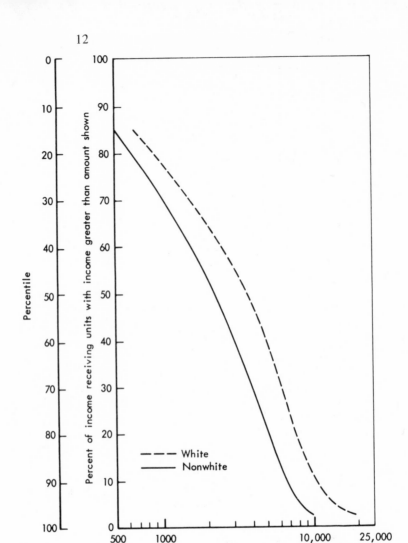

Figure 1-2. Distribution of Total Money Income to Persons, 1967.

range, the distance between the two curves narrows with increasing levels of income—that is, the nonwhite to white ratio tends to increase. All of this behavior is more clearly visible in the income-ratio-at-quantiles curve shown in Figure 1-3, which is derived by taking the nonwhite to white income ratio at selected percentiles and plotting the ratio against the percentiles. These changes, however, are not monotonic and their behavior at the tails in particular is quite different. For 1967, for example, in the lowest and highest fifths, the ratios decline with increasing income. Moreover, for the case of income to persons, for the distribution on the whole, there is no tendency toward increased ratios with increasing income such as is shown in the modal range of family income and the relative

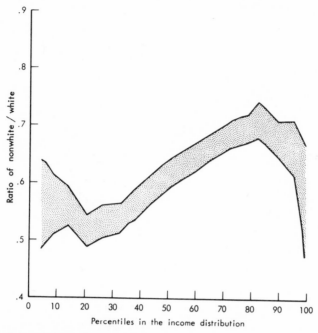

Figure 1–3. Ratio-at-Quantiles of the Income Distribution for Families (95% confidence limits), 1967.

decline in the bottom and top percentiles is plain (see Figure 1-4).

The Ends of the Distribution

There are good reasons to expect the two ends of these relative distributions to behave differently from the middle. At the bottom, income maintenance programs, despite their many familiar limitations, tend to put at least a low floor under nonwhite as well as white income and so to raise low-level nonwhite relative to low-level white income. Moreover, the lower the position in the nonwhite income distribution, the more one would expect these income supports to decrease nonwhite economic disadvantage relative to whites at the corresponding position in the white distribution. This effect would be even stronger with more generous income maintenance programs but is quite visible with current ones.

At the other end, nonwhites run into a variety of obstacles lost from view in averages and totals. Even though young whites and nonwhites have come closer together in median years of schooling, they are still very far apart in the advanced education associated with high income. In the older groups the schooling

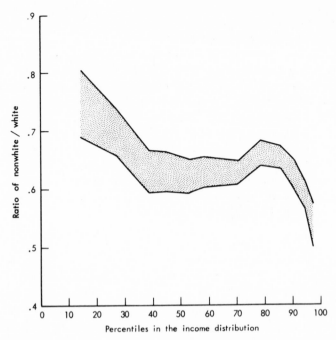

Figure 1-4. Ratio-at-Quantiles of the Income Distribution for Persons (95% confidence limits), 1967.

differences are larger. Moreover, even allowing for differences in years of schooling and in occupational structure, many social hurdles apparently make it particularly hard for nonwhites in top-level communication and decision networks, a particular white prejudice against nonwhites in supervisory and other authoritative roles (Blummer, 1961: 219; Siegel, 1965: 41-57). Such expectations about the two ends of the distribution are confirmed by the analyses (summarized in Sections III and IV) of the changes over time in money income distributions and their components and by the analysis of the effects of schooling and occupational distributions.

Patterns of the Income Ratio Curves

In fact, the behavior of the income-ratio-at-quantiles curves exhibit quite consistent patterns in recent years. The 1967 curve (Figure 1-3) is quite typical for families. It is neither linear nor monotonic. It does appear that there are three distinct segments of the curve, each of which may be approximately linear. Fitting straight lines to each of the three segments (that is, 0 to 21st percentile, 21st to 83 percentile, and 83rd to 100th percentile) gives strong evidence that these three parts of the distribution follow quite different patterns. The slopes for the nonwhite to white income ratios against quantiles of the distribution are negative for the two end segments and positive for the middle one. (The positive slope for families in the modal range appears to be associated with a greater tendency in nonwhite middle income families for wives to work as well as husbands and perhaps with the positive association of wives' job qualifications with husbands'.) The data points are also very close to linear over the middle segment.[6] In Figure 1-4, the segments of the relative distribution for persons (using 0 to 38th percentiles, 38th to 79th percentiles, and 79th to 100th percentiles) are not as clearly linear as for families, but the change in behavior of the curve is quite pronounced over these three parts of the distribution. And the evidence is particularly strong for a negative slope in the last segment (the upper part of the distribution).[7]

The Meaning of "Equal Opportunity"

The relevance of the low end of the distribution is clear, but why should anyone bother with higher percentiles, especially the top ones? There are good reasons for wanting to put the same floor under the income of nonwhites and whites. But to focus only on the lowest quantiles is to neglect the fact that there is a lower statistical ceiling over nonwhite income, one that is hard to penetrate. It may suggest a kind of settlement-house attitude, as distinct from the wider range of concerns indicated by the goal of equal opportunity. First, it should be observed that even the top 1 percent of nonwhite income receivers are hardly rich beyond the wildest dreams of avarice. The top 1 percent of nonwhite males who had income in 1966 received at least $12,000 (see Figure 1-5). The top 10 percent of white males, however, received at least $12,000,[8] and the top 1 percent of white males received at least $26,000. It seems only reasonable for nonwhites to want to have as much as a chance as whites to get $12,000 in annual income, or $26,000. This seems a natural interpretation of the phrase, "equality of opportunity." The phrase clearly covers an equal chance to exceed the poverty line, but getting an even chance with whites at middle and higher incomes seems to be implied as well. It may provide not only the symbolism of top nonwhite earners (such as top athletes or top politicians) but also useful incentives for those in lower ordinal groups to aim that high: even if they do not reach top income levels, they may get more than if they had not had that incentive. Finally, the growth of the nonwhite middle class and of a class of high-level managers, professionals, or entrepreneurs who make, say, $26,000 or more, might be directly associated with the economic improvement of other nonwhites—through savings and investment, by helping to build information networks, and through key positions of influence that affect entry, promotion, and profit in higher-paying occupations.

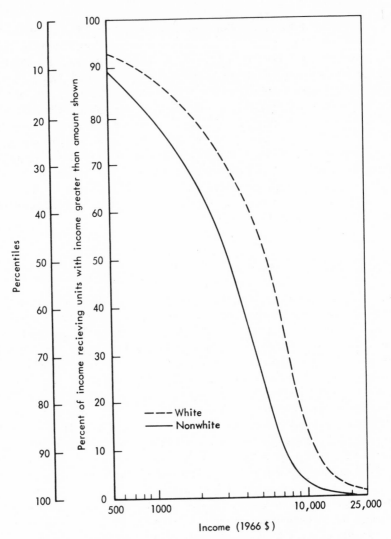

Figure 1-5. Distributions of Total Money Income to Men, 1966.

Of course, none of the above disparages the importance of lifting the low end of the nonwhite distribution. Rather, it stresses that the problems of discrimination apply to all of the distribution; that some useful aids to solving the troubles at the low end are not independent of progress at the middle and at the top; and finally, that slogans of "equal economic opportunity," if they mean what they say, imply for nonwhites an even chance with whites—not simply at scraping by above some arbitrary minimum, but at doing moderately well, and with a fair chance at making it big.

ng nonwhites, men have higher incomes than women, but the differ-
aller than that between white men and women.

e, of course, the principal breadwinners and for that reason the ob-
ore study; and the "status" of women, on the other hand, is often
o be primarily determined by the income, occupation, and education
usbands. It is also true that more data are published about men than
nd this tends to further focus research on male income. This in turn
ced by several traditions of research. For example, S.M. Lipset has
to us that the sociologists' familiar methods of studying occupation-
ty by relating the occupational status of the son to occupation of the
of clear interest for men but has no ready correlative for women. Be
it may, many studies focus exclusively on comparisons of white and
e men yet sometimes draw conclusions about nonwhites in general.
gure 1-6, however, we can see that men and women have quite different
, and any inference from one to the sum of the two (or in the reverse
n) requires caution. This caution has not always been observed and it has
nferences about changes over time.

is it justified, in spite of the principal importance for family welfare of
come, to focus *only* on male income and to neglect the incomes of white
nwhite women. This might be done on the premise that, in the case of
vomen, low incomes are almost entirely a matter of unconstrained choice,
hite women who participate less or receive smaller rewards in the labor
o so only because they are married to rich men and are not interested in
or high level jobs. That premise, however, may be doubted even by some
e not charter members of Women's Lib. First, for nonwhite compared
hite women, the ratio of the medians of year-round full-time earnings is
rger than that for all earnings, part- and full-time (in 1967, .761 compared
688; see Table 1-2). Second, even when the husband's income is high,
ite wives participate more than whites. "Among families where the hus-
yearly income was $10,000 or more, about half of the Negro wives com-
with a third of the white wives were working or looking for work" (Wald-
1970: 12) in March 1969. Since the interval is not bounded above and
ite husbands are undoubtedly clustered nearer the lower limit, this second
is suggestive rather than conclusive. Third, the income contribution of
, in any case, bears no simple inverse relation to the income of their hus-
. For nonwhites in the middle ranges, as we suggested earlier (p. 15), wives'
es are positively correlated with their husbands' income. Finally, the will-
ss to work of both white and nonwhite women is related not only to pay,
lso to the nonmonetary rewards of the work available—its interest, the
s it confers, and so on. An abundance of evidence suggests that (in parallel,
shall observe with nonwhite minorities) women find it especially hard to
uthoritative, high-paying jobs that call for high levels of education (see
ibald, 1970).

The greater disparity between whites and n
for aggregate persons (Figure 1-2) implies
between white and nonwhite women. The
nonwhite women are illustrated in Figure 1
men. Here we see that income to both wh
than income to either white or nonwhite m
for women are closer to each other than ar
means nonwhite to white income ratios are

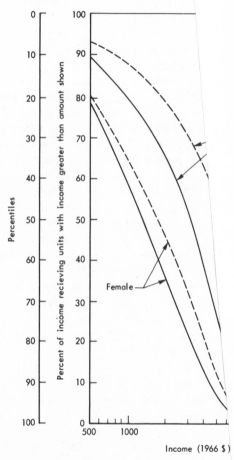

Figure 1-6. Distribution of Total Money Income
1967.

Thus, am
ence is sn
Men a
ject of m
thought
of their
women a
is reinfo
suggested
al mobil
father is
that as
nonwhit
From F
incomes
directio
misled i
Nor
male in
and no
white
that w
force
middle
who a
with w
even l
with
nonwl
band'
pared
man,
nonw
point
wives
band
inco
ingn
but
statu
as w
get
Arc

Both nonwhite and white women are discriminated against, though discrimination by reason of sex is even harder to disentangle and quantify than color discrimination. One needs to separate not only unequal pay for equal work from nonmarket discrimination in the opportunities to acquire skills, but also inequalities in opportunity available to women who want to and can perform the same job as well as men from educational choices and income differences due to differing social functions, capabilities, and preferences. The annals of prosecution under the Fair Labor Standards Acts, as well as common observation, make clear that some substantial part of the difference is discriminatory.

Regional and Farm-Nonfarm Comparisons

There are various ways of decomposing income distributions other than by sex. For example, for families we can look at income differences over different regions of the country or by farm-nonfarm residence. Figure 1-7 compares the ratio-at-quantiles curves for the South[9] and for the non-South for 1967. For both whites and nonwhites incomes are lower in the South than in the rest of the country. Notice, however, that the difference is greater for nonwhites than for whites. Thus, southern nonwhites have lower incomes relative to southern whites than have nonwhites living outside the South compared with whites outside the South. This greater income disparity in the South is very important for the overall picture, because at present about half of all nonwhite families live in the South, whereas only about one-quarter of white families do.

We find even greater disparities between white and nonwhite incomes for families who live on farms. The effect on the overall income distribution is small, however, since only a small proportion of families live on farms and today proportionately fewer nonwhites than whites. In 1967 about 5.5 percent of white families lived on farms, while about 4.4 percent of nonwhite families did.

The intersections of some of these unfavored categories show even larger contrasts in nonwhite to white ratios.

III. Changes Over Time

General impressions of decline or stagnation of nonwhite income relative to white income vary in meaning from nonwhite absolute decline from a previous nonwhite position to the view that the growth rates of nonwhite income have been positive but no larger than for whites.

Cyclical Instability of Nonwhite Relative Income

The graph in Figure 1-8 shows year-to-year percentage changes in both white and nonwhite median family income from 1947 to 1967 (in 1966 prices). The per-

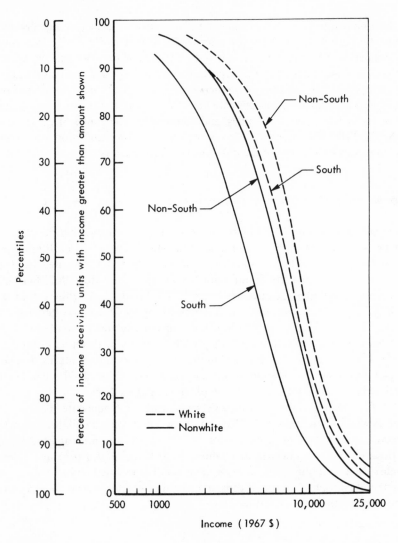

Figure 1-7. Distribution of Family Income, South and Non-South, 1967.

centage changes for the entire 20-year period and for three subperiods are illustrated in Figure 1-9a. From Figures 1-8 and 1-9a several points can be made. First, the annual average percentage improvement in nonwhite family median income, adjusted for price changes, has been greater than that for white families: 3.8 percent and 2.8 percent, respectively. Second, the fluctuations in both the subperiod trends and in the year-to-year changes are greater for nonwhites than for whites. These relatively larger nonwhite rises and falls in income appear to reflect changes in the tightness of the labor market and roughly to parallel busi-

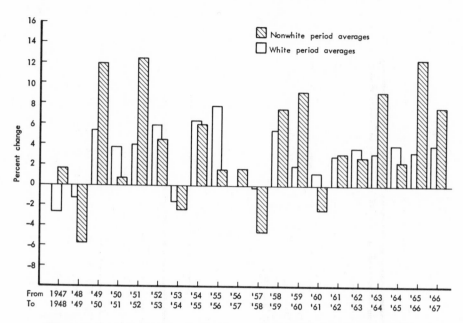

Figure 1-8. Annual Growth Rates in Median Family Income (1966 prices), 1947-1967.

ness cycle expansions and contractions.[10] The greater cyclical instability of nonwhite income is related to the fact that during the business cycle, in general, wages fluctuate most, the general run of salaries less, and professional and executive salaries least (Creamer, 1956), and nonwhite income has a disproportionately large share of some of the sorts of earnings that fluctuate most widely. The relatively larger short-term fluctuations of nonwhite income also offer a certain amount of support for some variants of a queuing model for nonwhite earnings. If (in Gary Becker's terms) employers' prejudices are measured by a discrimination coefficient that in effect makes employers act as if the real costs of hiring or promoting a Negro exceed the money costs by some percentage, then the scarcity and the rising costs of white labor can make the employer willing to pay that extra nonmonetary price in using nonwhites. When the market slackens it may not seem worth it to him. The evidence of unemployment rates, according to Harry Gilman's study of three business cycles from 1953 through 1961, did not support the hypothesis that nonwhites are the last to be hired and the first to be fired: in particular, the amplitude of the fluctuation of nonwhite unemployment rates was no greater than that of whites (though of course the levels were higher).[11] However matters stand so far as the relative instability of nonwhite compared with white unemployment rates is concerned, for nonwhite in-

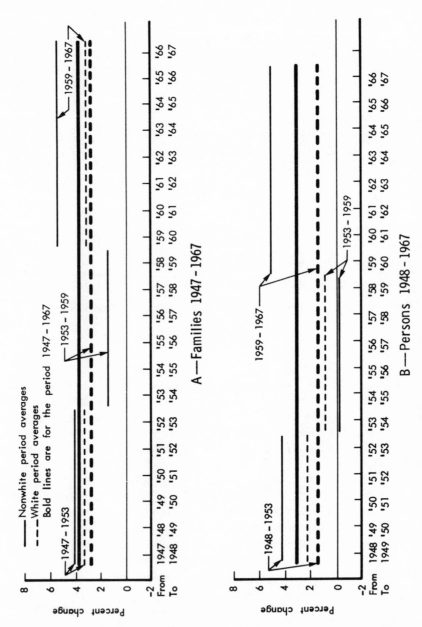

Figure 1-9. Total and Subperiod Growth Rates in Median Income (1966 prices).

come the case is quite clear. Nonwhite income fluctuates much more widely. And if nonwhite money income, whose fluctuations are tempered by money transfers, is more sensitive to short-term changes in the labor market, we would surmise that nonwhite earnings as distinct from income are even more variable.

Figure 1-10 is like Figure 1-8 except that it deals with income to persons, not families. It shows annual percentage changes in median income to persons from 1948 to 1967.[12] The percentage changes for the 19-year period and three sub-periods are shown in Figure 1-9b. The pattern of movement for persons is very much like that for families, except that both the long-term percentage gains and the cyclical fluctuations are even wider for income to nonwhite persons. These points are rather clear in the graphs for the total postwar period and the three subperiod trends.

The greater cyclical instability of nonwhite income can be seen more precisely by removing the trend effect and comparing the residuals of the year-to-year percentage changes in median income. When the income levels are taken into account, the deviations from the trend (measured by the sum of the squares of

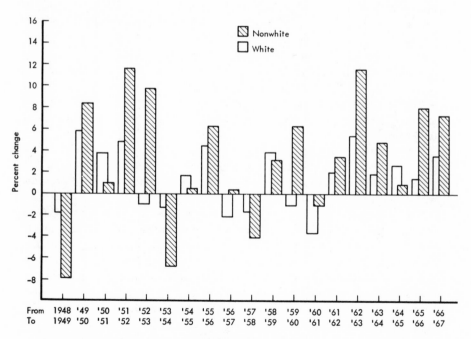

Figure 1-10. Annual Growth Rates for Median Income of Persons, 1948-1967.

the residual over the predicted income) are about 4 times higher for nonwhites in the case of persons and about 4-1/3 times higher for nonwhites in the case of families. These greater deviations for nonwhites exceed sampling error easily. The great instability of nonwhite family income and, even more, of income to nonwhite persons has, of course, direct implications for hardship— an aspect of welfare that is not adequately reflected in the usual measurement of the present value of earnings or the smoothed curves of lifetime earnings.

The greater instability of nonwhite income may be related to the fragmentary data often referred to in relative income or in permanent income theories of the consumption function (see Brady and Friedman, 1947; Duesenberry, 1948; Tobin, 1951; Duesenberry, 1962; and Friedman, 1957). These data indicate that nonwhites at any given income level save a larger percentage of their income than whites. Joseph Newhouse has suggested to us that the greater instability of nonwhite measured income biases downward estimates of marginal propensity and average propensity to consume more for nonwhites than for whites.[13] We would add that, even where a nonwhite and a white have identical lifetime incomes and therefore the same permanent incomes, the fact that the nonwhite receipts fluctuate much more widely would make it reasonable for the nonwhite as a rule to consume less in order to even out the sequence of feast and famine. This is so given the imperfection of capital markets, particularly for nonwhites, and the uncertainties as to the periods and amplitudes of the fluctuations. Nonwhites who want to avoid the risks of very low consumption would have to maintain reserves that would reduce their lifetime consumption. If the nonwhites do *not* steadily save more and consume less (and the data, despite their very frequent use in analyses of the consumption function, are piecemeal and ambiguous) they are worse off than whites, not merely because their lifetime income and consumption are generally lower, but because these are also much unsteadier.

The result of these considerations is to reinforce the judgment that the greater instability of nonwhite income makes nonwhites worse off compared with whites than the comparisons of their averages and totals accumulated over time would indicate.

For both nonwhites and whites, the growth rates of income to persons are generally lower than those of family income since both white and nonwhite women increased their participation in the labor force and their contribution to family income. White women participate less, but in the postwar period increased their participation more than nonwhites. Participation was 12 percentage points lower for white women in March 1969, but was as much as 20 points lower in past decades (U.S. Department of Labor, June 1970: 12). As a result, the *relative* (to white) growth rate of income to nonwhite persons (the aggregate of men and women) is higher than the *relative* growth of nonwhite family income. The growth rate of nonwhite income to persons was more than double that of white (3.1 percent per year compared with 1.5). The growth rate of nonwhite family income was about one-third higher than white (3.8 percent per year compared with 2.8 percent).

Short-term ups and downs in the labor market have long-term effects on race differences in income. Slack markets reduce incentives for employers to train unskilled labor for more highly skilled, better-paying jobs, and reduce the rewards to employees for investing time and money in acquiring skills (see Johnson, 1966). Labor markets that are tight enough and last long enough have the reverse effect. Employer prejudice may be overridden by the gap between the demand for and the short supply of the favored kind of labor. And there are net incentives for minorities to migrate to higher-income regions, occupations, and industries. Tight labor markets not only alter and increase a minority's productive potential by offering it job training and experience in higher-level skills; they also, as John McCall suggests, provide employers with information as to what that potential is and so can modify stereotyped underestimates.[14] The Korean war and again the Vietnam war were the times of greatest improvement since World War II in nonwhite median income. (The more fragmentary evidence on World War II gains for nonwhites shows the same. The changes for white as well as nonwhite women during World War II may be the most familiar example of the immediate short-term and the residual long-term effects of a very tight labor market.) Income to nonwhite persons has not returned to pre—Korean troughs either in absolute terms or relative to white.

Relative Nonwhite and White Distributional
Changes in Total Money Income

But again, we are concerned not only with changes over time in median incomes but with changes at other quantiles as well. To consider changes along the entire income distribution, we start with the semi-log curves shown in Figure 1-2 for persons in 1967. Then we add to them the similar curves for white and nonwhite persons in 1949. These are all shown together in Figure 1-11. At all percentiles both white and nonwhite incomes have improved. (Incomes for both years are given in 1967 dollars.) For many purposes, we have found more revealing another way of comparing white and nonwhite incomes for the two years. Here we use the income levels at each quantile for each year to form the ratio of nonwhite to white income at each quantile for each of the two years, and then plot a new graph of nonwhite to white income ratios against quantiles in the income distributions. This is illustrated in Figure 1-12. which shows that the income ratio has improved for all quantiles, but the improvement is generally greater at lower quantiles. This is more easily seen by subtracting the nonwhite to white income ratios for 1949 from those of 1967 to get the curve of ratio differences shown in Figure 1-13. Figure 1-13 also takes account of sampling variability in the income data, and the lower boundary of the shaded area represents the ratio difference

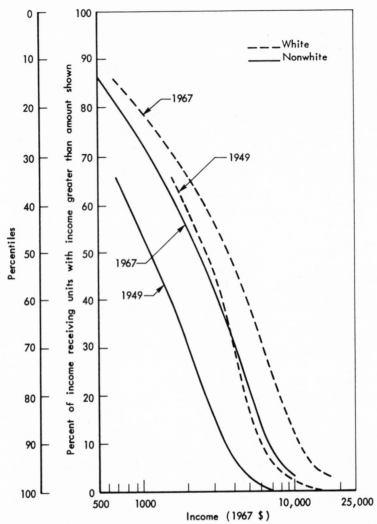

Figure 1-11. Distribution of Total Money Income to Persons, 1967 and 1949.

at each percentile for which we have about 95 percent confidence that the true value is equal to or greater than the amount shown.

This again helps to clarify and distinguish possible objectives. We observe that nonwhite median income has improved at a greater rate than white median income for both persons and families and that in relative terms the improvement for nonwhites has been greatest at the low percentiles for persons. Thus, efforts to achieve the distinct though related and useful goals of reducing poverty and hardcore unemployment would be directed at those parts of the income distribu-

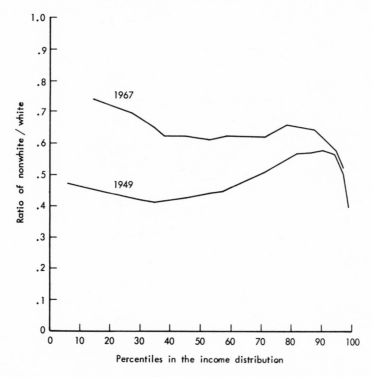

Figure 1-12. Ratio-at-Quantiles Comparison for Persons, 1949 and 1967.

tion where the greatest nonwhite relative improvement has already occurred, leaving the higher percentiles relatively unaffected. Notice that in Figure 1-13 it is only in the upper 10 percent of the income distribution that we are not at least 95 percent confident that nonwhite income has improved relative to white income. And in the upper 10 percent, we are talking not just about millionaires: income to nonwhite persons at the 90th percentile in 1967 was only about $6,796. Thus, a substantial effort aimed at the higher and middle percentiles as well as at the lower ones will be required in order to equalize white and nonwhite income distributions.

The pattern of relative nonwhite improvement in income position for families is more dependent on the choice of years than in the case of persons. The trend of greater improvement for lower percentiles is clear for persons when any earlier year for which CPS data are available is compared with either 1966, 1967, or 1968. In the case of families, however, we find this pattern occurring in a comparison of either 1945 or 1949 with 1967, but not for either 1947 or 1948 with 1967. Figure 1-14 illustrates the 1947 to 1967 comparison for families. We find a horn-like opening at the lowest percentiles but roughly equal improvement from about the 50th to the 80th percentiles, so that overall the improvement is slightly greater for the upper half of the distribution than for the lower half for families since 1947.[15]

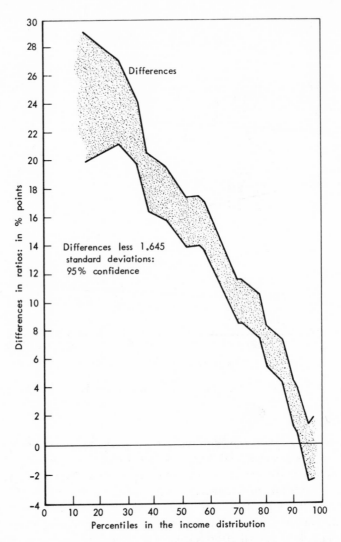

Figure 1-13. Total Money Income to Persons, Differences in Ratios of Nonwhite to White Incomes at Selected Percentiles, 1949–1967.

The greater relative improvement in total money income at the lower percentiles displays the effect of the increase in transfer payments since World War II (an increase that has, of course, been neither steady over time nor uniform in its effect on all categories of low income groups). In fact, as Figure 1-15 shows, the personal income ratio-at-quantiles curves have tended to rotate clockwise since the late 1940s, with the upper percentiles as a fixed pivot.

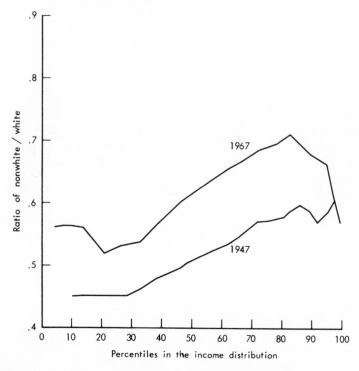

Figure 1-14. Ratio-at-Quantiles Comparison for Families, 1947 and 1967.

The short-run behavior at the low percentiles might be expected to exhibit the combined effect of this nonuniform trend of increase in transfer payments and a cyclical instability even greater than that at the median. And, in fact, in periods of cyclical expansion such as the long period of of growth from 1958 to 1967, the nonwhite to white income ratios grew more rapidly at the lower percentiles than at the median but declined less, or even grew, in comparison with the median at the lower quantiles during contractions such as that between 1948 and 1949.

Relative Distributional Changes Since 1939 in Wages and Salaries

The preceding paragraphs talk of postwar changes beginning with 1947 for family income and starting a year or two later for income to persons (the starting points for the continuous CPS time series on income by color). For earlier times income data by color are hard to come by, and income distributions by

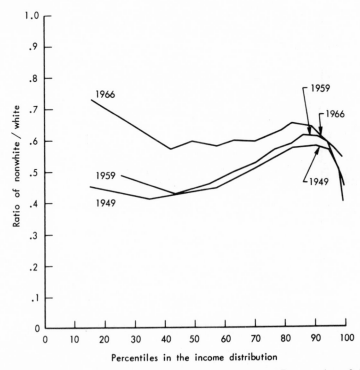

Figure 1-15. Ratios of Income to Persons at Selected Percentiles of the Income Distribution, 1949, 1959, and 1966. Source: Current *Population Survey* and unpublished Census materials.

color especially so. The 1935-36 Consumer Purchases Study (U.S. National Resources Committee, 1938) offers some distributions by color, but they represent the Negro population inadequately and cover only some parts of the country, include income in kind as well as money income, exclude direct relief payments, and are not comparable to data for the postwar years. Estimates for earlier periods are based on the decennial censuses of occupation and are constructed by using wages and salaries or earnings or total money income weights from a later period and applying these weights to very large classes of occupations. (Gary Becker, for example, applies 1939 wage and salary weights to a three-category classification: skilled, semiskilled, and unskilled.) No data exist on relative changes of nonwhite income within occupations.

Using unpublished census data, we have been able to make a comparison between white and nonwhite wage and salary distributions in 1939 and 1967. This 28-year span seems the longest permitting any confident comparison. Figure 1-16 shows the wage and salary ratios for the two years, both for full-time and part-time workers.

It is quite clear from this graph that for about 80 to 90 percent of the wage

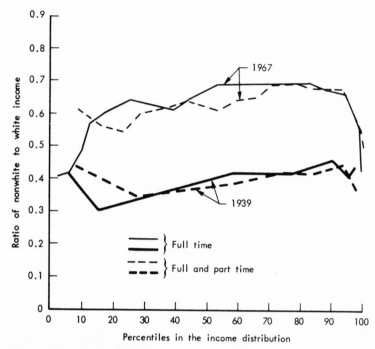

Figure 1-16. Ratios of Wage and Salary Income of all Wage and Salary Workers and of Year-Round Full-Time Workers, 1939 and 1967. Source: Current *Population Survey* and unpublished Census materials.

and salary distribution, the nonwhite to white ratios have roughly doubled in the 28-year period. The trend of greater improvement in lower percentiles noted earlier in the case of total money income to persons is not present in the case of wage and salary income to persons—a confirmation that improved welfare arrangements benefiting nonwhites in the lowest percentiles rather than higher earnings account for the greater closing of the gap at that end of the distribution. (Detailed data recently made available by color on types of income other than earnings for 1968 strengthen this conclusion.)

Changes Since 1967

The nonwhite to white ratio of median incomes changed very little from 1967 to 1969 for families, increasing from .621 to .625. The ratio changes across the distribution are generally small (mostly less than 2 or 3 percent), though the slope of the ratio-at-quantiles curve is somewhat smaller in the middle of the distribution, and the decline at the top appears to be somewhat sharper. The ratio at the median for persons did increase somewhat, from .623 in 1967 to

.642 in 1969. The persons ratio curve for 1969 is more consistently above that for 1967 than in the case of families, though for both persons and families they intersect several times.

Why Do These Results Differ From
Some of the More Common Statements?

1. Choice of Years. For one thing, the changes over time observed in such statements depend on the time covered, and many of the comparisons measure the difference between two rather accidentally chosen years. Given the relatively extreme fluctuations of nonwhite income, this has a very large effect. The most pessimistic conclusions stem from comparing the Korean highs with pre-Vietnam low points. But even the two most recent decennial censuses can mislead. They deal with income in 1949 and 1959, two recession years, and this has strongly influenced the results of many investigations. The censuses are a unique, invaluable, and much-used source of detailed income data but are not unaffected by their arbitrary position in the business cycle. This has biased not only longitudinal studies but cross-sectional ones as well.

To illustrate, consider the three ratio-at-quantiles curves for persons in 1949, 1959, and 1966 shown in Figure 1-15. Here we can see that the improvement for nonwhites relative to whites between 1959 and 1966 greatly exceeds that between 1949 and 1959. The use of 1959 data without corrections based on other years may bias conclusions from cross-sectional studies as well. To take an example, prospective lifetime earnings and relative marginal returns to schooling of whites and nonwhites are often estimated by use of only the 1959 income of various age cohorts in that year. This neglects trends as well as cyclical effects— and, as we have seen, the long-term percentage rate of growth in median income for nonwhites substantially exceeds that for whites, and nonwhite income relative to white is particularly low in recession years.

2. Focus on Income to Men. A second thing that has frequently misled inference in the field is the focus on income to men. A good many studies deal with male income but draw conclusions about the total nonwhite population. Figure 1-17 suggests the combined biases than can result from the arbitrary choice of years and an exclusive focus on men. It shows the ratio-at-quantiles curves for men in 1949, 1959, and 1966. The improvement to 1966 for males is clearly less dramatic than for aggregate persons, and from 1949 to 1959 the income ratios decline for many percentiles. This indicates that the improvement for females would be even greater than that for aggregate persons. Unfortunately, the median income for nonwhite females in 1949 fell within the lowest income interval published so that no income ratios could be computed for the lower half of the distribution.

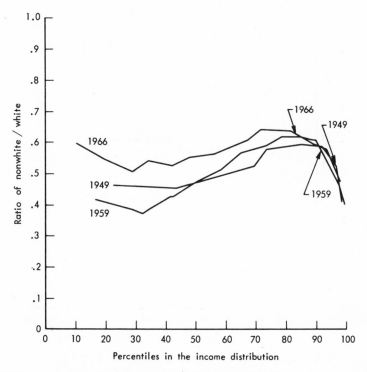

Figure 1-17. Ratios of Income at Selected Percentiles of the Income Distribution for Men, 1949, 1959, and 1966.

3. The Use of Averages Rather than Distributions. A third difference between the results we have presented and many more familiar statements it that the latter tend to use only the median or mean or just a few points on the distribution. The possible misleading effects of such a limitation are illustrated neatly by Figure 1-18, the ratio-at-quantiles comparison for families in 1945 and 1952. The two curves cross just about at the median, so that a comparison of ratios of median incomes only for the two years would lead one to conclude that there had been no change in the income position of nonwhites relative to whites. As can be seen from this graph, however, there were relative changes at all parts of the distribution *except* the median. The ratios improved in the lower half of the distribution and declined in the upper half. This is, of course, an extreme case, but it illustrates nicely the need to consider the complete distribution of income rather than only the median.

The 1945 to 1952 comparison serves as a reminder also that the starting points for the continuous series on income after the war—in 1947 in the case of families and in 1948 in the case of income to persons—are accidental. This puts at hazard some of the familiar generalizations about subtrends within the postwar period. The Current Population Survey of income got underway in 1944 and

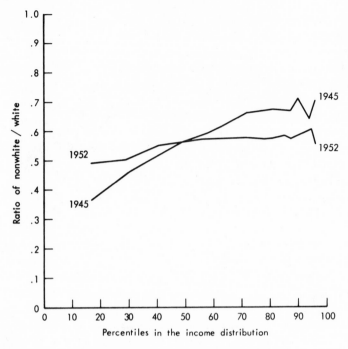

Figure 1-18. Ratio-at-Quantiles Comparison for Families, 1945 and 1952.

information by color has been put out regularly only since 1947. However, distributions can be obtained for total income to families in 1945, and we have used them in Figure 1-18. The CPS sample at that time was much smaller than the current one (8,000 households compared with about 50,000 households in 1968), and the sampling error is larger. More serious (since, we can take account of the sampling errors), there may be some undisclosed systematic bias limiting the use of the 1946 survey of 1945 income. For example, we do not know what the effects of the inclusion and exclusion of members of the armed forces were, and this could be important for the year 1945. Nonetheless, this and other evidence suggest that most of the improvement from 1939 to 1947 took place between 1941 and 1945.[16] Statements that divide the postwar period into two subperiods—a Golden Age followed by a Fall[17]—are dubious for their start as well as their finish.

4. Problems in Exclusive Use of Family Income. Fourth, most of the common statements refer to nonwhite relative family income and, as we have seen, family income is a more rubbery unit subject to alteration with changes in family structure. Nonwhite relative family income grew more slowly than income to persons.

5. Income Differences Versus Income Ratios. Fifth, several of the familiar statements refer to increasing dollar differences between whites and nonwhites.[18] We have taken ratios or percentage differences or logarithms or the like as more appropriate measures from a welfare standpoint.[19] If one regards the absolute dollar difference as defining the problem, then it would appear that Negro male wage and salary earners were much better off in 1939 compared with whites than they are today. The median of their wages and salaries was $460, 41 percent of whites, and $652 less. In 1967 Negro median wages and salaries were about 64 percent of whites and $2,464 less ($4,369 compared with $6,833). If we adjust the 1939 wage and salary income to 1967 dollars,[20] we get median nonwhite and white incomes of approximately $1,095 and $2,650, for an income difference of about $1,555. If the nonwhite median had been about 77 percent of the white median in 1967, the dollar difference would have been about the same as in 1939. Eliminating a $1,550 difference would then mean a 29 percent increase in income for nonwhites in 1967, whereas in 1939 it would have meant more than doubling nonwhite income. It seems implausible to suppose the marginal utility of the dollar difference is the same in both cases. In fact, while appropriate in some circumstances, the use of absolute or dollar differences here (as in the case of discussions of the economic development of the Third World and the gap between the rich and poor countries), tends to serve a hortatory rather than an analytic function. (The Japanese per capita GNP tripled in the decade beginning 1953, while that of the United States increased by less than 50 percent. The Japanese lost ground in dollars but most of us, including the Japanese, think they are catching up.) Welfare considerations aside, even for purposes of prediction, percentage rates of change have an obvious relevance to economic growth. One would expect that a $1,550 increase would take a good deal longer starting from a $1,095 base than starting from a $4,400 base. It is because the rate of change or amount of growth at a given date is related to size at that date that exponential functions are generally useful in forming our expectations about growth.

6. Comparison of Population Proportions at Fixed Income Levels. Sixth, the ratio of proportions[21] at a given income is frequently used in comparing white and nonwhite proportions above or below a poverty line or some given income levels. Aside from the troubles that can stem from focusing on one or two arbitrary dividing points in the distribution, however, such ratios of cumulative percentages do not directly measure relative income and, as we suggested earlier, can be quite misleading. Consider the case of the poverty line for families: 56.0 percent of nonwhite families and 16.5 percent of white families were below the poverty line in 1959, giving a ratio of .295 for the white to nonwhite incidence of poverty. In 1968, 32.4 percent of nonwhite families and 8.4 percent of white families were below the poverty line, giving a white to nonwhite ratio of .259. The white to nonwhite ratio, then, decreased, suggesting that in relative terms things improved *more for whites* than for nonwhites. If we compare proportions *above* the poverty line, however, we find that the nonwhite to white ratio increased from .527 in 1959 (44.0 percent for nonwhites and 83.5 percent for whites) to .738 in 1968 (67.6 percent and 91.6 percent for nonwhites and whites respectively). The nonwhite to white ratio of proportions of families above the poverty line, then, increased, suggesting that in relative terms things improved *more for nonwhites* than for whites (U.S. Bureau of the Census, 1969: Table D).

The results are similar when we compare proportions above and below $8,000. The nonwhite to white ratio of proportions of families above $8,000 (price adjusted, in 1967 dollars) was .278 in 1947 (5 percent of nonwhite families and 18 percent of white families) and .509 in 1967 (27 percent of nonwhite families and 53 percent of white families). This suggests that in relative terms the situation improved more for nonwhites. The white to nonwhite ratio of proportions below $8,000 decreased from .863 in 1947 to .644 in 1967, indicating greater relative improvement for whites (U.S. Bureau of the Census, 1968: 8).

The reason for this apparent contradiction is indicated by the curves shown in Figure 1-19. If we have two curves of identical shape but differing only by a translation along the horizontal (income) scale, we find that income differences would be the same for all quantiles (Figure 1-19a). Or, if the horizontal scale were log income, we would find that income ratios would be the same for all quantiles. But with either income or log income, the use of the ratio of proportions measure would indicate increasing nonwhite to white ratios if we compare proportions (or quantiles) below incomes, and decreasing nonwhite to white ratios for proportions above incomes. Extending this to changes over time, even if the translations over time for the income distributions were the same for whites and nonwhites (Figure 1-19b) on the income scale (or on the log income scale), we would still find that white to nonwhite ratios of proportions below any income figure (low income or high) would decrease, and nonwhite to white ratios of proportions above any income figure would increase. Of course, the nonwhite and white curves do not differ only by a translation on either the income scale or the log income scale, nor have changes over time preserved the shapes of either income curve. But the point here is that ratios of proportions above or below given income levels may reveal little or nothing about relative improvement over time of white and nonwhite incomes.

7. Migration and "The Reverse Harvard-Yale Paradox." A seventh point that has sometimes misled inference has to do with a phenomenon we have thought of as "The Reverse Harvard-Yale Paradox," a title suggested by the familiar story of a student who transferred from Yale to Harvard (or vice versa, depending on whether a Yale or Harvard man tells the story) and raised the average in both places. The reverse statistical phenomenon may work to reduce income ratios when we infer them from subgroup changes over time. In fact, it may have some-

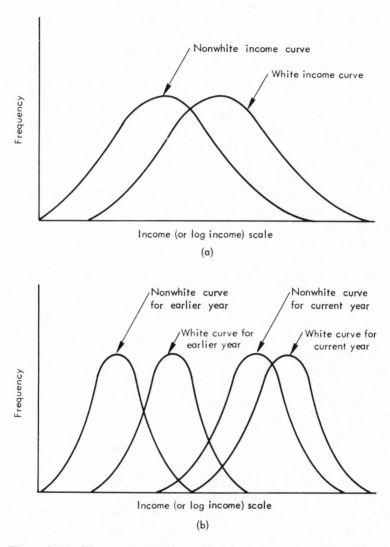

Figure 1-19. Illustrations for Case Where the White minus Nonwhite Income Differences (or for Log Scale the Nonwhite to White Income Ratios) are the Same for all Quantiles.

thing essential to do with the dynamics of relative growth; with shifts of minorities from low-income regions, occupations, and industries to higher-income regions, occupations, and industries. One might expect to find that: (1) the ones who make the shift are generally better educated, are more enterprising, and have higher incomes than the average in the places that they leave; and (2) as a result of the shift, the move, on the average, will raise their own incomes; but (3) the level will not immediately rise to the average level at their destination. From a national standpoint, that is from a standpoint including all those involved both at the starting point and at the destination, there is then a net relative improvement. But looking at the starting point and at the end point separately, relative income at each place may decline. More generally, the relative improvement in the national aggregate could be expected to be larger than those displayed in the subtotals.

This has happened in the case of geographical migration. There has been a very large migration of nonwhites from the South to the North and West. There is substantial evidence that the migrants were younger and better educated than the average (see Newman, 1966). Between 1955 and 1960 the South lost one-fifth of all the nonwhite men 25 to 29 years old who had some college training, but lost only 6 percent of those with elementary schooling. In fact, the regional ratios between the two census years show declines in the income of Negro men while the overall ratio was static (see Batchelder, 1964), and in the surge since 1959 the improvement has been larger for the total than would be inferred from the subgroups. The smaller the geographical subunit, the more misleading the subunit income ratios may be; so the trouble is likely to be even more acute for cities or neighborhoods than for regions.

A migration that means a net improvement from the standpoint of the aggregate of those involved at the starting and end points of the migration is all to the good if one is interested in people. If one is interested in places rather than people, on the other hand, the story may be very different. And, as Harry Johnson points out, politicians tend to come attached to places.

As our formulation above suggests, this problem in comparing subgroups affects not only geographical migration, but also shifts to higher-income job categories or higher-income industries. To take the case of occupations, the lower relative income of nonwhites is a product of two components: an underrepresentation of nonwhites among job categories that pay high average incomes, and a lower than average income for nonwhites within the job categories.[22] A shift in the proportion of nonwhites toward the higher-paying job categories, then, can be accompanied by a transient lowering of nonwhite relative pay within the job category. To overcome the large remaining gap between nonwhite and white income, however, it is plain that ultimately there will have to be large improvements in both components of the product, that is, in the relative distributions of nonwhites in jobs and their relative rate of pay within the job categories.

8. Occupational Shifts Understate Income Changes. An eighth point about estimates of changes over time in nonwhite relative income specifically affects those estimates of very long term trends that have been made using the occupational distributions in the decennial censuses with fixed wage and salary or other income weights. Such estimates do not reflect the relative improvements in nonwhite real incomes within job categories, but only the improvements in the distribution of nonwhites among jobs. They estimate only one of the two components of the product that measures changes in relative nonwhite income. Moreover, some of the best known of these use extremely broad categories.[23] The effects of past and current discrimination in the job market, however, are displayed not only in the distribution among jobs but also in differences in the rate of pay within jobs. The analogy sometimes suggested with indexes of output where one wants to eliminate the effects of price change does not apply. In estimating the changes in relative nonwhite income, one needs to take into account changes in *real* income relative to whites *within* occupations. Gary Becker (1957: 114) notes,

A decrease in discrimination could increase merely the relative income of Negroes within an occupational category and not change their relative occupational distribution. However, since discrimination against Negroes has been greater in the more skilled occupations, a large decrease in discrimination would probably also increase their opportunities in these occupations.

Supposing this is true, the magnitude of a total reduction in discrimination has nonetheless to be measured as a product of the two components.

Relative Improvement Has Clearly
Taken Place

A good many other statements suggesting that there has been no significant improvement of nonwhite income over time have been based on less complex inadequacies than those we have discussed. For charity's sake, we shall not expand on the simpler errors. In any case, the evidence for relative improvement over time (in the last two decades, since the Korean peak, in the last decade, and so on) of the nonwhite income distributions as a whole is quite plain. Such evidence can be summarized by measures using the area between the income-ratio-at-quantiles curves for a recent and for an earlier year and taking sampling errors explicitly into account. In the case of income to persons, we have better than .999 confidence that there was relative improvement for nonwhites from any of the years before 1960 considered to 1967. The evidence is nearly as strong for family income. And even when we take very short periods such as 1963 to 1967, for example, the confidence levels for improvement are still .998 for both families and persons. Nonwhite income has plainly improved more than white income. That, however, hardly means that the problem of race discrimination in income will soon be solved.

But We Are Still Far From Closing
the Income Gap

As we conclude this discussion of changes over time, two points need emphasis. They suggest strongly that, though there have clearly been sizable absolute and relative improvements, these can hardly be the basis for unclouded optimism. First, that nonwhite relative income has been extremely sensitive to the tightness of the labor market suggests that without a well-calculated and executed policy to avoid a setback after Vietnam, such a setback is quite likely. That the relative income of nonwhites did not return to pre-Korean troughs is only a little comfort. It did decline quite a bit after the Korean peak.[24]

Given the present large disparities, convergence will require a drastic improvement in the relative distribution of nonwhites among occupations and an improvement of their relative income within occupations. This in turn will require changes in education but not only that. In the next section we consider the effects of job distribution and years of schooling, as well as the effects of the age structures of the two populations.

IV. Some Components of the Income Disparities

Age Structure

The criterion for policy that has been implicit in the analysis so far assumes that it is a reasonable aim from the standpoint of equity that nonwhites overtake whites in the level and distribution of income, subject to a very few qualifications affecting such demographic traits as age distributions or family structure. As for the qualifications, take the example of age. Some differences in earnings can be accounted for by differences in the age structures of the nonwhite and white populations and would persist even if the level and patterns of individual lifetime earnings were the same in the two populations, so long as the age structures continued to differ. A 20 year old near the start of his career does not in general expect to receive as much income as he will receive at the age of 40: individuals characteristically tend to increase their ability to do work, reach some peak, and then decline as the composite result of changes in their knowledge, strength, energy, and so forth. So two individuals in the same line of work at different stages in their life cycles would expect to receive different incomes if equal work is paid equally and their lifetime earnings are equal.

In fact, the nonwhite population has a very different age structure from that of whites. For example, in 1967 the median age for Negroes (who make up the overwhelming bulk of the nonwhite population) was 21.1 compared with 29.1 for whites. The median age for Negro men was 19.7 compared with 28 for whites. These relationships apparently have been altering drastically in recent years, and it seems that race differences in median ages used to be considerably smaller. At any rate, they are smaller now for the part of the population that is over 14 years old and receives income: in 1967 Negro men *with income* had a median age of 38.9 compared with 41.8 for white men. As a consequence of the differing age structures of income receivers, if Negro men had the same lifetime earnings—that is, the same earnings as whites for each age group—then median income would be some 98 percent of white median income, and income levels would be lower than those of whites for most of the income distribution, especially at the low end. Near the 7th percentile, for example, it would be less than 84 percent of whites. (This calculation was made by taking white incomes at each age group and assigning these incomes to a population with the Negro age structure.) Yet these do not appear to be welfare differences or, therefore, differences in welfare resulting from discrimination. With such a transformation, there would still be inequalities but not necessarily inequities. In fact, it seems likely that such income equalities due to differences in age structure may continue to increase for the next few years. This, at any rate, is suggested by the greater disparity between the age structures of the Negro and white populations as a whole, as distinct from the age disparity of the populations of working age with income.

However, if the adjustment is made the other way around—that is, if instead of assigning white incomes to Negro age cohorts, one used the white age structure with Negro incomes—then this hypothetically older Negro population would experience, as the result of that artificial advance to later stages in lifetime earning careers, little or no improvement in income for most of the distribution. For men, the improvement in the ratio of median incomes would be only 1/4 of 1 percentage point and would average about 1 percentage point across the distribution. It is of interest that this adjustment shows a more sizable improvement at the lowest percentiles. For example, it makes a ratio difference of .07 near the 11th percentile, but less than .01 for all of the upper two-thirds of the distribution (see Figure 1-20). For women, the ratio of median incomes would actually drop by about 8 percentage points with this adjustment.

The results of this second statistical adjustment are of substantive significance. The difference between assigning white incomes to the black age distribution and assigning black income to the white age distribution means that the life pattern of earnings for blacks is very different from that of whites; that, in particular, the payoff to increased age and experience is less for blacks.[25] Blacks are concentrated in less skilled jobs where, in general, long experience contributes less to productivity. Even where they are in jobs where experience would count, they are likely to have come to these jobs with less of the formal schooling that

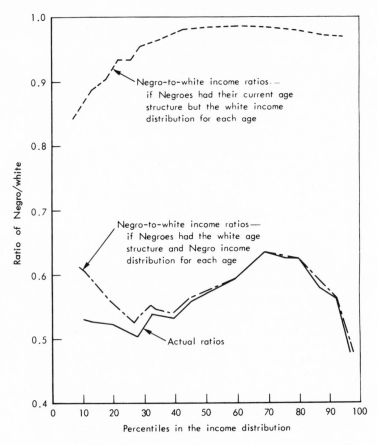

Figure 1-20. Relative Male Income Adjusted for Age, 1967.

would enable them to benefit from on-the-job training, to receive less on-the-job training, and to be rewarded less for the training and education that they have received. The data, however, do not permit separating these complementary factors.

We observed above that the difference in white and black median ages for income receivers is less than the difference for median ages of the two entire populations. This suggests that measuring changes over time for distributions adjusted for age differences for men would show a greater relative improvement than in the case of the unadjusted distributions and particularly at the low end. This is in fact the case, as shown in Figure 1-21, which compares adjusted distributions for men for the years 1949 and 1967.[26] This result confirms and amplifies our earlier observations about improvements at the low end of the income distribution based on data not controlled for age.

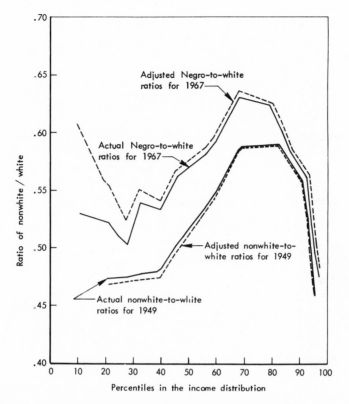

Figure 1-21. Changes over Time in Age Adjusted Relative Income for Men, 1949 and 1967.

Present and Past Discrimination,
Genetics, and So On

It is a fact of common observation that discrimination exists in the labor market today. Quite frequently nonwhites do not get paid equally for equal work. It is also obvious, however, that this is only part of the problem. In many cases, members of a minority receive less money because they do not do equal work, and they do not do equal work because they did not have an equal opportunity to acquire the relevant formal schooling or informal training. This is not a case of *current* discrimination by an employer against an employee: the current difference is the result of a *past* discrimination that narrowed the earlier educational choices available to the minority. Moreover, the difference in educational advantage may have to do not merely with the number of years spent in school, or even the "quality" of the schooling, but with its content. Some members of a minority may have gone to school the same number of years in schools measurably no worse than the majority schools, but the schooling may be less relevant for maximizing earnings.[27] Or the informal education that takes place outside the school in the extended family or among peers or on the job may have been poorer for that purpose.

Moreover, these various disabilities interact. The chances for benefiting from years in school are likely to be limited by disadvantages in the knowledge and motivations gained outside of school. The combined disadvantage, therefore, is not simply a sum but, as Thurow suggests, more like a product of many separate disadvantages. Finally, many of the factors are hard to define or measure. "Education," especially "informal education," covers not only the transfer of information but the instilling of motives or values that improve the chances for doing productive work in our society; the quality of formal schooling is not measured adequately by the pay of teachers or the cost of school buildings or scores in reading or arithmetic; and the inadequacies of measurement both in respect to quality and content seem likely to increase with the increasing numbers of years of schooling measured. And on many of the component factors there are few or no data.

These examples suggest how hard it is to disentangle the effects of current discrimination in the marketplace from the various results of multiple past discriminations that may in turn have made it unlikely that a minority can compete currently on equal terms. While the fact of current as well as past discrimination is clear enough, the precise magnitudes involved are not clear and, it appears to us, given our present state of knowledge, they are likely to resist exact determination. The proportion of the current income differences that is attributable to current discrimination in the marketplace is extremely difficult to determine and, in spite of several attempts, does not seem to us to have been measured convincingly.

Paradoxically, the logical structure of many models that have been used to measure current discrimination against nonwhites has been almost identical with that of models used to measure a supposed nonwhite innately inferior productivity. In both cases, the model builder attempts to show that only part of the difference in the reward or achievement can be explained as a result of some list of factors explicitly treated. The fact that the model leaves a sizable part of the variance unexplained may be taken in the one case as a measure of discrimination, and in the other as a measure of the genetic difference between races. This odd logical identity was illustrated recently in Arthur Jensen's (1969) well-known controversial article, "How Much Can We Boost IQ and Scholastic Achievement?" Jensen mustered a miscellany of study results that he interprets as evidence for innately lower Negro average intelligence, scholastic performance, and, apparently (the article is not precise in this respect), occupational status and differential earnings of men with the same schooling in the same line of work. The cited miscellany included studies of quite a few scholars who themselves interpret their results as measuring the effects of discrimination: James Coleman, Otis Dudley Duncan, Rashi Fein, and Daniel P. Moynihan.

We are not arguing against the use of simple models. Our view is that simple models are fine and, to the extent that they work, the simpler the better. But if a model does not provide an adequate explanation of a complex process, there is no logical basis to use its inadequacies as if they explained and precisely measured something not actually included in the model.

The logical problem is quite analogous to that affecting some economic models designed in the past ten or fifteen years to show the contribution of a specified list of inputs to the measured growth in output. There was a tendency, especially early on, to identify the residual growth of output not explained by changes in input quantities as an increase in the productivity of the inputs and, specifically, as a measure of the contribution of "new knowledge" to increases in output. But, of course, the residuals included errors in estimates of the influence on growth of those factors taken into account, and the influence of all factors not taken into account; the simpler and more inadequate the model the larger the apparent influence of "new knowledge."

Careful attempts to explain differences in earnings between various groups, say between professional and nonprofessional workers, run into quite analogous problems. The careful, early investigation of Friedman and Kuznets (1945) into professional incomes before World War II estimated that: (1) professionals earned on the average between 85 percent and 180 percent more than nonprofessionals; but (2) the extra costs, direct and indirect, of the long training needed for professional work would have called for, at most, a 70 percent extra return to make professional and nonprofessional pursuits equally attractive financially. A very plausible explanation of at least part of this difference between extra returns and extra costs is that the professions are "noncompeting groups." (Young men are not equally able to finance professional training, are not equally aware of opportunities for professional work, and social and economic stratification makes it much easier for some to enter professions and to succeed in them.) But it is also not implausible to assume, for example, that professional work attracts people with higher-level abilities than nonprofessional work. Inference from this analysis had to be qualified accordingly.

It is plain that both public and private institutions have offered nonwhites lesser opportunities than whites to get productive training and education, and that nonwhites have had a much more restricted range of choice among occupations. Further, it is clear that the prejudices of customers, employers, and fellow workers reduce nonwhite productivity in many jobs. Color prejudice, then, has much the same effect on the earnings of nonwhites as would a difference in ability. But the economic and educational processes involved in this result are enormously complicated and the forces that affect learning and the ability to earn money in the marketplace are highly confounded. Our understanding is quite limited. The empirical models available employ, for the most part, variance or correlation analysis or regressions with rather crude linear or sometimes log linear relations, a rather short list of quite coarse variables, and with a good many relevant variables left out of account altogether.

When we say, for example, that we are "controlling for" (or "adjusting for," or "holding constant") "occupation" or "education," it is important to bear in mind that we are not literally talking of " . . . men with the same schooling and in the same line of work" (Jensen, 1969: 16) who exhibit differences in income or employment rates, or the like. Rather, so far as occupation is concerned, we are talking about people within some very broad category of disparate jobs, one of a small number of sets of jobs into which we have partitioned gainful work. Becker (1957) uses 3 categories; Hiestand (1964), 7; Gilman (1963), 10 (as do we in the occupational adjustments presented below); Blau and Duncan (1967), 17; and so on for larger numbers of still heterogeneous sets. But even in a 17-occupation breakdown of males, a "single line of work," such as "salaried professionals," includes physicians and surgeons as well as primary and secondary school teachers. In 1968, the mean earnings of the former were $16,273, nearly double that of the $8,240 mean for the teachers. And of course nonwhites are much scarcer among physicians and surgeons than they are among teachers. The distinction between occupational differences and differences in skill and reward within the same occupation is to a considerable extent arbitrary, even when jobs are quite narrowly defined. But the broad categories of jobs for which relevant current data are available neglect a variety of differences that need to be controlled for a moderately convincing analysis of either the effects of current market discrimination or of differences in ability, to say nothing of distinguishing between the effects of discrimination and those of ability.

Analogous comments, of course, apply to controlling for years of schooling as a surrogate for education; and for a good many other variables that figure in the familiar models. And these are only some of the limitations of the familiar models. (1) Some models regress income on variables such as "occupational status" as well as schooling, but determine "occupational status" as a linear function of income and schooling in some past year. (2) The forms of regression used, in general, lend themselves mainly or solely to the use of a summary statistic for the dependent variable (for example, mean or median incomes or the non-white to white ratio of means or medians), even though comparisons at other points in the distribution are quite relevant to the policy points at issue. It is not surprising, then, that in general a substantial part of the variance in nonwhite-white income differences (or unemployment rates or scholastic achievement or IQ) is not associated with the coarse variables of the models.[28]

Fortunately, policy choices need not wait for complete understanding. We do not have to know the exact dividing line between the effects of past and current discrimination to support programs to reduce both. It is plain that both are very substantial and that they reinforce each other.

As for possible genetic difference, our view is not unlike that of Eckland (1967: 173-94) and of Duncan (1969), and, even more, that of the geneticists James F. Crow (1969: 153-61) and Joshua Lederberg (1969 a, b, and c). There are, of course, native differences among individuals in abilities of various sorts.

So far as race differences are concerned, however, genetic theory does not imply that each of the various traits associated with skin color has persisted because it has had a survival value in past environments, nor that the effects are immutable. And genetic theory has even less to say about the relation of race differences to the complexities of contributing to the product of a modern industrial society. The mischief to be done by rejecting a true hypothesis that there are no substantial genetic factors disabling nonwhites from contributing on a par with whites is so large compared with the consequences of accepting that hypothesis if it is false, that the null hypothesis seems the appropriate one on moral and political grounds as well as scientific ones. The appropriateness of this stance is reinforced by a candid and realistic view of the many limitations in our studies and in our understanding of these matters.[29]

With these caveats in mind, we turn to a summary of preliminary work on white-nonwhite differences in income distributions associated with differences in the distribution of major occupations and years of schooling.

Occupational Distributions

Nonwhites are greatly overrepresented in some jobs and underrepresented in others, a kind of occupational segregation. Many studies have measured this dissimilarity of the nonwhite and white occupational distributions (see Hare, 1962; Hodge and Hodge, 1965; Taeuber, Taeuber, and Cain, 1966).

While a very substantial occupational dissimilarity appears to be bad in itself, as are segregated housing and schools, the mere fact of dissimilarity does not offhand appear to explain why nonwhites have lower incomes than whites. It is conceivable that occupations might be "separate but equal" so far as income is concerned. The relation of dissimilarity, in fact, is symmetrical with respect to whites and nonwhites. Nonwhites may be scarce in "white occupations" because they are excluded. Whites may be scarce in "nonwhite occupations" because they regard them as nonwhite and inferior. Whatever the reasons for the segregation, the effects might be the same. A nonwhite in the jobs accessible to him has to compete with an extra supply of nonwhites who are capable of working in "white occupations" but are excluded from them. And he is free from the competition of the whites who chose to work elsewhere. A white, on the other hand, would experience a parallel extra competition from members of his own race whose prejudices limit their choice, and would benefit by freedom from the competition of the excluded nonwhites.

The earnings disparity stems from the fact that nonwhites find it specifically hard to get into higher-paying occupations and seem to be disproportionately limited to a range of occupations in which they can produce less and are paid less at the margin than whites.

There has been a considerable reduction in occupational dissimilarity in the last decade and a shift of nonwhites to higher-paying occupations. The improvement by 1967 was larger than had been anticipated, for example, in the National Planning Association projection made early in the 1960s for the year 1972. Many shifts expected by 1972 (see Northrup and Rowan, 1965: 30, Table I) had occurred by 1967 (Hodge, 1969: 20 ff), and the others were ahead of schedule. Nonetheless, in 1967 nonwhites were greatly underrepresented in high-paying occupations.

In Table 1-1 comparing white and nonwhite earnings for men in 1967 by major occupational categories, we note first that the relative status of nonwhites within occupations (as measured by the ratios of nonwhite to white median earnings) varies across different occupations. Second, the ratio of overall nonwhite to white median earnings is lower than any of the ratios for component occupation groups, with the exception of farmers and farm managers. The lower overall ratio is a result of the difference in the occupational distributions of whites and nonwhites. Nonwhites are proportionately overrepresented in occupational categories such as operatives, laborers, and service workers, and underrepresented in generally better-paying categories such as professional and technical workers; managers, officials, and proprietors; craftsmen and foremen; and sales workers.

We would like to separate the effects of broadly different occupational distributions from the effects of different earnings within major occupation groups. To be sure, we have already stressed that the "within-occupation" differences for the ten major occupations reflect large contrasts in jobs within each category. Among "professional, technical, and kindred workers," independent professionals receive much higher incomes than salaried professionals and may perform rather different functions. And, once again, the salaried professionals include poor ministers as well as rich surgeons.

*The Effects of Improving the Job
Distribution of Nonwhite Men*

To estimate the effect of the different occupational distributions (using the categories given in Table 1-1) on the overall earnings differences, we make an adjustment on nonwhite male earnings as follows. We calculate a new nonwhite earnings distribution from the actual earnings distribution by "reassigning" nonwhites among the ten occupational classes so that the proportion of nonwhites in each occupational class is the same as that of whites (that is, in effect, we make white and nonwhite occupational distributions operationally equal), but nonwhites are assigned the same earnings within each category as they now receive. The result of this adjustment is an increase in the nonwhite to white earnings ratio of about 12 percentage points at the median (that is, it would increase from .601 to about .723). The effect of this adjustment also, however, is different for points below the median than for points above the median (see Figure

Table 1-1
Ratio-at-Quantiles for Males Who Had Earnings, by Occupation Group of Longest Job[a] by Color, 1967

Occupation Group	Medians			Means			Proportions[b]	
	W	NW	NW/W	W	NW	NW/W	W	NW
Professional, technical, and kindred	$9090	$5971	.657	$9667	$6197	.641	.135	.073
Farmers and farm managers	2804	970	.346	4053	2155	.532	.041	.019
Managers, officials, and proprietors	8897	5831	.655	10144	6846	.675	.136	.037
Clerical and kindred	6088	5104	.838	5722	4803	.839	.072	.069
Sales workers	6103	4665	.764	6404	4714	.736	.063	.019
Craftsmen, foremen, and kindred	7089	5019	.708	6929	4907	.708	.198	.121
Operatives and kindred workers	5677	4423	.779	5443	4440	.816	.192	.243
Service workers, except private household	3886	3148	.810	4160	3244	.780	.066	.150
Farm laborers and foremen	885	681	.769	1639	1085	.662	.026	.073
Laborers, except farm and mine	2472	2915	1.179	3192	3071	.962	.070	.193
Total	$6290	$3780	.601	$6621	$4009	.605	1.000	1.000
Total for year-round full-time	7396	4964	.671	8131	5125	.630		

[a]10.1 percent of men who had earnings in 1967 were nonwhite.
[b]Proportions for occupations are proportion of earners who belong to that occupation group.

1-22). The increase in the nonwhite to white ratio averages about 18 percentage points in the lower half of the distribution and about 11 percentage points in the upper half. Therefore the ratio curve declines at the top even when the earnings distribution is adjusted for the current differences between the distribution of whites and nonwhites among major occupations. While such a redistribution does more for nonwhites at the low end, the ratios that would result from this adjustment are still substantially below 100 percent throughout the entire earnings distribution. The average proportion of the ratio disparity closed by the adjustment based on these 10 categories is about one-third.

The Effects of Improving the Job
Distribution of Nonwhite Women

In the case of earnings to women in 1967, we again find that the nonwhite to white ratio of median earnings in the aggregate is lower than any of the ratios for component occupational groups (see Table 1-2). In fact, the ratios are above 100 percent in about half of the categories. The most substantial difference, however, is in the white and nonwhite distributions among the occupational categories. Fourteen and one-tenth percent of white women were professional and technical workers, and 33.8 percent of white women were in the category clerical and kindred workers, while only 8.8 percent and 16.4 percent of nonwhite women were in these two categories, respectively. On the other hand, 23.5 per-

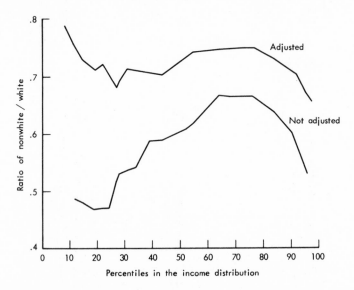

Figure 1-22. Ratio-at-Quantiles of the Income Distribution for Men, with Adjustment for (10-class) Occupational Categories, 1967.

Table 1-2
Ratio-at-Quantiles for Females Who Had Earnings, by Occupation Group of Longest Job[a] by Color, 1967

Occupation Group	Medians			Means			Proportions[b]	
	W	NW	NW/W	W	NW	NW/W	W	NW
Professional, technical, and kindred	$4481	$5148	1.149	$4513	$4941	1.095	.141	.088
Clerical and kindred	3362	3014	.896	3252	3026	.931	.338	.164
Sales workers	1335	1980	1.483	1791	2166	1.209	.078	.023
Operatives and kindred	2785	2384	.856	2709	2319	.856	.153	.174
Private household workers	371	821	2.213	636	1012	1.591	.056	.235
Service workers, except private household	1335	1844	1.381	1749	2037	1.165	.154	.227
Farm laborers and foremen	398	325	.817	693	390	.563	.013	.051
Total	$2461	$1694	.688	$2863	$2209	.772	1.000	1.000
Total for year-round full-time	4279	3258	.761	4457	3454	.775		

[a]12.9 percent of women who had earnings in 1967 were nonwhite.
[b]Proportions for occupations are proportion of earners who belong to that occupation group.

cent of nonwhite women who had earnings were private household workers, while only 5.6 percent of white women were. So it appears that most of the earnings disparities between white and nonwhite women could be closed with an occupational redistribution.

Performing the same kind of adjustment for women that has already been described in the case of men, we find support for the above statement. With the occupational adjustment, the ratio of nonwhite to white median earnings for females improves from about 69 percent to about 99 percent. The adjustment puts the ratio above unity for the lower half of the distribution (averaging about 108 percent) and close to unity in the upper half (averaging about 97 percent). Only at the top of the last decile does the adjustment yield little or no improvement (see Figure 1-23). Differences in the distribution among major occupations, then, account for nearly all of the disparities for women, except at the highest income percentiles.

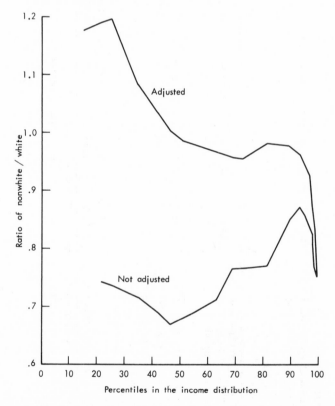

Figure 1-23. Ratio-at-Quantiles of the Income Distribution for women, with Adjustment for (7-class) Occupational Categories, 1967.

The Distribution of Schooling

The difference between nonwhite or Negro and white median years of schooling for those 25 years and older has been decreasing in recent years but it is still sizable: in 1967 the median was 12.2 for white and 9.4 for Negro men. For 25 to 29 year olds, the gap at the median appears by 1967 to have almost vanished (12.6 for whites and 12.2 for Negroes).

As in the case of income, however, so with years of schooling; the use of medians alone can be deceptive. The distributions of schooling remain very different; even for 25 to 29 year olds it appears that, while the medians are very close, all this means is that most nonwhites as well as whites finish high school.[30] In the upper half of the distribution of whites, however, much larger numbers go on to graduate school or at least graduate from college. In the case of men aged 25 to 29, 75.5 percent of whites and 58.1 of blacks had completed 12 or more years of schooling; the proportions that had completed 13 or more years are only 34.3 percent and 14.5 percent respectively. Among those who completed high school, then, a much smaller proportion of blacks than whites received any additional schooling. The higher black dropout rate occurs at all schooling levels. The proportions that completed 16 or more years of schooling were 19.1 percent and 5.3 percent, and for 17 or more years they were 7.9 percent and 1.0 percent.

While the difference in years of schooling completed at the 50th percentile (the median) is only .4 years, the difference at the 80th percentile is 2.8 years (12.9 and 15.7 years for blacks and whites respectively). And even for the lower end, the differences are all larger than .4. For example, at the 20th percentile the difference is 1.5 years (9.6 and 11.1 years, respectively).[31]

Increased schooling is clearly useful for raising nonwhite dollar income in absolute terms and is plausible for increasing the overall relative income of the nonwhite working population compared with whites. But the income of nonwhites with a given level of schooling need not thereby rise compared with the income of whites with an equal number of years of schooling. In fact it is commonplace in the literature to suggest that as nonwhites become better educated (or at least acquire more years of formal schooling), they increasingly find themselves with *lower* relative income than whites of equal education (or at any rate the same number of years of schooling). In this sense, nonwhite "relative poverty" might be expected to worsen as nonwhites catch up with whites in schooling and even as the nonwhite population *as a whole* gains on whites in income.

Marginal Returns to Schooling for
Whites and Nonwhites

Several studies indicate that nonwhite marginal returns to extra years of schooling are smaller than white. These studies are only in part comparable. Some measure "returns" as increased occupational status as in Blau and Duncan (1967: 207-41; Duncan and Duncan, n.d.), or earnings as in Hanoch (1965; 1967: 310-29), and in Herman Miller (1966: 123-67), or a reduced index of occupational dissimilarity between nonwhites and whites as in both Hare (1962: 118-19) and Siegel (1965: 41-57), or total money income as in S.M. Miller and Roby (1968; 1967: 16-52), or money wages and salaries as in Zeman (1955). The categories used for years of schooling cannot be exactly matched, and graduation years plainly contrast in importance to adjacent years when dropouts occur. Beyond high school, in some of these studies the data permit only the category "13 or more years of schooling"; in other studies "13 to 15" and "16 years and over." In still others, graduate level education is separable in a category of 17 years and over. Finally, these studies refer to different points in time: Zeman to 1939, Hanoch to 1959, Hare to 1939 and 1949, and so on. Nonetheless, they appear to agree in finding that returns, variously measured, increase with increasing years of schooling less for nonwhites than for whites, generally through the level of one or more years of college. At least a few commentators have taken this apparent relative decline with increased schooling as arguing against the current stress on formal education for nonwhites.

But first it should be noted that if education were more evenly distributed as between whites and nonwhites, such an income decline relative to whites with the same years of schooling, as schooling increases, would nonetheless go along with a very sizable increase not only in the absolute dollar income of nonwhites but also in the relative income of the nonwhite population as a whole.

Second, a decline in the nonwhite to white income ratios with increasing levels of formal schooling might in good part be accounted for by the relatively small investment made in on-the-job training for nonwhites. This would argue not against increased schooling for nonwhites but in favor of following investments in increased formal schooling, as in the case of whites, with a larger investment in on-the-job training, enabling nonwhites to make better use of their schooling. Mincer (1962) estimates that for a nonwhite man with college level education in 1949, investment in formal schooling averaged $13,200, and investment in on-the-job training came to $7,870. The corresponding per capita investments for all men in the United States were $15,900 and $24,300, about one-fifth higher in the case of schooling and more than three times as high for on-the-job training. Mincer's estimates very likely overstate nonwhite to white differences in on-the-job training.[32] Nonetheless, the differences are surely substantial, and reducing these differences will complement a relative improvement in nonwhite formal schooling. The returns to the latter will be higher if these joint effects are not ignored.

Third, it should be observed that none of the studies cited show that the relative marginal returns to nonwhites decrease *steadily* with higher education. For example, Hanoch, whose inquiry on earnings and schooling is the most elaborate and carefully qualified, shows a much higher relative increment for nonwhites than for whites at the graduate level (17 years of schooling and over). Miller's data (1966: Table VI-3) show some increased marginal return at 17 or more years of schooling for the 18 to 64 year olds (the nonwhite to white earnings ratios were .576 for 5 years or more of college as distinct from .521 for 4 years) and this is even clearer for the 35 to 44 year olds (where the ratios are .612 by comparison with .527). Hare found college graduates less dissimilar than college students and college students less than high school graduates. The largest marginal change in Siegel's occupational distributions was a sharp decrease in dissimilarity between those with 3 years of college and those with 4 years or more. Blau and Duncan suggest that though there is a marginal decline in relative occupational status for nonwhites with increasing education, their educational investment does begin to pay off with graduate studies.

Fourth, the gross figures for the population 25 years or over confound the difference between returns to education for given population cohorts of whites and nonwhites and differences due to an increased weight for nonwhites by comparison with whites of the younger cohorts. The more educated nonwhites are, on the average, at an early phase of their lifetime earnings cycle. They are farther from their peak income than the whites. The figures presented here do not correct for this.

Fifth, with notable exceptions, such as the studies of Hanoch and Mincer, most of the inquiries cited have examined the gross relative returns to schooling without any explicit consideration of costs. But both direct costs such as tuition, and indirect opportunity costs in the form of earnings forgone or postponed during the years of schooling, appear to be lower for nonwhites. The relevant cost data are scarce, and they are extremely hard to estimate. Yet they have a quite critical influence on computations of private net internal rates of return. Hanoch (1966: 71, 84) emphasizes that his estimates of the marginal internal rates are most sensitive to errors in the rather arbitrarily estimated initial segments of his age profiles of earnings. Such estimates for nonwhites are particularly doubtful.[33]

Sixth, the earnings forgone, omitted from the gross figures on marginal returns to schooling, can be expected to affect the college and graduate level especially. It is only in the last years of high school, in college, or in graduate school that either whites or nonwhites have earnings to forgo, and one might expect the difference between nonwhite and white earnings to increase with an increase in schooling. Therefore, not only do gross returns to schooling in general understate net returns of nonwhites compared with whites, but the bias very probably increases with increasing years of schooling.

Seventh, even reliably estimated net private money returns would not be decisive either for an individual or for public choice. For the individual, the financial investment model of education only catches some of its major values; education is also a consumer good that may be directly enjoyed, and it offers positions in society that may be valued variously by different individuals and different ethnic groups at a given time. Moreover, a more nearly even distribution of education between whites and nonwhites has social as well as private returns.

None of the foregoing comments, moreover, take into account all the relevant variations in quality and content of schooling, and other inadequacies of our controls.

Finally, it appears that the gross returns to schooling are changing rapidly and it is not safe to generalize from a few years. Using a single year, say a decennial census date or a recent Current Population Survey year, is particularly hazardous. For example, comparing 1966 and 1967, using three categories for years of schooling, there were improvements for males at all levels but particularly at the college level. The nonwhite to white ratios of median income in 1966 were .705, .701, and .653 for the elementary, high school, and college levels, respectively, and in 1967 the corresponding figures were .734, .712, and .751. The improvement at the college level was statistically significant considering sampling errors, but the others were not. This is an important matter, however, because it has been suggested that returns were small at the college level for nonwhite men compared with white men. For both years the ratio for all males 25 and over (.574 in 1966, .604 in 1967) was lower than for each of the three component classes because of the larger proportion of nonwhites in the lower educational groups and the higher proportion of whites in the higher educational classes. About 47 percent of nonwhite males in 1967 had only elementary school training whereas only about 28 percent of white males were at this level. The college level includes about 25 percent of whites and only 12 percent of nonwhites.

Finer breakdowns of income by years of schooling completed in 1967 show that the nonwhite to white ratio of median incomes for men is *not* a monotonic function of years of schooling, although more often than not the ratio does decline with increasing years of schooling. There is improvement in the ratio with the 12th year of schooling, and again for 13 to 15 years of schooling, but the marginal change in the ratio is negative for all of the other schooling categories (see Table 1-3). The marginal changes between adjacent categories are not statistically significant for any, but fitting a straight line to these data results in a negative coefficient for years of schooling. This fit is also not statistically significant, however; it is not possible to make any strong statement about the relative marginal returns to schooling at the median for white and nonwhite men.[34]

Inferences about marginal returns to schooling, however, are usually based on mean incomes rather than medians. For the data points available, the ratio of nonwhite to white mean incomes declined steadily with increased schooling (again, see Table 1-3). Fitting these data to a straight line results in a negative coefficient for years of schooling, and a much better fit than in the case of medians.[35]

Straight line fits on income by years of schooling are not warranted, since a year of schooling is not a uniform unit. The 8th, 12th, and 16th years are gradu-

Table 1-3

Income for Males 25 and Over by Years of Schooling and Color, 1967

Years of schooling	Medians				Means				Proportions	
	W	NW	NW/W	Marginal change in ratio	W	NW	NW/W	Marginal change in ratio	W	NW
Elementary	$3936	$2889	.734		$4533	$3269	.721		.283	.473
High school	7047	5015	.712	−.022	7352	5047	.686	−.035	.470	.410
College	9463	7110	.751	.039	10792	7271	.674	−.012	.247	.117
Less than 8	3118	2570	.824		3758	3073	.818		.139	.372
8	4881	3711	.760	−.064	5278	3992	.756	−.062	.144	.101
9 to 11	6408	4545	.709	−.051	6558	4627	.706	−.050	.166	.203
12	7378	5427	.736	.027	7787	5461	.701	−.005	.303	.207
13 to 15	8299	6418	.773	.037	8994	6267	.697	−.004	.104	.057
16 or more	10740	7868	.733	−.040	12089	8223	.680	−.017	.144	.060
Total	$ 6732	$4064	.604		$ 7404	$4467	.603			

ation years and are thus critical points. The marginal income returns for these particular years should be expected to be higher than for other years. A straight line fit simply averages everything out and thus cannot give an accurate picture of relative white and nonwhite marginal returns to additional years of schooling. Using the nonwhite to white ratios in the regression fit at least handles the problem of the nonuniformity of years of schooling, and the fit on ratios of mean incomes indicates that nonwhite and white marginal returns to schooling follow different patterns— that is, nonwhites have a lower marginal return to additional years of schooling. The differences in the fits for medians and for means suggest the importance of looking at income distributions.

The Effects of Relative Increases in
Years of Schooling for Nonwhite Men

In estimating the effects of differences in nonwhite and white years of schooling completed on the relative income standing of nonwhites, we perform an adjustment analogous to that used for major occupations as follows: we use current nonwhite income levels within each of the six categories of years of schooling but change the weights given to each. The new weights given to nonwhite incomes are the current proportions of whites in each year of schooling category. The result is then an income distribution determined by white schooling levels but nonwhite returns for each level of schooling; that is, we have adjusted nonwhite income for the differences in the number of years of schooling completed by whites and nonwhites. This adjustment shows that the nonwhite to white income ratios for men improve more for the low and middle income percentiles than for the high income percentiles. The average improvement in the nonwhite to white income ratio for the lower half of the distribution is about 17 percentage points while the average improvement in the upper half of the distribution is a more modest 10 percentage points (see Figure 1-24). This suggests again the particular difficulty nonwhites have in getting high incomes, even when years of schooling have been equalized. It should be pointed out here, as can be seen in Figure 1-24, that the ratios are still substantially below 100 percent after the adjustment. The average proportion of the ratio disparity closed by the adjustment for years of schooling for men is roughly the same as in the case of the adjustment for occupations—about one-third.

Relative income by schooling categories improved between 1967 and 1968, although not as dramatically as between 1966 and 1967. The largest change in the Negro to white ratio of median incomes for men occurred for the 13 to 15 years of schooling group, with the ratio increasing from .747 in 1967 to .808 in 1968. There was also a large improvement for those with 8 years of schooling from .765 to .822. The ratio was more stable for the other schooling categories. But perhaps the most important change was in the distribution among the differ-

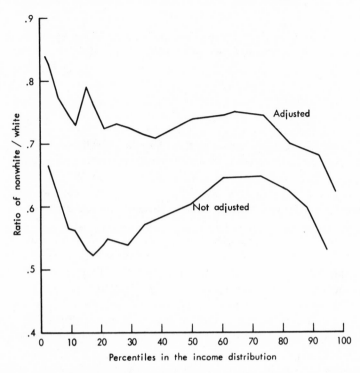

Figure 1–24. Ratio-at-Quantiles of the Income Distribution for Men 25 and Over, with Adjustment for Years of Schooling Completed, 1967.

ent levels of schooling. The number of black men 25 years old and over with four or more years of college increased from 162,000 in 1967 to 271,000 in 1968, an increase of about 34 percent in one year. The corresponding increase in the number of white men with four or more years of college was only 2 percent. And looking back at the number of blacks now in college, we find that the number increased by 85 percent between 1964 and 1968. This change will not show up in the income figures for those 25 and over for several years yet.

The changes from 1967 to 1968 in the nonwhite to white ratios of median incomes for men by schooling categories resemble those for the Negro to white ratios, except at the college level. The nonwhite to white ratio for all men with one or more years of college hardly changed at all from 1967 to 1968, going from .751 to .753, but it did confirm the large change from 1966 to 1967. Moreover, the corresponding Negro to white ratio improved from .691 in 1967 to .731 in 1968. The increase in the total of all nonwhite men 25 and over with four or more years of college was about half that for black men, 18 percent compared with 34 percent. The number of nonwhite men with one or more years of college increased by 74,000 in that one year, and about 65,000, or 88 percent, of those were Negroes. This is a higher percentage of Negroes among nonwhites at the college level than in previous years.

Effects of Relative Increase in Years
of Schooling for Nonwhite Women

In the case of women, in 1966 we find that the nonwhite to white ratios of median incomes improve with additional years of schooling. The same trend is present for 1967. There is improvement from 1966 to 1967 in the ratios for both the elementary and high school levels, but the ratio for the college level, although above 100 percent for both years, declines slightly for 1967. The ratios for 1966 were .803, .850, and 1.126 for the elementary, high school, and college levels, respectively. The corresponding ratios for 1967 were .865, .922, and 1.097. Finer breakdowns on the years of schooling categories for 1967 show improvement in the ratios with additional years of schooling with the exception of the 12th year of schooling (see Table 1-4). Fitting straight lines to these data for women results in better fits than for men for both medians and means. The regression coefficient for years of schooling is positive for women, indicating a larger (proportional) marginal return to schooling for nonwhite women than for white women.[36]

Using an adjustment on the nonwhite income distribution for women similar to that used for men, we find that for the lower half of the distribution the ratios improve by an average of 22 percentage points, which puts the average ratio above unity in the lower half of the distribution. In the upper half of the distribution, however, the adjusted ratios are again higher (by about 16 percentage points) than the unadjusted ratios, but they average about 93 percent (see Figure 1-25). We find, therefore, that an adjustment for years of schooling brings about a much greater improvement in the income ratios for women than for men, although in both cases the improvement is considerably greater for the lower income levels than for the higher ones.

So, for both occupational differences and years of schooling, we find nearly all of the income disparity accounted for in the case of women, while for men each factor separately accounts for roughly a third of the income disparity. Since years of schooling have a substantial influence on the occupational distribution, the two factors do overlap, so that the joint effect would not be a sum of the two. We are now in the process of analyzing data for 1966 from the Survey of Economic Opportunity and tapes for 1966 and 1968 from the CPS. These data, which have recently become available (in particular the CPS tapes), permit us to take account of the joint effect of occupation, schooling, age, and other variables on the entire income distributions of whites and nonwhites.

Table 1-4
Income for Females 25 and Over by Years of Schooling and Color, 1967

Years of schooling	Medians				Means				Proportions	
	W	NW	NW/W	Marginal change in ratio	W	NW	NW/W	Marginal change in ratio	W	NW
Elementary	$1250	$1081	.865		$1839	$1446	.786		.277	.444
High school	2543	2345	.922	.057	2963	2584	.872	.086	.527	.444
College	3898	4275	1.097	.175	4496	4377	.974	.102	.196	.112
Less than 8	1121	989	.882	.080	1640	1324	.807	.062	.132	.319
8	1385	1332	.962	.031	2021	1757	.869	.012	.145	.125
9 to 11	2043	2028	.993	−.042	2546	2242	.881	.047	.173	.226
12	2924	2782	.951	.051	3167	2939	.928	−.002	.354	.218
13 to 15	3082	3089	1.002	.089	3732	3454	.926	.054	.100	.053
16 or more	5126	5594	1.091		5300	5192	.980		.095	.060
Total	$2178	$1700	.781		$2952	$2281	.773			

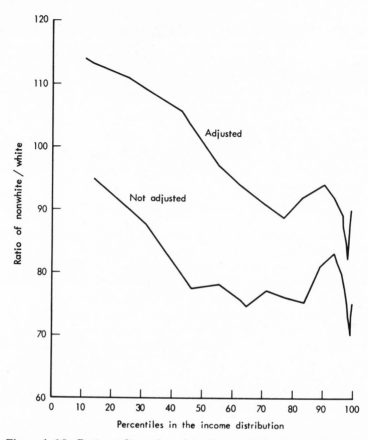

Figure 1-25. Ratio-at-Quantiles of the Income Distribution for women, 25 and Over, with Adjustment for Years of Schooling Completed, 1967.

Concluding Comments on Schooling and
Jobs and the Income Ratios at
Higher Quantiles

Nonwhite relative income would be raised very substantially if we equalized years of schooling between the races, even if the quality and content of schooling were unaltered. And the same goes for equalizing the distribution of non-whites and whites among the major occupations, even if the distributions of detailed occupations were not improved and there were no improvement in non-white to white income ratios within occupations. But each of these changes would leave most of the present gap unclosed and would help the lower more than the upper half of the nonwhite distribution. The top quantiles would show little relative improvement.

Nonwhite to white income ratios tend to be lower for the higher categories of years of schooling and for the higher-paid occupations, though we have seen that these tendencies are not uniform and moreover appear to be changing in recent years. Where nonwhite to white income does decline with increased schooling or increased occupational status, there are at least two ways of looking at the phenomenon.

First, barriers to entry and promotion may be higher at these higher reaches of society. Prejudice, as many have noted, may be particularly strong against admitting nonwhites to positions involving supervision or authoritative decision or high prestige. Whatever its quantitative extent, it is plausible that something like this phenomenon has been at work.

A second way of looking at it is connected to, although it is not identical with, our earlier comments on unexplained residuals and the inadequacies in our standardization of the factors we use in explaining income disparities. Here we would observe that the shaky equivalence of "same years of schooling" and "same education," and the shaky equation of "same census occupation" with "same line of work," get even shakier with increased years of schooling and increasingly high-paid categories of occupation.

Take education, and consider first educational "quality." There has been much controversy since the Coleman report, *Equality of Educational Opportunity*, about the effects of school quality on scholastic achievement. We do not propose to enter the lists in that battle. It is worth observing, however, that a recent analysis by Alex Mood (1969: Tables 1 and 2) of the data gathered for the report shows that the proportion of the variance in achievement between schools associated with indexes of school quality and peer quality increases with increasing grades of school through the 12th grade. Mood's concern is to point out that most of the variance removed can be associated with either the peer or school characteristics and that essentially all of the school effect can be associated with the index of teacher quality. For our own purposes, the fact that the squared correlation coefficients generally increase with increased schooling—that is, that an increased proportion of the variance (the total variance in achievement being almost constant over years of schooling) is associated with either peer quality or teacher quality or other school effects— is of particular interest. For it suggests that the higher the number of years of schooling, the less reliable are "years of schooling" as a measure of "education" or as a predictor of scholastic achievement.

All of Mood's data refer to general education in the elementary and secondary schools. Higher education poses larger conceptual problems for measuring quality and achievement. On these grounds alone, one would suspect the standardization implied in "same years of schooling" to be more doubtful for college and graduate schools.

In fact, while the content of the curriculum in the lower schools may for many practical purposes be taken as one among many aspects of "school quality" to be covered by a single index, this makes less sense at the college level or above. Education increases in differentiation as one goes from grade school to graduate school. Reading, writing, and arithmetic vary between regions, but they are being taught in grade schools in all regions, and nationwide scholastic achievement tests are feasible in principle. It is hard to think of a sensible, common measure or standardized achievement test for the progress of art historians and dentists. It strains usage to identify fine arts or English lit or classics as taught at Harvard as of a lower "quality" than engineering or business administration or medicine at the same institution. (It may strain Harvard usage especially.) Nonetheless, engineers, doctors, and business majors may in general make more money. For explaining disparities in income, "years of schooling," taken without qualification, is likely to lose explanatory force more or less steadily with the increasing level and differentiation of education.

Something like the foregoing comments about schooling at higher levels might apply to an increased shakiness in equating "same census occupational category" and "same line of work" for the higher-paying categories. Within major occupational groups, nonwhites are in detailed occupations that require less training and skill and "for this reason their earnings as well as earnings of the white incumbents of those (detailed) occupations will be low" (Taeuber, Taeuber, and Cain, 1966: 274). Moreover, the low-paid work of the laborer or the household service worker seem much less differentiated than the highly varied skills of the professionals and managers. There is some evidence that there is a greater income variability among professional (and especially independent professional) than among nonprofessional workers,[37] but our own preliminary analysis of recent income data (along with a new measure of internal inequality)[38] suggest that this may not be so. Whether or not the income of professionals has a wider spread, their precise lines of work do.

The inadequacies in standardization of the education and occupation variables appear, then, to make for understanding the gains that might result from a more even distribution of nonwhites and whites among jobs and schooling categories. The increased differentiation of schooling and work at higher levels, however, has some implications for policy: attempts to reduce the income disparity along the entire income distribution might aim more precisely at the kinds of formal and informal education and training best calculated to prepare nonwhites for a substantially higher-paying range of occupations. And, so far as jobs are concerned, private as well as governmental efforts need to focus not simply on entry level jobs capable of barely lifting nonwhites out of poverty but on increased representation in those detailed occupations that might give them an even chance with whites for middle and higher incomes. It may be rather hard to apply fair employment practice laws to promotions for merit within a given line of work. But the more narrowly defined an occupation, the less troubling this may be and the more precisely the nonwhites may aim and prepare to earn higher incomes. This does not eliminate the problem of prejudice against nonwhites in supervisory jobs but it may circumscribe it somewhat.

Finally, we have stressed that the tendency for nonwhite to white income ratios to decline with higher categories of years of schooling has not in the past been uniform. And it appears now to be in the process of change. Hanoch, for example, believes that the reversal at the graduate level of the relative decline in his estimated nonwhite marginal returns to years of schooling may be quite meaningful in spite of all the uncertainties of the estimates. And we suspect he is right, given the analogous improvements at higher levels found in a number of independent studies.[39]

We might conjecture several explanations for such an improvement at the graduate level in past decennial census years. First, it is possible that nonwhite graduate schooling, much more than schooling at the college level or below, took place at predominantly white schools. Up to recently, no all-Negro college awarded PhDs, most did not confer any graduate degrees or had been doing so only for a short while, or had been offering graduate as well as undergraduate training in a range of professions with relatively low prospects for lifetime earnings. (This could be so partly because they were professionals servicing the low-income Negro community or because they were professions that in general paid less.) Assuming this were so:

1. It would have implications not only for the content but for the quality of the schooling (the teachers and the facilities) and for a good deal else that may be linked to higher income. The quality of graduate training would have been much closer to that of whites than the quality of undergraduate training.
2. The improved quality of classroom work would be reinforced by the prior training of the other students who presumably will have come from better colleges. This would help provide some informal learning as well as a taste of the competition with whites to be faced later in jobs.
3. Such predominantly white graduate schools could establish a lot of the connections and information networks useful in obtaining   work in more highly paid occupations later.

The road to top incomes, W. Arthur Lewis (1969) has suggested, runs through a rather select list of white majority schools.

Scientists, research workers, engineers, accountants, lawyers, financial administrators, Presidential advisers—all these people are recruited from the university. And indeed nearly all of the top people are taken from a very small number of colleges—from not more than some 50 or 60 of the 2,000 degree-granting institutions in the United States. The Afro-American could not make it to the top so long as he was effectively excluded from this small number of select institutions. The break-through of the Afro-American into these colleges is therefore absolutely fundamental to the larger economic strategy of black power.

Lewis does not mean of course that top incomes should be the sole target. In fact, he suggests, entry into training programs in the building and printing and publishing industries and others is essential if there are to be relative improvements in the middle range.

The schooling and training of nonwhites in recent years has been changing in content and quality as well as amount. Estimates of the return to further increases in schooling and training need to take these changes into account. Even more, the social return to increased investment in nonwhite schooling and post-school training and to the occupational redistribution of nonwhites depends on the appropriate aims of policy—whether simply to keep unemployment rates low or to reduce the number below a fixed or changing poverty line, or also to even the chances of nonwhites and whites to obtain middle and high income.

Summary and Conclusions

1. From the 1966, 1967, and 1968 data, the most powerful conclusion to be drawn is that nonwhite family and personal incomes are much inferior to white incomes along the entire distributions of each. It is not simply a matter of the middle of the distribution. Still less is the trouble confined to the low ends. The differences are pervasive and they are displayed most sharply in the existence of upper limits that tend to bound nonwhite personal income.

2. "Inequality" among nonwhites, measured in standard ways, is not much different from "inequality" among whites. In the case of families, nonwhite income is slightly more unequal. Nonwhite income to persons is slightly less unequal.

3. Nonwhite income is cyclically more unstable than white. But theory suggests that tight labor markets, like slack ones, have persistent effects; and in fact lasting gains have been made, especially during the very tight labor markets of World War II, Korea, and Vietnam.

4. The ratio of nonwhite to white income to persons did not return to prewar troughs after World War II and Korea, but it did decline with the loosening of the labor market. After Vietnam, it may do so once more, unless a well-aimed and executed policy prevents it.

5. Nonwhite family income has grown relatively faster than white income since before World War II and since the end of it. At the median, nonwhite family income has increased about one-third more rapidly since 1947, and nonwhite income to persons has increased twice as fast as white since 1948—the starting year for continuous (unpublished) annual data on income to persons.

6. Nonetheless, even at these rates, convergence would take place only in a distant future—even for median income to persons at some time near the end of the century.

7. Relative gains over time have been largest at the low end of the distribution. In fact, compared with white, there has been little or no change in nonwhite income at the top.

8. This conclusion is emphasized if one takes into account the sizable differences in the current age structure of nonwhite and white populations and in their relative changes over time. Some of the income difference in the lower percentiles is accounted for by the larger proportion of young people among nonwhites. And, since this age difference has increased in the postwar years, the improvements at the bottom end are larger when income is controlled for age. On the other hand, the fact that such age adjustments do not significantly affect the middle and upper end of the distribution confirms the hypothesis that nonwhites get much lower money returns to increasing age and experience.

9. Adjusting nonwhite earnings for differences in distribution among major occupations improves the nonwhite to white income ratios for both men and women. For men it removes about a third of the disparity on the average throughout the distribution and almost half the disparity in the lowest fifth. For women, where the disparity is smaller, it is erased altogether in the lower half of the distribution. (In fact, the ratio is greater than unity there.) It does less in the high end of the distribution for women as well as for men. Nonetheless, the ratio at the high end for women is close to unity except in the last decile, the top of which is almost unaffected by the occupational adjustment.

10. Adjustments for differences in years of schooling show much the same character: for men they eliminate about a third of the disparity on the average, less than this at the upper and more at the lower half. In the case of women they put the ratio well above unity for the lower half of the distribution and slightly below it for the top half. Both the occupational and the schooling adjustments exhibit the particular difficulty nonwhites have in receiving high income.

11. Equality in years of schooling, or jobs in the same broad occupational category, only very crudely approximate identities in education or line of work. A substantial part of race income disparities, variously measured, may be associated with a few such coarse variables by simple linear or log-linear rules. Not surprisingly, this generally is not so for a still larger fraction of the disparity, however defined. Models that try to use the disparity unexplained by such relationships to separate precisely the effects of present from past discrimination have in general the same logical structure and the same defects as those that take the unexplained disparity as genetic and possibly immutable. In one case the unexplained residuals are attributed to present race discrimination in the marketplace and in the other to race inferiority. But these residuals plainly have a great deal to do with inadequacies in the standardization of the variables, with factors left out, and with differences be-

68

tween the nonlinearities in reality and the simple relations assumed in the models.

12. Some related though distinct comments apply to generalizations about nonwhite relative returns to extra years of schooling. In past decennial census years, several inquiries have found that nonwhite marginal returns appear generally, though not steadily, to decrease relative to white returns with increased years of schooling. It appears, however, that the inadequate standardizations involved in equating years of schooling or broad job categories have become even less adequate as schooling and skill levels increase. This increased differentiation of higher education and higher-level skills (as well as prejudice against putting nonwhites in authoritative, supervisory, or decision-making positions) may account for the behavior of the earlier census data, and also might help to explain why in these past studies relative returns to schooling, after a decline, turn and increase at the graduate level. At the graduate level, nonwhites in the past more frequently obtained their training in white schools. Graduate schools also tend to train people for professional rather than supervisory careers.

13. These relations are changing, and for recent years we find any decreasing trend in gross relative marginal returns for nonwhite men quite weak. But even if the returns to schooling were smaller for nonwhites, this would not imply that more schooling is unimportant for either the relative or the absolute income of the nonwhite population as a whole. The returns to schooling for nonwhites, whether smaller or larger than for whites, are nonetheless positive, and nonwhites are less schooled than whites. Equalizing the schooling distribution (as stated in point 10 above) closes the average income gap by about one-third. In the case of women it appears that nonwhite marginal returns are higher than white.

14. Some final comments on implications for policy. (These comments are based on a larger study of which this monograph is a part.) A good many aims of policy that are loosely connected with the problem of race differences in income have been confounded with it: reducing inequality in society as a whole, poverty, unemployment, ghetto riots, among others. These are all worthy or plausible goals but they are not the same goals.

   a. Eliminating the differences in income between whites and nonwhites need not affect inequality in society as a whole. In fact, if nonwhite men were given the same level and distribution of income as white, this would in recent years have increased inequality (measured by the relative standard deviation or the variance of the natural logarithms) for the aggregate of whites and nonwhites.

   b. Although nonwhites are disproportionately poor, two-thirds of nonwhites are not poor, and most poor are white.

   c. If nonwhite unemployment rates were the same as those for whites, this would help some specific categories of nonwhites (teenagers and women especially) but would have very little direct effect on nonwhite income in the aggregate. In 1966 it would have increased it by less than 2 percent. On the other hand, of the 60 percent increase needed to close the gap, nearly half would be achieved if nonwhites were distributed among the major job categories in the same proportions as whites. And, even if there was no change in occupational distribution, more than half of the gap would be closed if nonwhites received the same rate of pay in each occupational category.

d. Such a convergence of the income distributions of nonwhites with whites can be justified on grounds of equity. It has quite uncertain relations, however, to the problem of reducing the incidence of riots and of increasing public order in the short run. The unsophisticated views that men riot because they are poor or getting poorer are plainly inadequate, but the more sophisticated and paradoxical theories that men riot because things are getting better are not much more persuasive as generalizations. Past and present theories of "relative deprivation" specify in advance too little about the reference group taken as standard to be proved wrong, or to provide much information about the effects on public tranquility of future decreases in the disparity in rewards to nonwhites and whites. Grounds of equity are quite adequate and offer the most persuasive justification for reducing race differences in income.

Notes

1. For the most part we have used annual data for whites and nonwhites since these are available since the 1940s. For purposes of the Census, the nonwhite population is primarily (over 90 percent) the black population. Other nonwhites are mainly Orientals and American Indians. Orientals receive more and Indians less income than blacks. Both an upward and a downward bias, then, affect inferences from white-nonwhite income disparities to white-black differences. The biases do not substantially affect the largest aggregates but are important, for example, in regional comparisons: Orientals and Indians make up nearly half the nonwhites in the West, while in the South almost all nonwhites are black.

2. For full citations, see bibliography at end of article.

3. The term "family" as used here refers to a group of two or more persons related by blood, marriage, or adoption or residing together.

4. See T.P. Schultz, *The Distribution of Personal Income*, Washington, D.C.: Subcommittee on Economic Statistics of the Joint Economic Committee, Congress of the United States, 1965, p. 7, which stresses the variable size, structure, and wants of the family unit and therefore the greater ambiguity of family income data compared with data on personal income.

5. Some of the reasons for our extensive use of logarithms, percentage differences, and the like are given on page 35.

6. Let X = quantiles of the distribution, and Y = the nonwhite to white income ratio for families. Then the straight line fits are $Y = .599 - .376X$ for $0 < X \leqslant .209$ with R^2 .826, $Y = .441 + .336X$ for $.209 \leqslant X < .826$ with $R^2 = .991$, $Y = 1.182 - .565X$ for a $.826 \leqslant X < 1$ with $R^2 = .829$. The slopes for all three fits are significantly different at the 5 percent level from the slope of .1567, which results from fitting a line to the whole distribution. All three fits took account of the sampling errors for each point, that is, each point had a weight inversely proportional to the variance in the estimate at that point.

7. Let X = quantiles of the distribution, and Y = the nonwhite to white income ratio for persons. Then the straight line fits are $Y = .832 - .530X$ for $0 < X \leqslant .382$ with $R^2 = .971$, $Y = .580 + .085X$ for $.382 \leqslant X \leqslant .787$ with $R^2 = .503$, and $Y = 1.116 - .560X$ for $.787 \leqslant X < 1$ with $R^2 = .808$. All three slopes are significantly different at the 5 percent level from the slope of $-.1379$, which results from fitting a straight line to the whole distribution, and the last slope is significantly below zero at the 5 percent level. All three fits took account of the sampling errors for each point, that is, each point had a weight inversely proportional to the variance in the estimate at that point.

8. Forming the nonwhite to white ratio of these proportions with income above $12,000 (that is, 1 percent/10 percent) as a measure of nonwhite disadvantage at that income level has an obvious intuitive appeal. The variation of such ratios with increasing income levels at a given date and the variation over time of such ratios above a given dollar income level have both been suggested to us as useful measures of changing nonwhite disadvantage. In fact, in 1967 nonwhite relative proportions with income above various dollar amounts declined linearly with income from .963 at $500 to .233 at $10,000, suggesting a steady and drastic worsening of nonwhite relative disadvantage with higher income levels. The regression, moreover, was statistically significant at the .001 level. But its substantive significance is slender. The ratios *below* various dollar levels suggest the opposite: a steady relative improvement with increasing income. Something like this measure is rather popular for indicating changes over time and is equally misleading for this purpose. We comment on it in Section III.

9. The South as used here includes, besides the District of Columbia, 16 states: Maryland, Delaware, Virginia, West Virginia, North Carolina, South Carolina, Georgia, Florida, Kentucky, Tennessee, Alabama, Mississippi, Louisiana, Arkansas, Oklahoma, and Texas.

10. The business cycle peaks and troughs as set by the National Bureau of Economic Research for the period are: peak November 1948, trough October 1949; peak July 1953, trough August 1954; peak July 1957, trough April 1958; peak May 1960, trough February 1961. See Geoffrey H. Moore and

Julius Shiskin, *Indicators of Business Expansions and Contractions* (New York: National Bureau of Economic Research, 1967), p. 25. The income figures are, of course, annual totals and therefore tend to hide or distort short-term fluctuations that peak at various other times of the year.

11. See Harry J. Gilman, "Discrimination and the White-Nonwhite Unemployment Differentials," PhD Dissertation, Department of Economics, University of Chicago, August 1963, Chapter 3. Bergmann and Kaun, on the other hand, did find support for the "last hired" hypothesis in their study of Negro unemployment. See Barbara Bergmann and David Kaun, *Structural Unemployment in the United States* (Washington, D.C.: U.S. Department of Commerce, 1966), pp. 90-99.

12. Here and in the analyses of the changes of income distribution over time, we have used unpublished census data to extend the CPS income to persons series back from 1953 to 1948.

13. The marginal propensity to consume, k, can be estimated from income, y, and consumption, c, with the equation $c = k\,y + e$. If we take account of cyclical variation in income, the equation becomes $c = k' \, (y_p + y_t) + e'$, where y_p represents permanent income and y_t represents transient income. y_t has zero mean and some positive variance and is independent of y_p. The regression coefficient for the second equation is estimated as

$$\hat{k}' = \frac{\text{Cov}\,(y_p + y_t, c)}{\text{Var}\,(y_p + y_t)} = \frac{k\,\text{Var}\,(y_p)}{[\text{Var}\,(y_p) + \text{Var}\,(y_t)]} \,.$$

$\hat{k}'$ is therefore an unbiased estimate of k' only when $\text{Var}(y_t) = 0$, but otherwise it will underestimate marginal propensity to consume.

14. See John J. McCall, *Racial Discrimination in the Job Market: The Role of Information and Search*, RM-6162-OEO (Santa Monica, Calif.: The Rand Corporation, January 1970). Also Chapter 7 of this volume. McCall's work, done independently and in parallel with our own, used different methods (a Markov mover-stayer model) and different data (Social Security Administration work history information). It reaches a similar conclusion about the greater instability of nonwhite incomes. See also the articles by Arrow (Chapter 2) and Kosters and Welch (Chapter 3) in this volume, which contain arguments and evidence consistent with these points.

15. From 1945 to 1967 the improvement in family income in the lower half is triple that in the top half. For possible limitations in the 1945 data, see pages 29-30.

16. In fact by 1944: 1945 was a year of recession from the wartime peak.

17. See, for example, the statements of Tobin and of Ross quoted on pp. 5, 6.

18. Fein and Michelson hold the problem is that "the absolute spread between white and nonwhite median family income is rising." Rashi Fein and

Steven Michelson, *The Washington Post*, 14 January, 1968. Vivian W. Henderson writes, "The real predicament" of Negroes is that they are "losing rather than gaining ground in reaching dollar parity," and "People do not spend or save percentages. They spend and save dollars." Vivian W. Henderson, "Regions, Race, and Jobs," in Arthur M. Ross and Herbert Hill, eds., *Employment, Race and Poverty* (New York: Harcourt, Brace and World, 1967), pp. 76-104.

19. The use of differences in this context seems to rest on the assumption that utility is proportional to income, or at least that the slope of utility as a function of income is constant and that prudent persons maximize expected income. At least since Daniel Bernoulli and Gabriel Cramer in the eighteenth century, however, it has been clear that such a rule of behavior is inconsistent with observed practices both of insurance and fair gambling. Cramer and Bernoulli indicated that not expected income but the expected utility of income is maximized. And the utility of an increment in income depends on the amount of income to which the increment is added. While plausible utility functions may differ from each other for extreme values of income, the logarithm of income is the most widely accepted approximation for the moderate ranges of income that include all the income distributions considered in this study. For an excellent historical and critical comment on these matters, see L.J. Savage, *The Foundations of Statistics* (New York: Wiley, 1954), pp. 91ff.

20. The adjustment is actually based on the change in the price index between 1940 and 1967, since the value of the index for 1939 could not be found.

21. See footnote 8, above.

22. The nonwhite to white income ratio $R = (G_n/G_n') \cdot (G_n'/G_w)$, where G_n and G_w are nonwhite and white incomes, respectively, and G_n' represents the income of a population that has the white job distribution but the nonwhite rates of pay within each job category. Thus, the factor G_n/G_n' is an index of relative job distributions with fixed nonwhite income weights, and the factor G_n'/G_w is an index of relative income within job categories, using fixed white job distribution as weights.

23. See, for example, Gary S. Becker, *The Economics of Discrimination* (Chicago: University of Chicago Press, 1957), Chapter 9. In this fruitful and pioneering theoretical work, Becker presented an index constructed by applying 1940 census estimates of 1939 wage and salary weights to three broad categories for whites and nonwhites: skilled, semiskilled, and unskilled.

Elton Rayack has criticized Becker's index for the use of fixed income weights and constructed an index of his own designed to reflect the fact that there is a narrowing of differentials between the average earnings of skilled workers of both races and the average of both races in unskilled occupations. (Elton Rayack, "Discrimination and the Occupational Progress of Negroes," *Review of Economics and Statistics* 43 (May 1961): 209; Gary S. Becker,

"Discrimination and the Occupational Progress of Negroes: A Comment," *Review of Economics and Statistics* 44 (May 1962): 214). Rayack's point, which Becker answers adequately, is quite different from our own. Becker's index measures improvements in job distribution among nonwhites, but it says nothing about changes in nonwhite relative income within job categories. Neither, however, does Rayack's index.

Some misunderstanding may be created by references to the supposed stability from 1910 to 1950 of such an index of the relative changes in the distribution of nonwhites among very broad job categories as implying that there was no change in market discrimination in those 40 years. "The average occupational position of Negroes has risen quite strikingly in both the North and South, but their position relative to whites has been remarkably stable; in the North this was only slightly higher in 1950 than in 1910, and in the South it was slightly lower in 1950 than in 1910. While many important and relevant changes may have taken place in both regions, a very tentative conclusion from this stability would be that neither striking increases nor striking decreases in discrimination against Negroes have occurred during the last four decades." See Becker, *The Economics of Discrimination*, p. 125. Compare also Alan Batchelder, "Decline in the Relative Income of Negro Men," *Quarterly Journal of Economics* 78 (November 1964): 527.

However, for the reasons given, as well as several others connected with problems of separating the effects of past discrimination in schooling and the like from current market discrimination, that index does not measure Becker's "Market discrimination coefficient," which Becker defines as the proportional difference between the equilibrium wage rates for whites and for nonwhites with and without discrimination—assuming white and nonwhite labor are perfect substitutes. A good many such inferences have been much less tentative than Professor Becker's.

24. As an indication of the possible effect, consider the relationship between the rate of change in GNP with the rate of change of white and nonwhite median incomes. Although the relationship is not very strong using only one independent variable, the regression results are nevertheless interesting. Letting x = the rate of change in GNP, and Y_1 = rate of change in median income to nonwhite persons, Y_2 = rate of change in median income to white persons, Y_3 = rate of change in median income to nonwhite families, and Y_4 = rate of change in median income to white families, we find the following equations:

$$Y_1 = -.0866 + .8464x, \ R^2 = .185,$$
$$Y_2 = -.8973 + .5963x, \ R^2 = .354,$$
$$Y_3 = -.2653 + 1.0448x, \ R^2 = .293,$$
$$Y_4 = .5126 + .5807x, \ R^2 = .350.$$

For both persons and families, the coefficient is higher for nonwhites than for whites, indicating that nonwhite income is more dependent on the general condition of the economy. The coefficients are significant at the 5 percent level for all but the first of these four regressions. The years used are 1948 to 1967 for persons and 1947 to 1967 for families.

25. Lester Thurow has studied the joint effects of education and experience for nonwhite and for white men, in 1959, and has found the payoff to experience much less for nonwhites. (Lester Thurow, "The Occupational Distribution of the Returns to Education and Experience for Whites and Negroes" (Washington, D.C.: Federal Programs for the Development of Human Resources, Subcommittee on Economic Progress of the Joint Economic Committee, Congress of the United States, 1968), vol. I, p. 267 ff.) He approximates experience by data on the age of individuals less a constant representing the typical school leaving age for a given number of years of schooling. He approximates education by years of schooling and occupation by ten broad occupational categories. All these approximations are admittedly rough. The use of age for work experience, to take one example, ignores the fact that some of the time after leaving school might have been spent out of employment or in jobs unrelated to the ones in which income was earned in 1959. And there is good reason to believe that this is a more important factor for nonwhites than for whites. That is, nonwhites may typically complete any given number of years of schooling at a later age than whites, and may have spent more time in jobs unrelated to their present work. Thurow's calculation of the return to training or experience assumes that all the remaining income differences by age groups after controlling for occupation and years of schooling are due to a return to experience. But, as he is aware, other factors affect income and several of these may vary as between nonwhites and whites. (See footnote 32, below, for a related comment on circularities in the of lower nonwhite investment in training, measured by lower earnings forgone, to explain lower nonwhite income.) Thurow, moreover, measures the differences in payoff in absolute dollar terms, and the increasing gaps he refers to are dollar gaps.

26. Income by race and age was not available from the CPS for 1949. The data used for the 1949 age adjustment were obtained from the 1950 Census.

27. This point needs emphasizing. It differs from the matter of the quality of schooling that has been much in controversy since the Coleman report. It applies particularly to higher education where one would expect a larger diversity of curricula. In the past most Negroes who went to college were enrolled at Negro colleges: in 1947, 85 percent. (See Gary S. Becker, *Human Capital* (New York: National Bureau of Economic Research, 1964), p. 94n.) While this has changed drastically in recent times, it is reported to be still true of some 90 percent of Southern Negroes. The curriculum was adapted especially to preparing for the two professions in which Negroes had relatively easy access—the ministry and teaching in elementary and secondary schools. And "teaching and preaching" are among the lowest paid professions. Recently there has been a large shift among Negroes toward preparation for careers in business. See *The New York Times*, 22 December, 1969, p. 19.

28. Anthony H. Pascal and Leonard A. Rapping's "Racial Discrimination in Organized Baseball," Chapter 4 of this volume, may be a unique example of a

study that convincingly analyzes the results of current discrimination in the market place, separating its effects from others. For baseball it was possible for them to measure precise line of work, ability, and reward independently.

29. Jensen himself warns that " . . . no adequate heritability studies have been based on samples of the Negro population of the United States," but nonetheless favors a genetic explanation of race differences in achievement. On this Lederberg comments: "This position will be difficult to confirm or refute by any experiments that I can foresee as realistically possible in the face of existing cultural alienation. Large segments of either community refuse to be color blind. How then can we discuss experiments like adoption of black children into white families, with any realistic expectations of their answering such subtle questions as the genetic basis of the development on the brain? We part company on the impact of racial alienation on intellectual development. I believe this is quite sufficient to account for the statistical observations without having to speculate about other genetic factors. Jensen fails to see enough difference in early environments of children he believes to be in comparable economic strata, to account for later school difficulties. We must point out that 'comparable' groups have never been standardized even for simple, physical health or for nutrition during pregnancy." *The Washington Post*, 29 March, 1969a.

30. Years of schooling are recorded in integer values only. But it is assumed that all of those reported as having completed 12 years of schooling, for example, are uniformly distributed between 12.0 and 12.9. A median of 12.2, then, means that the 50th percentile is .2 of the distance between the percentiles for those with less than 12 years of schooling and those with 12 or less years.

31. We use differences at percentiles rather than ratios of proportions for reasons similar to those discussed in Section III on the limitations of such proportions for measuring income differences.

32. Mincer's model, like some other human resources models, does not escape the problems of inadequate standardization involved, for example, in the use of years of schooling as a surrogate for education. Such models attribute differences in earnings of persons of the same age and sex with the same number of years of schooling to differences in "experience." But these lower returns to "experience" actually reflect also lower quality of schooling, less relevant curricula, and a good deal else. "Experience" here is a catchall for many factors that cause nonwhite income to be lower in each age and year of schooling class.

Investment in training or experience defined in this context is measured by capitalizing earnings forgone. In the past it would be lower for nonwhites even if they had experienced the same physical and social processes of training and learning by doing as whites, since nonwhites would have forgone less. That is, their alternative earnings are generally poorer in each age, sex, and schooling class. To use differences in investment so defined to explain income disparities between nonwhites and whites of the same age, sex, and schooling (as some have done) is then circular. On the other hand, while the physical investment in training and experience is hard to measure directly, it is clear that it has been very substantially less for nonwhites than for whites.

33. Hanoch makes clear that his estimated rates of return do not take account of "expected secular growth in incomes, . . . improvements over time in productivity and in the quality of schooling, . . . cyclical variations in earnings, . . . expected changes in relative supply and demand of various skills, . . . the progressive taxation of earnings, and . . . differences in the cost of living." Giora Hanoch, "An Economic Analysis of Earnings and Schooling," *The Journal of Human Resources* 2, no. 3 (1967): 324. Several of these omissions may strongly bias the comparisons between nonwhites and whites.

34. The resulting regression equation is $Y = .8125 - .0052X$ where $X =$ years of schooling for males in 1967, and $Y =$ the nonwhite to white ratio of median incomes. But under the null hypothesis that the coefficient is 0, a value this extreme in either direction could be expected to occur 50 percent of the time, so that this fit is not a very good one. $R^2 = .355$.

35. The resulting regression equation is $Y = .8402 - .0105X$, where $X =$ years of schooling for males in 1967, and $Y =$ the nonwhite to white ratio of mean incomes. Under the null hypothesis that the coefficient is 0, a value this extreme in either direction could be expected to occur about 7 percent of the time. $R^2 = .868$.

36. The resulting regression equations are $Y = .8324 + .0136X$, where $X =$ years of schooling for females in 1967, and $Y =$ the nonwhite to white ratio of median incomes, and $Z = .7593 + .0129X$, where X is as above and $Z =$ the nonwhite to white ratio of mean incomes. Using a 0 coefficient as the null hypothesis for both fits, a value as extreme as the first could be expected to occur about 10 percent of the time, but less than 1 percent of the time for the second fit (on ratios of means). The R^2s are respectively .822 and .972.

37. See Milton Friedman and Simon Kuznets, *Income from Independent Professional Practice* (New York: National Bureau of Economic Research, 1954), especially pp. 71 ff. and p. 390. " . . . the evidence presented, while certainly insufficient to demonstrate that the incomes of independent professional men are more variable than those of any other occupational group, does seem to warrant the conclusion that earnings from independent professional practice display greater relative variability than earnings from all pursuits combined and probably than earnings from most other pursuits taken separately. A similar but more equivocal conclusion is probably justified about the earnings of all professional workers, salaried and independent." p. 80.

38. We form the ratios of "income to professionals" to "income for the total of all occupations" at corresponding percentiles of the distribution in a manner exactly analogous to the method used to obtain the nonwhite to white income ratios. An increasing slope in this curve indicates greater inequality in the numerator group, and a decreasing slope (as was observed in the above example) indicates less inequality in the numerator group. This is easier to see in the case of a

year-to-year income ratio curve. Letting the later year be the numerator, a decreasing slope would indicate that the lower percentiles had increased their income by a larger percentage than the higher percentiles, meaning less inequality in the later year. And vice versa for an increasing slope.

The income intervals in the published data used are not very well chosen for revealing inequalities in the top half of the distribution of high-income occupations such as professionals, and especially for self-employed professionals. We hope to be able to obtain more appropriate data for this purpose from CPS tapes.

39. See pp. 55 and 56.

References

Archibald, Kathleen. *Sex and the Public Service: A Report to the Public Service Commission of Canada*. Ottawa, 1970.

Banfield, Edward C. *The Unheavenly City*. Boston: Little, Brown, 1970.

Batchelder, Alan. "Decline in the Relative Income of Negro Men." *Quarterly Journal of Economics* 78 (November 1964).

Becker, Gary S. *The Economics of Discrimination*. Chicago: University of Chicago Press, 1957.

Becker, Gary S. "Discrimination and the Occupational Progress of Negroes: A Comment." *Review of Economics and Statistics* 44, no. 2 (May 1962).

Becker, Gary S. *Human Capital*. New York: National Bureau of Economic Research, 1964.

Bergmann, Barbara, and David Kaun. *Structural Employment in the United States*. Washington, D.C.: U.S. Department of Commerce, 1966.

Blau, Peter M., and Otis Dudley Duncan. *The American Occupational Structure*. New York: Wiley, 1967.

Blumer, Herbert. "Race Prejudice as a Sense of Group Position." In Jitsuichi Masouka and Preston Valien, eds., *Race Relations: Problems and Theory*. Chapel Hill: University of North Carolina Press, 1961.

Brady, Dorothy S., and Rose D. Friedman. "Savings and the Income Distribution." *Studies in Income and Wealth*, vol. 10. New York: National Bureau of Economic Research, 1947.

Caplan, Nathan S., and Jeffrey M. Paige. "A Study of Ghetto Rioters." *Scientific American* 219, no. 2 (August 1968).

Carmichael, Stokely, and Charles V. Hamilton. *Black Power: The Politics of Liberation in America*. New York: Random House, 1968.

Coleman, James S. *Equality of Educational Opportunity*. Washington, D.C.: National Center for Educational Statistics, U.S. Office of Education, U.S. Department of Health, Education, and Welfare, 1966.

Creamer, Daniel. *Personal Income During Business Cycles*. Princeton, N.J.: National Bureau of Economic Research, 1956.

Crow, James F. "Genetic Theories and Influences: Comments on the Value of Diversity." *Environment, Heredity and Intelligence*. Cambridge, Mass.: Reprint Series no. 2 compiled from the *Harvard Educational Review*, 1969.

Duberman, Martin. "Black Power in America." *Partisan Review* 35, no. 1 (Winter 1968).

Duesenberry, James S. "Income-Consumption Relations and Their Implications." *Income, Employment and Public Policy*. New York: Norton, 1948.

Duesenberry, James S. *Income, Saving and the Theory of Consumer Behavior*. Cambridge, Mass.: Harvard University Press, 1962.

Duncan, Beverly, and Otis Dudley Duncan. "Minorities and the Process of Stratification." Unpublished paper prepared under Contract no. OE-5-85-072 with the U.S. Office of Education as a part of project no. 5-0074 (EO-191), "Socioeconomic Background and Occupational Achivement: Extensions of a Basic Model." Ann Arbor: University of Michigan.

Duncan, Otis Dudley. "Inheritance of Poverty or Inheritance of Race?" In Daniel P. Moynihan, ed., *On Understanding Poverty*. New York: Basic Books, 1969.

Eckland, Bruce K. "Genetics and Sociology: A Reconsideration." *American Sociological Review* 32 (April 1967).

Faltermayer, Edmund K. "More Dollars and More Diplomas." *Fortune* 77 (January 1968).

Fein, Rashi. "An Economic and Social Profile of the Negro American." In Talcott Parsons, ed., *The Negro American*. Boston: Beacon Press, 1967.

Fein, Rashi, and Stephan Michelson. Article in *The Washington Post*, 14 January 1968.

Friedman, Milton. *A Theory of the Consumption Function*. Princeton, N.J.: National Bureau of Economic Research, 1957.

Friedman, Milton, and Simon Kuznets. *Income from Independent Professional Practice*. New York: National Bureau of Economic Research, 1954.

Gilman, Harry J. "Discrimination and the White-Nonwhite Unemployment Differentials." PhD Dissertation, Department of Economics, University of Chicago, August 1963.

Guthrie, Harold. "The Prospect for Income Equality Between Whites and Nonwhites." Unpublished study for the Office of Economic Opportunity, 1969.

Hanoch, Giora. "Personal Earnings and Investment in Schooling." PhD Dissertation, University of Chicago, December 1965.

Hanoch, Giora. "An Economic Analysis of Earnings and Schooling." *The Journal of Human Resources* 2, no. 3 (1967).

Hare, Nathaniel. "The Changing Occupation Status of the Negro in the United States: An Intracohort Analysis." PhD Dissertation, Department of Sociology, University of Chicago, December 1962.

Henderson, Vivian W. "Regions, Race, and Jobs." In Arthur M. Ross and Herbert Hill, eds., *Employment, Race and Poverty*. New York: Harcourt, Brace and World, 1967.

Hiestand, Dale L. *Economic Growth and Employment Opportunities for Minorities*. New York: Columbia University Press, 1964.

Hodge, Claire C. "The Negro Job Situation: Has It Improved?" *Monthly Labor Review* (January 1969).

Hodge, Robert W., and Patricia Hodge. "Occupational Assimilation as a Competitive Process." *The American Journal of Sociology* 71, no. 3 (November 1965). Also appears in *Occupational Assimilation as a Competitive Process: Two Views*. Madison: Reprint 11, Institute for Research on Poverty, University of Wisconsin.

Jensen, Arthur. "How Much Can We Boost IQ and Scholastic Achievement?" *Environment, Heredity, and Intelligence*. Cambridge, Mass.: Reprint Series no. 2 compiled from the *Harvard Educational Review*, 1969.

Johnson, Harry G. "Unemployment and Poverty." In Leo Fishman, ed., *Poverty Amid Affluence*. New Haven, Conn.: Yale University Press, 1966.

Kain, John F., ed. *Race and Poverty*. Englewood Cliffs, N.J.: Prentice-Hall, 1969.

Lederberg, Joshua. "The Meaning of Dr. Jensen's Study of IQ Disparities." *The Washington Post*, 29 March 1969a.

Lederberg, Joshua. "Genetics Can Be as Exciting as Astrology if You Ignore Subtleties of How Genes Act." *The Washington Post*, 5 April 1969b.

Lederberg, Joshua. "Race and Intelligence." *The Stanford Daily*, 21 October 1969c. Reprinted in the *Congressional Record*, 5 November 1969, p. E9 399.

Lewis, W. Arthur. "The Road to the Top is Through Higher Education—Not Black Studies." *The New York Times Magazine* (May 11, 1969). Reprinted from *University* (a Princeton Quarterly).

McCall, John J. *Racial Discrimination in the Job Market: The Role of Information and Search*, RM-6162-OEO. Santa Monica, Calif.: The Rand Corporation, January 1970. Also Chapter 7 of this volume.

McGraw-Hill Special Report No. 2005. "Business and the Urban Crisis." *Business Week* (February 3, 1968).

Miller, Herman P. *Income Distribution in the United States*. Washington, D.C.: U.S. Bureau of the Census, 1966.

Miller, S.M., and Pamela Roby. "Poverty, Inequality, and Conflict." *The Annals* 373 (September 1967).

Miller, S.M., and Pamela Roby. "Education and Redistribution: The Limits of a Strategy." Unpublished essay, 1968.

Mincer, Jacob. "On-the-Job Training: Costs, Returns, and Some Implications." *Journal of Political Economy* 70 suppl. (1962).

Mood, Alex M. "Analysis of the American Educational System." *Journal of the Operations Research Society of America* 17 (Spring 1969).

Moore, Geoffrey H., and Julius Shiskin. *Indicators of Business Expansions and Contractions*. New York: National Bureau of Economic Research, 1967.

Moynihan, Daniel P. "Employment, Income and the Ordeal of the Negro Family." In Talcott Parsons, ed., *The Negro American*. Boston: Beacon Press, 1967.

National Advisory Commission on Civil Disorders. *Report of the National Advisory Commission on Civil Disorders (Kerner Report)*. New York: Bantam Books, 1968.

Newman, Dorothy K. *The Negroes in the United States, Their Economic and Social Situation*, Bulletin no. 1511. Washington, D.C.: U.S. Department of Labor, Bureau of Labor Statistics, June 1966.

Northrup, Herbert R., and Richard L. Rowan, eds. *The Negro and Employment Opportunity: Problems and Practices*. Ann Arbor: Bureau of Industrial Relations, Graduate School of Business Administration, University of Michigan, 1965.

Pascal, Anthony H., and Leonard A. Rapping. *The Economics of Race Discrimination in Organized Baseball*, RM-6227-RC. Santa Monica, Calif.: The Rand Corporation, December 1970. Also Chapter 4 of this volume.

Rayack, Elton. "Discrimination and the Occupational Progress of Negroes." *Review of Economics and Statistics* 43 (May 1961).

Ross, Arthur M. "The Negro in the American Economy." In Arthur M. Ross and Herbert Hill, eds., *Employment, Race and Poverty*. New York: Harcourt, Brace and World, 1967.

Rustin, Bayard. " 'Black Power' and Coalition Politics." *Commentary* 42, no. 3 (September 1966).

Savage, L.J. *The Foundations of Statistics*. New York: Wiley, 1954.

Schultz, T.P. *The Distribution of Personal Income*. Washington, D.C.: Subcommittee on Economic Statistics of the Joint Economic Committee, Congress of the United States, 1965.

Siegel, Paul M. "On the Cost of Being a Negro." *Sociological Inquiry* 35, no. 1 (Winter 1965). Also excerpted in John F. Kain, ed., *Race and Poverty*. Englewood Cliffs, N.J.: Prentice-Hall, 1969.

Taeuber, Alma F., Karl E. Taeuber, and Glen G. Cain. "Occupational Assimilation and the Competitive Process: A Reanalysis." *The American Journal of Sociology* 72, no. 3 (November 1966). Also appears in *Occupational Assimilation as a Competitive Process: Two Views*. Madison: Reprint 11, Institute for Research on Poverty, University of Wisconsin.

Thurow, Lester. "The Occupational Distribution of the Returns to Education and Experience for Whites and Negroes." Washington, D.C.: Federal Programs for the Development of Human Resources, Subcommittee on Economic Progress of the Joint Economic Committee, Congress of the United States, vol. 1, 1968.

Thurow, Lester. *Poverty and Discrimination*. Washington, D.C.: Studies in Social Economics, The Brookings Institution, 1969.

Tobin, James. "On Improving the Economic Status of the Negro." In Talcott Parsons, ed., *The Negro American*. Boston: Beacon Press, 1967.

Tobin, James. "Relative Income, Absolute Income, and Saving." In H.G. Johnson, *Money, Trade and Economic Growth (In Honor of John Henry Williams)*. Cambridge, Mass.: Harvard University Press, 1951.

U.S. Bureau of the Census. *Current Population Reports*. Series P-23, no. 26, BLS Report no. 347. "Recent Trends in Social and Economic Conditions of Negroes in the United States." (July 1968).

U.S. Bureau of the Census. *Current Population Reports*. Series P-23, no. 28. "Revision in Poverty Statistics, 1959 to 1968." (August 12, 1969).

U.S. Department of Labor, Bureau of Labor Statistics. *Monthly Labor Review* (June 1970).

U.S. National Resources Committee. *Consumer Incomes in the United States: Their Distribution in 1935-1936*. Washington, D.C., 1938.

Waldman, Elizabeth. "Women at Work: Changes in the Labor Force Activity of Women." *Monthly Labor Review* 93, no. 6 (June 1970).

Zeman, Morton. "A Quantitative Analysis of White-Nonwhite Income Differentials in the United States." PhD Dissertation, University of Chicago, September 1955.

2 Models of Job Discrimination

Kenneth J. Arrow

Some Models of Racial Discrimination
in the Labor Market

The real subject of this chapter is economic theory itself or, more precisely, the use and meaning of neoclassical price theory in application to the allocation of resources and the distribution of income in the real world. More specifically, these are some reflections that have grown out of attempts to analyze the differentials in income between blacks and whites in the United States with the tools of economic theory. The phenomenon of income differentials is, after all, an economic phenomenon, however much it may be linked with other social dimensions. There is no reason to impose the burden of a full explanation upon economic theory, but it should provide insight into the links between the social, cultural, and individual facts on the one hand and the economic facts on the other just as the theory of production is supposed to provide a link between the facts of technology and the uses and rewards of factors.

My discussion will therefore be a programmatic and methodological one rather than a confident analysis. My intention is to present the deficiencies of neoclassical analysis, as brought out by the attempt to use it as a tool for the analysis of racial discrimination in the economic sphere, and by so doing to suggest the areas in which further research may be more fruitful.

To avoid misunderstanding, let me make clear my general attitude toward the fruitfulness and value of marginal analysis. On one hand, I believe its clarifying value in social thought is great. Especially when dealing with problems central to economics, the difference in approach between trained economists and others, however able, is enormous. The importance of the search for possible alternatives, the value of consistency in different contexts as a guide to judgment, and, above all, the appreciation that the workings of institutions may be such that the outcomes are very different from the intentions of the agents are among the lessons of economic theory. So long as scarcity is an issue and social organizations for coping with it are complex, these principles and their logical elaboration and empirical implementation will be important. Though this is not the place for an elaborate defense, I reject, on both logical and historical grounds, the widespread suspicion that neoclassical economics is simply an apology for the *status quo*.

On the other hand, everyone knows that neoclassical economics is seriously deficient in two directions: (1) its implications, though often exemplified in the real world, are also often falsified (mass unemployment and failures in economic development are the most conspicuous examples); and (2) the implications of neoclassical economics are frequently very weak. Consequently, neoclassical economics says nothing about important economic phenomena. Thus, a highly disaggregated Walrasian model implies a distribution of income; but it would be difficult indeed to say if the observed facts are or are not compatible with the model.

Let us turn to the case at hand. Today, mean earnings of blacks in the United States are about 65 percent of those of whites. This ratio has varied over time; it is certainly cyclical, being higher in prosperity than in recession, and seems to show a very slow upward trend, though one cannot be sure. The tight labor markets of World War II brought a sharp rise of about ten percentage points; the ratio remained near that level until the slackening of employment in the 1950s, after which there was a decline until about 1963 (*Economic Report of the President*, 1970: 200, Table C-20). The present higher levels may be due to the change in political climate, through fair unemployment laws and through changes in attitudes by economic agents, employers, unions, and individual employees, or again it may simply be due to a high demand for labor. We really do not know.

There are differences in unemployment rates partly because of the concentration of blacks in occupations with high-employment rates, but a good part of the difference remains even after correction for the occupational distribution (Gilman, 1965). Nevertheless, the differential unemployment rates are not a major explanation for black-white income differentials. If the unemployment rates were equalized, the earnings differentials would be reduced by only a few percentage points. The bulk of the difference is accounted for by differences in wage rates, partly because blacks are concentrated in low-income occupations and partly because they receive lower wages even within given occupations, at least as conventionally classified (see Chapter 1). In what follows, I will therefore speak of racial discrimination in the labor market as being evidenced only through wage differentials.

What would a disciple of Marshall and Walras have to say by way of economic analysis? The most obvious explanation goes back to Cairnes' noncompeting groups; that is, it concerns the supply. For one reason or another, it can be argued, the marginal productivity of black labor is lower than that of white on the average. Some supply factors indisputably exist. The educational level of blacks in the labor force is lower, and we know from many studies that earnings are correlated with educational level. (As an aside, I am not persuaded that differences of earnings with educational level are entirely due to increases in productivity, but that is a different story.) The educational gap is being rapidly reduced; indeed, there is only about a six-month difference in the median numbers of years of education between the races among those leaving school today (see Chapter 1). But of course this change has not yet had time to have much effect on the comparative average educational levels of the entire labor force. It is also undoubtedly true that the quality of education received by blacks is inferior, though understanding of this fact is not easy to come by. Age distribution is another supply factor; blacks are on the average younger, and, up to a certain point, age is a positive factor in earnings. Less well-known supply factors also have their role. More black families are headed by women. Black families are somewhat larger, and it is apparently a well-established fact that individuals with many siblings earn less.

Various authors have made corrections to the income differential based on these factors (Duncan, 1969: 98 and 106; Tables 4-3 and 4-4). The analysis is indeed reminiscent of sources of growth. The studies tend to show that these factors will, taken together, account for one-half or more of the observed income differential, but there remains at least 40 percent unexplained. No doubt failure to explain is not the same as proof of nonexplanation. There may easily be other supply factors overlooked or not easily quantifiable; motivational differences due to cultural variation and especially the heritage of slavery have often been cited by popular writers and by some social scientists, though the evidence is less than compelling. Thus, for instance, it is frequently held that blacks have, because of cultural and historical conditioning, a stronger tendency to discount the future and, because of this, a lower propensity to make investments in themselves. It may indeed be true that they make less personal commitment with a view toward later reward, and I will return to this point later, but I doubt that this behavior is due to a basic difference in attitude toward the future. If it were, it should also be reflected in lower propensities to save; but in fact repeated studies have shown that at any given income level blacks save, if anything, a higher proportion of their income than whites (Friedman, 1957: 70-85 and references).

Since it appears that supply considerations can explain only part of the black-white income differential, it is advisable to turn to the demand side, which is, in any case, what I am primarily interested in. There are some obvious positive reasons for expecting the demand for black labor to differ from that for white labor of the same productivity. For one thing, we have other evidence that on the average whites act as if they dislike association with blacks. Residential segregation is an obvious and well-documented example. No explanation exists, other than the desire of whites to avoid blacks. The only possible alternative hypothesis would be segregation by economic status, but comparison between blacks and whites of equal income shows conclusively that blacks are far more segregated (Taeuber and Taeuber, 1965; Pascal, 1967). Also, at least in the recent past, discrimination in some labor markets, particularly those where unions controlled entry, has been completely overt.

Another positive reason for arguing that a racial discrimination exists in the demand for labor is that the measured income differentials are greater at higher educational levels. For example, among males aged 35 to 44 in the northern

United States in 1959, the ratio of mean nonwhite to mean white income was 79 percent for those with elementary school education, 70 percent for those with high school education, and only 59 percent for those with college education. Indeed, the mean income of nonwhite college graduates is or was, as of 1959, no greater than that of white high school dropouts (Miller, 1966: 140, Table VI-3). (Incidentally, my shift in reference from "blacks" to "nonwhites" has no deep significance. The Census figures I have just been quoting give only the white-nonwhite breakdown, but in fact blacks constitute the overwhelming majority of nonwhites in the United States.) Since the successive stages of schooling select those most in tune with the needs of the dominant culture in all aspects, including the economic, it is hard to give any explanation for these figures based on supply considerations. It is most reasonable to explain them on the hypothesis of a racial discrimination in demand that is more intense for higher economic positions, the jobs into which the more educated ordinarily go.

From now on I will speak of black and white as being interchangeable in production, at least within given skill levels, so as to emphasize the demand determinants of wage differentials. The relevant theoretical literature is surprisingly small in view of the importance of the subject and the great attention it has received by the public. The main study is that of Gary Becker (1959) some thirteen years ago; still earlier, Edgeworth (1922) had written on some aspects of wage discrimination according to sex. The possible channels by which discriminatory attitudes come to affect wages are well stated by Becker, but what might be termed the general equilibrium aspects are largely ignored; that is, the effects of wage differentials on the stimulation of compensating behavior are slighted, and, as will be seen, these create a crucial dilemma for an appreciation of the value of economic theory.

The most natural starting point for analysis is to look at the proximate determinant of the demand for labor, the employer's decisions. If we assume away productivity differences between black and white employees, the simplest explanation of the existence of wage differences is the taste of the employer. Formally, we might suppose that the employer acts so as to maximize a utility function that depends not only on profits but also on the numbers of white and black employees (see Chapter 6, pp. 187-189). Presumably, other variables being held constant, the employer has a negative marginal utility for black labor. A positive marginal utility for white labor might also be expected, if only in some sense to offset and dilute the black labor. A specific version of this hypothesis would be that the employer's utility depends only on the ratio of black to white workers and is independent of the scale of operations of the firm.

Under these circumstances, the employer will hire white workers up to a point somewhat beyond where their marginal productivity equals their wage, since he is also rewarded through their positive marginal utility. Similarly, he will stop hiring black laborers at a point somewhat before the point that equates their marginal productivity to their wage. Under the assumption that the two

kinds of workers are perfect substitutes in production, the marginal productivities of the two kinds of workers are equal. Their common value depends only
on the total number of workers of both races hired. It follows, then, that equilibrium is possible only when the wages of white workers are above the marginal
product of labor and the wages of black workers below. To be precise, white
wages will exceed marginal product by the marginal rate of substitution between
white workers and profits, the rate being computed at the white-black ratio in
the labor force. A similar statement holds for black wages.

Under this model, it is clear that black workers incur a definite loss, as compared with the competitive level in the absence of discrimination. On the other
hand, white workers are likely gainers relative to the nondiscriminatory level. It
can be shown that aggregate output is unaffected if all employers discriminate
equally; otherwise there may be some efficiency loss in total output. Whether
employers gain or lose in the aggregate is a quantitative question about which a
priori theory gives no definite answer in general. However, in the special case
where it is assumed that an employer's utility depends only on the ratio of the
two kinds of workers, the employer neither gains nor loses, as compared with a
nondiscriminatory situation.

Once we start applying utility analysis to racially discriminatory behavior, we
may extend it to other members of the productive team. In those cases where
the entry of workers into jobs is controlled directly by unions, as in the building
trades, discriminatory attitudes by fellow workers become decisive. The results
are more apt to be total or partial exclusion rather than wage differentials. I am
more interested in pressures that work through the market, however.

Consider white workers who supply services complementary to those of another class of workers, for example, white foremen working with a floor force of
mixed race (see Chapter 6, pp. 189-191). If the foremen dislike working with
blacks, they may offer their services at a higher wage to those firms with higher
proportions of black workers. That is, given the choice of working for different
firms with different proportions of black workers and different wages, they will
choose according to some utility function that represents the trade-off between
wages and the number of white and black workers. The firm's offers of
employment to foremen will then have two dimensions, the wages and the
proportion of blacks in the floor force. But this in turn means that the firm will
have a different demand for black laborers than for white, even if they are
perfect substitutes in production and even if the employer himself has no discriminatory feelings.

It should be understood that the wage differentiation for foremen according
to the proportion of black floor workers may in practice appear in a disguised
form. The cost to the employer of increasing the number of blacks may be measured not in statistically observed higher wages for his foremen but in lower
morale, lower productivity, or simply lower quality of personnel.

If, parallel to our earlier assumption about the utility functions of employers, we assume that the discriminatory tastes of foremen are determined by the *ratio* of blacks to whites under them rather than by the amounts, it can be shown that in equilibrium the black workers lose, the white floor workers gain an equal amount, and neither the foreman nor the employers gain or lose money income.

I have spoken thus far of foremen and floor workers, but obviously the analysis applies to any two complementary forms of labor. A particularly interesting possibility is discrimination by lower-level workers against supervisors. That is, the costs of hiring labor may be higher if they have to work for black supervisors. Indeed, it may be expected that the effects of discrimination of this type are greater than the reverse, and this for two reasons. First, the resentment against working under a supervisor belonging to a despised group may be more intense than the simple dislike of having them close by. Indeed, sufficiently superior social status can certainly completely compensate for nearness, as in the master-servant relation. Second, effects of discrimination by lower echelons against higher may be greater than the reverse simply because there are so many more of the former. Thus, even if the wage compensation needed to work with blacks is the same in two situations, lower working with higher and vice versa, the cost to the employer is much greater in one case than the other.

I find this last observation especially interesting, because it explains why more highly educated blacks are more heavily discriminated against. They would expect to go into the higher-level jobs where the discrimination may be greater.

Parenthetically, let me say that I have omitted still another taste element in the explanation of discrimination, namely, discrimination by customers. If whites dislike associating with blacks in any capacity, they may in particular dislike dealing with them when purchasing goods. Several interesting questions arise here, particularly with regard to the exact social nature of the buyer-seller relation in different contexts, but in any case this aspect is irrelevant to the more normal situation in which those who make the goods do not meet buyers face to face.

At a certain level, then, we have a coherent and by no means implausible account of the economic implications of racial discrimination. In the grossest sense, it accounts for the known facts. For example, the fact that discrimination against blacks increases with the level of education implies that the rate of return to the investment in human capital is lower for blacks than for whites, explaining in turn why the proportion of blacks in college is lower than that of whites.

Still, I do not think this is satisfactory. To begin with, we can be troubled by the lack of specificity in the hypotheses being advanced. This is, of course, a defect common to all utility explanations of economic behavior. The theory does not give any quantitative clues. A marginal productivity theory of demand for labor, true or false, asserts a highly specific relation between the production function and the demand for labor, each of which is observable under ideal conditions. A utility theory in and of itself asserts much vaguer connections, usually of a qualitative nature and frequently not even that. To take a parallel case, we know that as per capita incomes increase, the proportions in which different commodities are purchased alters. This generalization about behavior is, in fact, of the greatest importance from the practical point of view. It can only be explained by invoking the nature of tastes, in technical language the nonhomotheticity of the indifference surfaces. Have we explained anything? I do not want to get involved in the meaning of explanation as an epistemological concept, but it is fair to say that the explanation in terms of tastes is not useless. If we add the assumption that the tastes of individuals are similar, at least in a statistical sense, then we may be able to make inferences from the history of demand patterns in one country to that of another. Similarly, in the case of racial discrimination, we may be able to infer from the behavior of employees of one type to those of another on the hypothesis that their tastes are similar.

The hypotheses of the theory lack specificity in a second sense. They invoke a dislike of association with blacks, but as I have already suggested, the dislike may depend upon the nature of the association. Physical proximity is probably significant only because of its implications for status and for feelings of superiority and of fear. The slave owner and his overseer felt no reluctance to work with an all-black labor force. Railroad and airline porters tend to be blacks. Still the matter is not just one of status; detailed studies show wage differences even in narrowly specified low-level occupations, though these differences are much smaller than the average in the economy. No doubt the general concept of association with blacks has to be broken down into several dimensions. But the fact that utility analysis leads to such more detailed questioning is, in my view, an evidence of its fruitfulness.

The excessive generality of utility hypotheses about economic behavior is, then, a drawback, but one that seems intrinsic in the nature of the case. There is a second objection to this and other utility explanations that I will discuss more briefly; namely, that we offer no explanation of racial discrimination but simply refer the problem to an unanalyzed realm. We all remember Molière's intellectual who explained that opium produces sleep because it contains a great deal of the dormitive principle. Yet in a sense, all scientific explanation involves the same process of musical chairs; all we ask is that the explanatory principles have some degree of generality and parsimony. In the context of racial discrimination, however, one may worry that this advice is too cheap. Explaining an economic phenomenon such as the impact of attitudes, taken as given, on the workings of the economic system is legitimate enough; but what if those attitudes are themselves the result of economic behavior? Specifically, and in more emotional language, what if racial discrimination and the tastes that underlie it are tools of economic exploitation?

I have mentioned two possible difficulties with accepting utility explanations. A third, which I wish to emphasize most strongly, is of a very different nature and has different implications. The question can be raised whether the economic system does not have other forces that counteract the tendency toward wage discrimination. Sherlock Holmes, a man much concerned with the formulation of hypotheses for the explanation of empirical behavior, once asked about the barking of a dog at night. The local police inspector, mystified as usual, noted that the dog had not barked at night. Holmes dryly noted that his silence was precisely the problem.

Have we some dog whose silence should be remarked? Yes; those vast forces of greed and aggressiveness that we are assured and assure students are the mainsprings of economic activity in a private enterprise economy; not the best but the strongest motives of humanity, as Marshall had said. For some employers, the trade-off between discrimination and profits is less than for others. There need be no assumption of higher morality; if interpersonal comparisons are admitted, it might simply be that some employers are greedier than others. Presumably, they will take advantage of the gap between black and white wages by demanding the black labor (see Chapter 6, pp. 191-193). In the long run, the less discriminatory will either drive the more discriminatory out of business or, if not, will cause the wage difference to fall. If we suppose that there are some actual or potential employers who do not discriminate at all, then the wage difference should, in the long run, fall to zero. The discriminating employers may possibly continue to operate, but they will employ only white labor.

This kind of argument is not unfamiliar in other fields of application. As soon as utility-maximizing behavior is introduced into the productive side of the economy, the question arises of its relation to profit-maximization and particularly to the role of competition. The theory of the firm, particularly under imperfect competition, has found a considerable, if fitful, place for tastes. Hicks (1935) noted that a monopolist might prefer a quiet life to maximum profits. Herbert Simon (1959) and his students, especially Oliver Williamson (1967), have suggested that entrepreneurs might seek to maximize a utility function in which other variables entered besides profits: the emoluments of the higher officers and the sheer size of the firm, as well as avoidance of decision making. Marris (1964) has taken up a dynamic version of the size theory; his entrepreneurs have tastes for growth as well as profits.

There has also been a countervailing current of opinion that argues, in effect, that the utility functions of entrepreneurs do not matter. Competition will force firms to maximize profits, since otherwise they will not survive. Even under imperfect competition, profit maximizers will find it profitable to take over firms from utility maximizers. I should note here that from the viewpoint of formal analysis, this case is not as different as might appear from the first; it still presupposes a considerable amount of competition in the capital market.

The prevailing opinion seems to be that the question of utility maximization can be raised only under conditions of imperfect competition. Those who defend the importances of tastes for size and growth usually are first concerned to argue that the firm has potential access to monopoly profits, and it is these that might be dissipated in seeking after nonpecuniary goals.

Upon reflection, I believe the relevant distinctions are wrongly drawn. Even under perfect competition, if I have a taste for size and derive pleasure from it, I might perfectly well accept a rate of return below the competitive level in order to indulge my tastes. Indeed, all the statistical evidence I know of suggests that self-employed businessmen in general are accepting less than a competitive rate of return (or alternatively less than their competitive wage) for such pleasures. A perfectly competitive equilibrium is compatible with utility maximization by entrepreneurs; of course, the price they have to pay for their tastes will depend on the tastes of others in the market, but they are not driven out as sharply as might be supposed.

I want to argue, however, that the hypothesis of competitive elimination might have more force in the case of racial discrimination. More generally, I would suggest, rather tentatively, that this hypothesis might be more likely to hold when the nonpecuniary variables have negative marginal utilities than when they have positive ones. The reason is simple enough: the employer can always avoid the negative utilities and still achieve a competitive rate of return by simply becoming a pure capitalist, a stockholder.

Before going into more details and qualifications, let me again draw an analogy, this time with the spread of innovations. In explaining a failure to introduce an innovation, historians frequently invoke a conservative spirit on the part of the entrepreneurs in question; for example, Landes (1969) in comparing English and French attitudes toward innovation at the end of the eighteenth century. Theorists find themselves puzzled. No doubt it is possible for French entrepreneurs to have, on the average, a utility function that has a negative weight for innovation. But if even a few entrepreneurs for some eccentric reason lack this distaste, they will introduce the innovation and the forces of competition will force the others to follow suit, at the peril of elimination. These competitive tendencies operate through the capital market as well as the product market, of course; new capital will flow to the successful innovators.

No doubt this argument has to be modified in the case where monopoly profits are earned. It will pay the firm to remain in business and indulge its distaste for innovation or for hiring blacks. But the fundamental point is that the competitive pressures, to the extent that they are decisive, work toward the elimination of racial differences in income, under the usual assumptions of economic theory.

Thus, after building up a more or less reasonable mechanism that gives a rationale for linking economic discrimination with other social attitudes, I now argue that if the logic of the competitive system is accepted, discrimination should still be undermined in the long run. This forces us to reconsider the meaning of long-run competition, which I do below. I must also call to your attention that the negative discussion has so far only concerned discrimination by employers. I must also ask whether discrimination by other employees is also eroded over time. This raises some other questions of a more technical nature.

A model in which white employers and employees were motivated by a dislike of association with blacks as well as more narrowly economic motives would give a satisfactory qualitative account of observed racial discrimination in wages but, at least as far as employers are concerned, it is hard to understand how discriminatory behavior could persist in the long run in the face of competitive pressures. Several assumptions have been made, implicitly or explicitly, and perhaps should be restated here: constant returns to scale in the long run, a sufficiently wide spectrum of tastes toward discrimination and in particular a sufficient number of actual or potential nondiscriminating employers, and an adequate freedom of entry. The last condition, let me stress, is consistent with a certain amount of imperfect competition. If there is enough entry by nondiscriminating entrepreneurs to absorb the entire black labor force and some more, then wages would be equalized, but the surviving discriminating firms would now be completely segregated. Obviously, the degree of freedom of entry necessary to eliminate racial wage differentials depends upon the proportion of blacks in the labor force. But, in the United States, the black workers constitute some fifteen percent of the labor force; if employer discrimination were the sole cause of wage differences, it is hard to believe that competitive forces are inadequate to eliminate racial wage differentials.

What then of employee discrimination? Let me take up a case not touched on explicitly before (see Chapter 6, pp. 193-194). Because of its extreme nature, it lends itself to simple analysis. I refer to discrimination by white employees who are perfect subsitutes for blacks. The discussion itself is due to Becker, but I want to draw attention to its wider implications.

Suppose for a simple model that there is only one kind of utility function expressing a trade-off between wages and the proportion of white workers in the labor force of the firm. Any employer can purchase black labor at a fixed price, but for white labor he must choose some point on an indifference curve between wages and the white proportion. A little reflection makes it obvious that if the wages required by whites for an all-white labor force are lower than black wages, total segregation for whites is optimum for the firm, while in the contrary case an all-black labor force is cheapest. We are, of course, still assuming equal productivity for the two races. At a general equilibrium with full employment of both types of labor, some firms must be segregated in one direction and some in the other. It would never pay a firm to have a mixed labor force, since they would have to raise the wages of their white workers above the level for the all-white option. The firms would also have to find the two types of segregation equally profitable; otherwise, they would all switch to one or the other. This requires that wages paid to whites in the all-white firms equal that paid to blacks in the all-black firms. There would be again no wage differentials.

The relation of this result to the possibility of discrimination by complementary types of labor will be discussed shortly, but the model and the kinds of processes of which it is symbolic deserve some attention. Obviously, we are concerned that we have drawn an implication—no wage differentials—that is contrary to observation. We also have drawn another implication—segregation—that is very much a fact. Indeed, some 70 percent of the small firms in Chicago have no black workers at all, although about 14 percent of the Chicago labor force is black. The evidence is that even in large firms blacks tend to be separated by department and by occupation (Baron and Hymer, 1968: 262-63; U.S. Department of Labor, 1969:44, Table 12). Thus, the pure theory turns up with tantalizing results, partly clearly false, partly yielding unusual insights.

The analysis just used, simple as it is, is not typical of economic theory. We tend to infer that conflicting forces will balance somewhere in the middle. Here, on the contrary, it is of the essence that firms prefer extreme alternatives to compromises. In technical language, we have a failure of convexity. The situation is similar to, though not identical with, a famous crux of economic theory, the relation between increasing returns and competitive equilibrium. Here too under competitive conditions the firms will either shut down completely or go to some high level of activity, possibly too high to be compatible with resource limitations.

The recognition of nonconvexities and their importance in economic life is hardly new; we all recall the central role that Adam Smith gave to division of labor and its relation to the size of the market. Indeed, Smith's ideas of specialization among individuals, firms, and even nations are exactly analogous in formal structure to the occurrence of racial segregation in production. But it has proved very difficult to incorporate nonconvexities in systematic general theories. Marx, for example, talks a good deal about concentration of ownership of capital, based on what we would call increasing returns; but his models of simple and expanded reproduction display perfectly orthodox constancy of returns. In the last 20 years, the increasing formalization of economic theory has made more prominent than ever the role of the convexity assumptions that literary economists have always used freely. There is now a growing body of literature, however, starting with Farrell's paper of 1959, that is seriously attempting to wrestle with the relaxation of convexity hypotheses. At least this much seems to be possible to assert: if the nonconvexities are small on the scale of the entire economy, then something like a competitive equilibrium is still possible. But the structure of that equilibrium may be different from what would obtain under convexity. There will be a tendency toward specialization, in the present context toward segregation. Though price levels may not be so much different than they would be in a comparable convex world, the distribution of individuals among occupations and of output among products may display much more concentration on widely separate positions.

Let me return to the problem at hand. The vision of firms rushing from one kind of segregation to another in response to small wage changes is troublesome, and I will come back to that point. Meanwhile, let us ask if the analysis of discriminatory feelings by perfect substitutes has any lessons for discrimination by complementary types of labor. I think the answer is clearly yes, if we suppose that there are black workers available at both higher and lower levels, for then the employer can exploit any racial wage differentials by hiring labor force that is black at all levels. If the proportions of the different skills in the black labor force are different from those desired, the resulting equilibrium will not necessarily equate wages at each level, but there will be a tendency to equate wages on the average. It is possible, for example, that black foremen, presumably scarce, will be paid more than their white counterparts because they are willing to work with a black floor force, which is cheaper to the employer.

We thus see that the structure of tastes that seems adequate to give a short-period explanation does not seem to resist the operations of competitive pressures in the long run. One might search for other and more stable explanatory structures, but I know of none that have been proposed or that seem at all credible. Instead, I propose that we look more closely at the long-run adjustment processes. In particular, as I have already suggested, when dealing with nonconvexities, the adjustment processes may have to be very rapid indeed. You must recall that in these circumstances marginal adjustments are punished, not rewarded. If the firm is to gain by a change, it has to go all the way. Intuitively, we are not surprised that a firm will hesitate to scrap its entire labor force and replace it with another. The problem is to give an acceptable formalization of this intuition.

In several different contexts, there has been a recognition that adjustment, even when convexity is not an issue, is costly in itself. Edith Penrose (1959) and Robin Marris (1964) have made costs of growth an intrinsic part of the dynamic theory of the firm. By this I mean that, if a firm grows in size and capital, the cost to the firm is the accumulation of capital plus an additional term that depends on the rate at which the firm grows. The latter can be explained in several different ways. One is that the organization of the firm has to alter with its size and there is a cost to acquiring new channels of communication and control within the firm. Another is that the firm needs to expand its markets; but a customer, once acquired, will remain one cheaply, so that the cost is that of acquiring the customer and therefore is determined by the rate of growth. Note that in both cases we are really saying that some kind of intangible capital goods is acquired—either communication channels within the firm or goodwill among customers—and these capital goods are costly.

The same principle—that capital costs of an unconventional kind play an important role in economic behavior and decisions—has been applied to the study of labor turnover, a problem more closely connected with ours. Operations researchers, in trying to draw up plans for the hiring of personnel, have incorporated in their models a fixed cost of hiring an individual. Sometimes it is also held that cost is attached to firing as well. These costs are partly in administration, partly in training. Even in the case of workers who have already been generally trained in the kind of work to be done, learning the ways of the particular firm is a necessity. This approach, it has been argued by some, has important general economic implications; it implies that firms should not adjust their labor force very rapidly to cyclical shifts in demand, since they may incur both hiring and firing costs if they do—costs that are avoided if the worker is retained during slack periods. This hypothesis provides some explanation for the well-known fact that the average productivity of labor falls in slack periods. Workers are being held in employment even though they contribute little to output to avoid the costs of rehiring them in the expected future boom. I do not myself know whether this explanation is in fact adequate but merely note that it is seriously considered.

I suggest that a similar consideration explains why the adjustments that would wipe out racial wage differentials do not occur or at least are greatly retarded (see Chapter 6, pp. 194-198). We have only to assume that the employer makes an investment, let us call it a *personnel investment*, every time a worker is hired. He makes this investment with the expectation of making a competitive return on it; if he himself has no racial feelings, the wage rate in full equilibrium will equal the marginal product of labor less the return on the personnel investment. Let us consider the simplest of the above models, that of discrimination by fellow employees who are perfect substitutes. If the firm starts with an all-white labor force, it will not find it profitable to fire that force, in which its personnel capital has already been sunk, and hire an all-black force in which a new investment has to be made simply because black wages are now slightly less than white wages. Of course, if the wage difference is large enough, it does pay to make the shift.

Obviously, in a situation where costs arise in the process of change, history matters a good deal. A full dynamic analysis appears to be very difficult, but some insight can be obtained by study of a very special case. Suppose that initially the labor force is devoid of blacks. Then some enter; at the same time an additional entry of whites occurs, and some new equilibrium emerges. Under the kinds of assumptions we have been making, a change, if it occurs at all, must be an extreme change, but three kinds of extremes, or corner maxima now exist. The typical firm may remain segregated white though possibly adding more white workers, it may switch entirely to a segregated black state, or it may find it best to keep its present white working force while adding black workers. In the last case, of course, it will have to increase the wages of the white workers to compensate for their feelings of dislike, but it may still find it profitable to do so because replacing the existing white workers by blacks means a personnel investment. If we stick closely to the model with all of its artificial conditions, we note that only the all-white firms are absorbing the additional supply of white workers, so there must be some of those in the new equilibrium situation. On the other hand, there must be some firms that are all black or else some integrated firms whose new workers are black in order to absorb the new black workers. It can be concluded in either case, however, that a wage difference between black and white workers will always remain in this model. Furthermore, there will be some segregated white firms. Whether the remaining firms will be segregated black or integrated will depend on the degree of discriminatory feeling by white workers against mixing with blacks.

I have not worked out the corresponding analysis for the case that has several types of workers with different degrees of discriminatory feelings against racial mixtures in the complementary types. Nevertheless, one easily surmises that similar conditions will prevail.

The generalization that may be hazarded on the basis of the discussion thus far can be stated as follows: if we start from a position where black workers enter an essentially all-white world, the social feelings of racialism by employers and by employees, both of the same and of complementary types, will lead to a difference in wages. The forces of competition and the tendency to profit-maximization operate to mitigate these differences. The basic fact of a personnel investment, however, prevents these counteracting tendencies from working with full force. In the end, we remain with wage differences coupled with tendencies to segregation.

This concludes what may be thought of as the central model. I cannot help but feel that still other factors exist. I have two suggestions to make, both of a very tentative nature. The first is that what I have referred to as the discriminator tastes of the employer might in fact be better described as a problem in perception (see Chapter 6, pp. 199-203 and Chapter 7, pp. 205-207, 213-218). That is, employers discriminate against blacks because they believe them to be inferior workers. Notice that in this view the physical prominence of skin color is highly significant. As an employer, I might have all sorts of views about the relative productivities of different kinds of workers. Determining what kind of a worker he is may be a costly operation in information gathering; even if I hold my beliefs strongly, it may not, in many circumstances, be worthwhile in my calculations to screen employees according to them. Skin color is a cheap source of information, however, and may therefore be used. In the United States today, I believe it fair to say that school diplomas are being widely used by employers for exactly that reason; it is believed that schooling has something to do with productivity, and asking for a diploma is an inexpensive operation.

The structure of this argument and the range of its applicability need to be carefully considered. It only applies if the employer incurs some personnel investment cost. Presumably after a worker is hired, his performance is or can easily be made to be a matter of known fact. If there were no personnel investment, the employer would hire everyone who applied and simply fire those unqualified. But presumably any testing operation, even a trial period, is some form of personnel investment.

The second assumption is that the qualities of the individual are not known to the employer beforehand. The most interesting case of that kind is one in which the worker must make some investment in himself but one which the employer can never be sure of. I am thinking here not of the conventional types of education or experience, which are easily observable, but more subtle types the employer cannot observe directly: the habits of action and thought that favor good performance in skilled jobs, steadiness, punctuality, responsiveness, and initiative. A worker who has made the requisite investment will be said to be *qualified*.

The inefficiency that arises here because employers do not know the qualifications of workers as well as the workers do, is the same in principle as that caused by "adverse selection" in insurance. The insured may represent different degrees of riskiness, and each may have some perception of his own degree, but in many cases the insurance companies have much poorer ability to differentiate. If the insurance companies set rates corresponding to average riskiness, the less risky will eliminate or curtail their purchase of insurance, so that the actual experience of the company will be less favorable than the mean in the population. The rates will have to be raised further, thereby eliminating still more of the favorable risks; either the given type of insurance will eventually be eliminated altogether, or an equilibrium will be reached that is inefficient relative to one in which different premiums are charged to those of different riskiness.

We have two primary elements in this model: the employer's investment of personnel capital will be wasted if the employee turns out not to have made his investment; and the employer cannot know beforehand whether or not the employee is qualified. The employer does know the race of the individual, however, and he holds some subjective beliefs about the respective probabilities that white and black workers are qualified. It is of course immediately obvious that if the subjective probability in the mind of an employer that a white worker is qualified is higher than that a black worker is qualified, there will have to be a wage difference if the employer is to hire any blacks at all.

The effects of this model are similar to those based on tastes, but the causes are different. We would still want to know why the subjective probabilities are different. The simplest explanation is prejudice, in the literal sense of that term; that is, a judgment about abilities made in advance of the evidence and not altered by it. Of course, the persistence of prejudice really should not be left unexplained. One possible explanation is to be found in theories of psychological equilibrium, such as Festinger's (1957) theory of cognitive dissonance. If an individual acts in a discriminatory fashion, he would, according to this theory, tend to have beliefs that justify his actions. Indeed, precisely the fact that discriminatory behavior is in conflict with an important segment of our ethical beliefs will, according to this theory, intensify the willingness to entertain cognitive beliefs that will supply a socially acceptable justification for this conduct.

Another model of this type is more narrowly economic. Suppose that employers do not misperceive, that they know correctly the proportions of black and white workers who are qualified. Suppose also that the acquisition of human capital in the form of qualifications by workers is costly and that they face an imperfect capital market in any effort to finance this acquisition. Then the actual proportion of whites who are qualified is a function of white wages and similarly with blacks. I assume here, as always, that blacks and whites are essentially identical, so these two functional relations are the same.

Clearly, a nondiscriminatory set of wages that will be an equilibrium is possible, but it is also possible that this equilibrium may not be stable. Suppose, to begin with, that the proportion of qualified whites is slightly higher than that of blacks. Then white wages will be higher. In response to this differential, there will be an incentive for whites to increase their qualifications relative to blacks, thereby accentuating the initial discrepancy.

This verbal argument is not conclusive, and the formal discussion is more complex. The stability of the nondiscriminatory equilibrium, however, depends on quantitative values of the parameters; that is, on the supply functions for qualified labor and on the personnel investments needed by the firms.

Since personnel investments are greater at higher levels, this model of personnel investment and uncertainty about qualifications also helps to explain the increasing discrimination against blacks in higher-level jobs. Indeed, the motive for developing the observed model was to explain the observation that much discrimination occurred in the form of a disproportionate representation of blacks in lower-wage occupations, analogous in many ways to the dual economies characteristic of underdeveloped countries. The analogy has been suggested by some who have made detailed studies of local labor markets; for example, Baron and Hymer (1968) for Chicago, and Doeringer and his students (Feldman, Gordon, and Reich, 1969) and Piore with reference to Boston. Without going into detailed discussion of the somewhat variant viewpoints, the common view is that blacks are largely, though not exclusively, confined to marginal jobs marked by low wages, low promotion possibilities, and instability of employment. The instability, incidentally, is in large part voluntary; it is interpreted as a rational response to limited opportunity, which both increases the value and decreases the cost of search.

In particular, both research groups feel that coexistence of segregation and discrimination is in some sense an equilibrium condition, that no employer or employee will find it individually profitable to depart from the existing situation. Within conventional deterministic models, it is hard to formalize this possibility, as indeed is true in dual economy models for underdeveloped countries; why does not competition from the victims of discrimination reduce wages in the preferred occupations and permit them to enter?

The foregoing model (as elaborated in Chapter 6) is designed to suggest a mechanism in terms of which partial occupational segregation is nevertheless an equilibrium condition. In view of its desperately oversimplified character, it is perhaps best thought of as a metaphor.

Finally, a comment on the question of group interests. It is certainly a common view that in some sense racial discrimination is a device by which the whites in the aggregate gain at the expense of the blacks. Hence, the whole problem is to be interpreted as an exploitative relation. A stable relation exists here; the values inherent in discrimination uphold a structure that is profitable to those holding those values.

On purely methodological grounds, I do not think such a view can be denied, provided it works, though it is contrary to the tradition of economics. Economic explanations for discrimination or other phenomena tend to run in individualistic terms, and the models presented earlier are no exception. Economists ask what motivates an employer or an individual worker. They tend not to accept as an explanation a statement that employers as a class would gain by discrimination, for they ask what would prevent an individual employer from refusing to discriminate if he prefers and thereby profit. Economists do indeed recognize group interests if they appear in legal form, as in tariffs, licensing, or legally enforced segregation. The distinction between the legal structure and other social pressures, however, is hardly a sharp dichotomy. If perceived group interests can lead to legislation, they can also lead to other social pressures.

I think something can be said for views of this kind, but their mechanism needs careful exploration. We must really ask who benefits, and how are the exploitative agreements carried out? In particular, how are the competitive pressures that would undermine them held in check? The exploitation of blacks can work only if the tendency of individual employers to buy the cheapest labor is somehow suppressed. Recall the great difficulty that producers of rubber and of coffee have had in their efforts to create a mutually beneficial monopoly.

Obviously, from the preceding analysis, the whites certainly gain by discrimination. I must add, though, that it seems very difficult to construct a model in which employers gain in any obvious way; the gains to the whites appear to accrue to white workers primarily. This fact, if it is one, already creates difficulties for the group interest hypothesis; after all, the employers are the most direct possible agents of exploitation, and it would be better for the theory if they were beneficiaries.

In any case, we are not to imagine conspiracies in which 170 million white Americans put their heads together. The process of communication by which the white race agrees on means to further its collective interests must operate unconsciously through its value-forming and allocating social institutions. The argument would have to be that the discriminatory tastes as given up to this point are themselves the mechanism by which discrimination profitable to the whites is carried out. These discriminatory values must be internalized and felt to be genuine by those holding them. It was an obligation of conscience for Huckleberry Finn to turn over the runaway slave, Jim, to the authorities for return to his master, and he resolved to do so for inner peace. Finally, Huck could not return his friend to such misery, but he well knew that his failure was only another proof of his fundamental depravity and that anyone with a stake in society would return a runaway slave rather than suffer the disutility of a failure to carry out his social duty. The process by which these discriminatory values are formed and transmitted is certainly complex and lengthy in time, and we may easily suppose that the exploitation that results is far from optimum for the exploiters.

Notice that the question at issue is not whether racist utility functions are socially conditioned. We accept that the tastes for material goods are affected by the surrounding culture; and how much more so tastes about status relations. The crucial question, to my mind still an open one, is whether the acceptance and preservation of racial attitudes are in some way related to their profitability to the group. One might hypothesize some sort of Darwinian process for utility functions in which those economically profitable for the group have a greater chance of survival. All this is at the moment merely speculative, at best a suggestion for research.

One further point should be made here. I do not see how the process of racial discrimination can begin in the economic sphere or out of purely economic motives. It always pays any group with enough power to discriminate against some other, but redheads or blue-eyed individuals do not seem to suffer much. Since color is seized on as a basis for discrimination, there must be an extra-economic origin, although it is not precluded that its economic profitability reinforces the discrimination once started.[1]

I have chosen a topic on which many of us feel the greatest moral outrage and have analyzed it most dispassionately. Neither the moral indignation nor the cool analysis is misplaced; their juxtaposition is one of those paradoxes inherent in the nature of human society of which only the naive are ignorant. Our mastery of ourselves as social beings needs all the reinforcement it can get from study of ourselves in all contexts. Indeed, in the absence of analysis from a self-imposed and sometimes painful distance, our moral feelings can lead us to actions whose effects are the opposite of those intended. This is not intended to imply that social action must wait on adequate analysis. Inaction may be, and in this case surely is, as dangerous as any likely alternative. Indeed, social action may be indispensable to increasing our knowledge when the consequences are subjected to adequate study. But a firm commitment to ends must not preclude a tentative, questioning attitude to particular means of achieving them.

Note

1. Hodge and Hodge advanced the hypothesis that, other things being equal, wages in an occupation were lower the greater the number of blacks and suggested this might make social barriers to entry of blacks a rational procedure and a possible cause of prejudice. (Their interpretation of the empirical evidence is far from conclusive, but that is another question.) In reply, Taeuber, Taeuber, and Cain argued that it would pay the members of any occupation to bar any

group of people; the selection of blacks as the target could be explained only on noneconomic grounds. (See Robert W. and Patricia Hodge, "Occupational Assimilation as a Competitive Process," *American Journal of Sociology* 71 (1965): 249-85; Alma F. Taeuber, Karl E. Taeuber, and Glen G. Cain, "Occupational Assimilation as a Competitive Process: A Reanalysis," *American Journal of Sociology* 72 (1966): 273-85. There seems to be considerable confusion in this controversy. An individual has many interests, and for each interest he may find a different set of other individuals who share them. Why certain kinds of groups perceive themselves as having common interests and not others is a question on which economics does not seem likely to throw much light. But *given* group identification, it is not so unreasonable that the members of the group will work together to promote group interests, even though it would pay any individual to depart from them.

References

Baron, H.M., and B. Hymer. "The Negroes in the Chicago Labor Market." In J. Jacobson, ed., *The Negro and the American Labor Movement*. Garden City, N.Y.: Anchor Books, 1968.

Becker, Gary S. *The Economics of Discrimination*. Chicago: University of Chicago Press, 1957.

Duncan, Otis Dudley. "Inheritance of Poverty or Inheritance of Race?" In Daniel P. Moynihan, ed., *On Understanding Poverty*. New York: Basic Books, 1969.

Economic Report of the President. Washington, D.C.: U.S. Government Printing Office, February 1970.

Edgeworth, F.Y. "Equal Pay to Men and Women for Equal Work." *Economic Journal* 31 (1922): 431-57.

Farrell, M.J. "The Convexity Assumption in the Theory of Competitive Markets." *Journal of Political Economy* 67 (1959).

Feldman, P.H., D.M. Gordon, and M. Reich in P. Doeringer, ed. "Low-income Markets and Urban Manpower Programs: A Critical Assessment." Discussion Paper no. 66, Harvard Institute of Economic Research, 1969.

Festinger, Leo. *A Theory of Cognitive Dissonance*. Palo Alto, Calif.: Stanford University Press, 1957.

Friedman, Milton. *A Theory of the Consumption Function*. Princeton, N.J.: National Bureau of Economic Research, 1957.

Gilman, Harry J. "Economic Discrimination and Unemployment." *American Economic Review* 55 (1965): 1077-95.

Hicks, J.R. "Annual Survey of Economic Theory: The Theory of Monopoly." *Econometrica* 3 (1935): 1-20.

Hodge, Robert W. and Patricia Hodge. "Occupational Assimilation as a Competitive Process." *American Journal of Sociology* 71, no. 3 (November 1965): 249-85.

Landes, David. *The Unbound Prometheus*. Cambridge: Cambridge University Press, 1969.

Marris, Robin. *The Economic Theory of "Managerial" Capitalism*. New York: The Free Press of Glencoe, 1964.

Miller, Herman P. *Income Distribution in the United States*. Washington, D.C.: U.S. Bureau of the Census, 1966.

Pascal, Anthony H. *The Economics of Housing Segregation*, RM-5510-RC. Santa Monica, Calif.: The Rand Corporation, November 1967.

Penrose, Edith. *The Theory of the Growth of the Firm*. Oxford: Oxford University Press, 1959.

Simon, Henry. "Theories of Decision-making in Economics and Behavioral Science." *American Economic Review* 49 (1959): 253-83.

Taeuber, Alma F., Karl E. Taeuber, and Glen G. Cain. "Occupational Assimilation as a Competitive Process: A Reanalysis." *American Journal of Sociology* 72, no. 3 (November 1966): 273-85.

Taeuber, Alma F., and Karl E. Taeuber. *Negroes in Cities: Residential Segregation and Neighborhood Change*. Chicago: Aldine, 1965.

U.S. Department of Labor. *Handbook of Labor Statistics*, Bulletin no. 163. Washington, D.C., 1969.

Williamson, Oliver E. *The Economic Theory of "Managerial" Capitalism*. Chicago: Markham, 1967.

3

The Effects of Minimum Wages by Race, Sex, and Age

MARVIN KOSTERS
FINIS WELCH

Introduction

This chapter analyzes differences in the impact of changes in aggregate employment in the U.S. economy between whites and nonwhites, between males and females, and between teenagers and adults. As the pace of economic activity varies, the effects are not uniformly distributed among industries; and within industries, the effects on various types of productive inputs are uneven. For example, employment of people will be likely to vary more than employment of machines, and purchases of machines may vary even more than employment of people. By tracing the pattern of employment fluctuation between worker classes—the color-age-sex groups—we improve our ability to predict the distribution of costs from economic instability.

Long-term changes in employment patterns of the various classes of workers are primarily a result of trends in labor force participation, the skill composition of the workforce, wages, and employment opportunities. Short-term changes in employment are influenced by the industrial, occupational, and skill composition of workers in different classes and short-term substitution possibilities. Short-term employment changes are distributed unevenly among industries, occupations, and skill classes as a result of compositional shifts in the demand for output and differences in substitution possibilities among input classes. Since capital employed by the firm is less sensitive to temporary fluctuations in product demand than employment, substitutability of various classes of labor for nonlabor inputs is a factor of obvious importance. To compensate for the relative fixity of capital, firms will concentrate employment changes in those classes that are most substitutable for capital.

The differential impact of short-term employment changes is also a result of differences in the amount and character of investment in the skills and capabilities of workers that are acquired in connection with employment. For highly routinized and short-term jobs, employment decisions and compensation will be governed almost entirely by expected current work performance. That is, workers with easily identifiable skills will be hired for the services they perform for whatever period these services are required. Little or no investment in upgrading or improving worker skill levels needs to be made and wages paid will reflect the marginal product of current labor services.

On the other hand, for workers employed for a potentially long duration for less routine work, the connection between compensation and the current productivity of their labor services will be loosened. Workers may be paid less than their current marginal product while acquiring investment, if such investment raises their productivity in other firms as much as in the firm in which they are employed. Investment of this type—in general human capital—can be profitably provided by firms if the worker's wage while he receives the training is sufficiently lower than current marginal product to compensate for training costs incurred by the firm. Wages equal to current marginal product can be paid when general training is provided only if the worker's ties to the firm can be strengthened so that investment costs can be recouped in the future over the worker's expected term of employment.

Employment for potentially long duration often entails investment that improves a worker's productivity within his firm by more than in other firms.[1] Workers acquiring firm-specific investment will typically receive wages higher than their marginal product in other firms as an incentive for them to remain with the firm. Wages need not reflect current marginal product in each period because investment costs incurred can be recouped over a worker's expected term of employment. Introducing specific training, therefore, results in abrogating equality of wages and marginal products in each period as an equilibrium condition, and it provides an important link between current and expected future labor productivity and wages. The firm's hiring and retention policies will reflect not only current wages and marginal products, but also the expected level of marginal product in the future.

Suppose that a firm experiences an increase in demand. Before it is convinced that the increase will be maintained, output expands because the firm purchases inputs whose costs can be quickly recouped. For example, the firm might defer purchasing new capital goods with long recoupment periods and hire laborers that are good substitutes for capital. It might also delay hiring persons in whom it would ordinarily invest in firm-specific skills and hire others instead. As it becomes convinced that the increased demand will be maintained, its input composition is adjusted to reflect more "normal" or longer-term patterns of input requirements. During this readjustment, "transitional" employees may be replaced by capital and other workers.

Similarly, if a firm previously in equilibrium is faced with a contraction in demand for its product, it may choose to hedge against the possibility that the change is temporary by laying off workers to whom it has only a short-term commitment instead of disposing of its capital assets. And it may retain laborers in whom it has substantial investment, to increase the probability of recoupment at a later date. If the contraction persists, it will of course adjust to more normal input combinations, reducing capital assets and laying off persons for whom it realizes that a "sunk" investment cannot be recouped. At the same time, it will rehire some of those originally laid off when it hedged against having to make the potentially more expensive reduction.

As the level of economic activity fluctuates, some classes of workers will share more than proportionately in the transitions between peaks and troughs in aggregate demand. Fluctuations in employment of these "marginal" workers will be exaggerated relative to the total, and employment extremes for these workers will occur before the extremes in the aggregate. For others, variations will be less than proportionate and the extremes will be belated.

At any point in time, there exists a level of employment consistent with the economy's long-term equilibrium path; call it normal employment. To the extent that realized employment differs from its long-term equilibrium, we can presume that the deviation, which we call transitional employment, reflects a short-term adjustment to unforeseen contingencies. Thus, actual employment at any point in time is viewed as normal employment plus transitional employment. If aggregate employment is below its long-term trend, transitional employment is negative; and if it is above the trend, transitional employment is positive. The model we use to estimate the distributional effects of fluctuations in employment is of the form

$$E_{it} = \gamma_{it} E_{pt} + \beta_{it} E_{\tau t} + u_{it}$$

where E_{it} corresponds to the number of persons in the ith color-sex-age class employed in the tth period. E_{pt} represents projected or normal aggregate employment in period t and is operationally defined as an extrapolation of the past. $E_{\tau t}$ is our measure of transitional employment and is defined as observed less projected employment. u_{it} is the omnipresent error. Viewed this way, γ_i is the fraction of normal aggregate employment accounted for by the ith class and the set of γs represents the distribution of the normal employment among the classes. Accordingly β_i is the fraction of transitional employment accounted for by the ith class.

It is clear that the γs and βs are not just a set of constants but are variables endogenous to an economic system. They reflect trends in labor force participation, the skill structure within and between the classes, substitutability of the various classes for other classes and nonlabor inputs, the industrial and occupational distributions of the classes, and other factors affecting long- and short-term supply and demand for labor such as unionism and minimum wage legislation.

The primary feature of the model is that it focuses only upon distributional effects of fluctuations and says nothing of factors determining the actual level of employment. Suppose that aggregate employment has been constant for long enough so that no transitional employment exists and all is normal. After this period, suppose that employment drops by $100a$ percent. Since normal employment is an extrapolation of the past, as the drop occurs, E_{pt} remains at its previous level and

$$E_{\tau t} = (1-a) E_{pt} - E_{pt} = -aE_{pt}$$

Prior to the change, we assume that the labor market was in long-term equilibrium and that $E_{it-1} = \gamma_i E_{pt-1} = \gamma_i E_{pt}$ and the $E_{\tau t-1} = 0$. Accompanying the change, E_{it} would fall to $\gamma_i E_{pt} + \beta_i (-aE_{pt})$ representing a decline in employment of $100 \frac{\beta_i}{\gamma_i}(a)$ percent, so that when aggregate employment changes from its long-run equilibrium, for each 1 percent change, employment in the ith class will change by $\frac{\beta_i}{\gamma_i}$ percent.[2] Thus, β_i/γ_i is an index of the marginality of the ith class to the workforce and called "the coefficient of marginality." If the effects of fluctuations in aggregate employment were uniformly distributed β_i would equal γ_i for all classes, implying that the composition of the work force would be invariant over fluctuations in aggregate employment. On the other hand, if a particular class accounts for a larger fraction of the transitional than the normal workforce, $\beta/\gamma > 1$, then as total employment varied about its long-term path, employment in the particular class would vary disproportionately to the total. If a class were intramarginal, $\beta/\gamma < 1$, its employment fluctuations would be damped relative to the total.

At any point in time, we observe only the number of persons employed in each of the groups, but these observations are not conveniently broken into normal and transitional. Our procedure is to select an operational definition of aggregate normal employment with its implied observations of transitional employment and then by variants of least-squares regression, we estimate the γs and βs. As our definition of normal employment, we use three projections. Observed employment one year ago is projected one year forward, and similarly for two and three years in the past; these projections are then averaged, with the largest weight going to the projection based on the most recent period. The operational definition is

$$E_{pt} = 1/2\, E_{t-4}\, (1+r)^4 + 1/3\, E_{t-8}\, (1+r)^8 + 1/6\, E_{t-12}\, (1+r)^{12}$$

where E_{t-i} represents aggregate employment in the $(t-i)$th quarter, and r is an estimate of the long-term quarterly growth rate in aggregate employment.

Using this definition of normal (now projected) employment, Figure 3-1 depicts employment in two classes, corresponding to $\beta_1/\gamma_1 = 2$ and $\beta_2/\gamma_2 = 1/2$, relative to observed total employment. In this illustration, we see that employment in class 1, the marginal class, not only fluctuates more violently than total employment, but it reaches its extremes sooner. The submarginal class realizes less drastic fluctuations and its extremes are belated. The over and undershooting reflect substitution between transitional and more permanent workers as underlying changes are expected to be maintained. One important feature of the model is that as aggregate employment "levels off" (the end of the sine curve in Figure 3-1) employment of marginal workers will fall as they are replaced by their intramarginal counterparts.

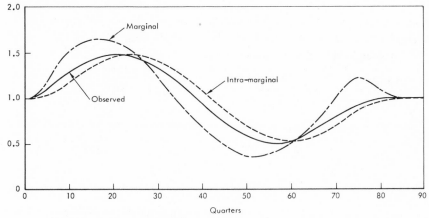

Note: For the marginal class $\beta/\gamma = 2$.
For the intramarginal class $\beta/\gamma = \frac{1}{2}$.

Figure 3-1. Hypothetical Relative Employment Patterns of Marginal and Intramarginal Classes Over a Cycle.

Employment Shares

Table 3-1 contains estimated employment shares, both for normal and transitional employment, for adults and teenagers. Although it would be preferable to analyze narrow age intervals within the class twenty and over, such data are not available. The estimates are averages based on quarterly employment data for the period 1954-68 and the estimation technique and regression results are provided in the Appendix on pp. 114-117.

We estimate that adult white males account for 57 percent of normal employment and 42 percent of transitional employment, so that as total employment falls by 1 percent, employment in this group will fall by only .75 percent. White females account for 27 percent of normal employment and nonwhite females for 4 percent, and each accounts for roughly the same proportion of transitional as for normal employment. That is, adult females experience employment fluctuations in proportion to those of the total economy. Within adult classes, only nonwhite adult males experience fluctuations in employment that are more severe than those of the total economy. They account for slightly less than 6 percent of normal employment and 8 percent of transitional, so that as total employment falls, employment in this group falls at a relative rate 1.3 times as large.

Because white adult males account for such a large share of adult employment and because their employment is not as cyclically sensitive as the aggregate, our estimates indicate that the employment of adults viewed as a single

Table 3-1

Average Shares of Normal and Transitional Employment and Average Coefficients of Marginality: Quarterly Average of U.S. Civilian Employment, 1954-68

Employee group	Normal employment, $\overline{\gamma}$	Transitional employment, $\overline{\beta}$*	Coefficient marginality, $\overline{\beta}/\overline{\gamma}$
Adults (20+)	.934	.823 (.779)	0.88 (0.83)
White males	.570	.449 (.425)	0.79 (0.75)
Nonwhite males	.058	.083 (.079)	1.42 (1.34)
White females	.269	.253 (.240)	0.94 (0.89)
Nonwhite females	.040	.038 (.036)	0.95 (0.90)
Teenagers (16-19)	.063	.233 (.221)	3.70 (3.51)
White males	.032	.124 (.117)	3.87 (3.66)
Nonwhite males	.004	.019 (.018)	4.81 (4.56)
White females	.025	.078 (.074)	3.12 (2.95)
Nonwhite females	.002	.012 (.011)	5.25 (4.97)

*The estimated shares for transitional employment sum to 1.056 instead of unity. Numbers in parentheses are normalized.

Source: U.S. Department of Labor, Bureau of Labor Statistics, *Employment and Earnings and Monthly Report on the Labor Force*, 15, no. 8 (February 1969).

class is relatively stable over the business cycle. Adults constitute 94 percent of normal employment and only 78 percent of transitional employment. Much of the brunt of the employment cycle is borne by teenagers who account for 6.3 percent of normal and 22.1 percent of transitional employment. Our estimate is that as aggregate employment falls 1 percent, adult employment will fall 0.83 percent and teenage employment will fall 3.51 percent.

At the sample mean, our estimate is that white teenage males account for 3.2 percent of normal employment and 11.7 percent of transitional employment, so that a 1 percent decline in aggregate employment will result in approximately 3.7 percent decline in employment within this group. Similar results are found for each of the teenage groups: alongside a 1 percent decline in aggregate employment, employment of nonwhite teenage males will decline in estimated 4.6 percent, nonwhite females by 5 percent, and white teenage females by an estimated 3 percent. Nonwhite teenagers appear more marginal to the workforce than whites. Teenagers absorb a phenomenally disproportionate share of aggregate employment fluctuations, varying on average by more than four times the percentage variation for adults.

Minimum Wages

The model used to estimate employment shares is formed to include effects of increasing minimum wages on those shares. The estimates show that, on balance, adult employment fluctuates less violently than teenage, which is as the theory of "specific" human capital predicts: teenagers are typically less skilled and experienced than adults.

Since teenagers are marginal to the work force, we would expect them to fare especially well during expansionary periods such as 1958-68, yet this is not reflected in their unemployment rates.[3] It is true that a large part of the sustained teenage unemployment during this period reflects the postwar baby boom. For example, between 1958 and 1968, the teenage population increased from 9.5 million to 14.2 million or by 49.5 percent. During this same period, the adult population rose by only 13.6 percent. Yet during this same period, changes in minimum wage legislation may have operated to the peculiar disadvantage of teenagers, and these changes, in and of themselves, may be capable of explaining a large part of the divergent trends in adult and teenage employment rates.

Between 1954 and 1968, legal minimum wages increased from $0.75 per hour to $1.60 per hour and relative to average hourly earnings in manufacturing, the minimum wage increased from .42 to .53. In addition, in 1954 only 46 percent of all employed persons worked in firms covered by minimum wage legislation; in 1968, 62 percent of aggregate employment was covered.

The direct effects of minimum wages are obvious. When an employer is faced with a legal minimum wage, if it exceeds the contribution of some employees to the firm's revenue, the firm can either lay these persons off or "subsidize" their employment.[4] Moreover, as the firm's demand for labor increases through time it will probably forego hiring some persons it otherwise would have hired, because hiring them would require a subsidy. On balance, we would therefore expect aggregate employment to be reduced by the introduction of a legal wage floor. An analysis of factors determining aggregate employment is beyond the scope of this study, which concentrates instead upon the impact of minimum wages on employment shares, and therefore upon the distribution of changes in total employment.

To illustrate the minimum wage effects, consider a distribution in which persons in the labor force are arrayed according to the value productivity of their labor services. Assuming strict profit-maximization and a perfectly competitive labor market, the distribution of wages offered by firms would coincide with the distribution of value productivity of labor. Assuming for simplicity that coverage is complete,[5] introducing a minimum wage would have the effect of truncating this distribution of wage offers. Wage offers below the legal minimum would not be made. The resulting employment loss represents the effect on aggregate employment of the minimum wage.

The impact on the distribution of employment among age-sex-color classes can be illustrated by considering separate value productivity distributions for each group. The largest effects on employment of introducing a minimum wage would be realized by those groups with larger proportions of their members whose productivity falls below the minimum wage. This is illustrated in Figure

3-2a for a given level of demand, where those in Skill class 2 have a larger proportion of workers with productivity below the minimum wage. For these groups, an increase in the minimum wage would decrease their share of normal employment. For groups in which the converse occurs—those with relatively few members whose productivity lies below the minimum wage—less than proportionate employment reductions would be realized, increasing their share of normal employment.

During the course of cyclic activity, the demand for labor increases and declines. This can be construed as simply shifting the labor productivity distributions back and forth along the labor productivity axis. Groups whose modal productivity lies near the minimum wage, exemplified by Skill class 2 in Figure 3-2, will experience larger employment changes as the minimum wage truncates the productivity distributions. In addition, groups with relatively low productivity tend to have relatively low hiring costs and little firm-specific investment. As a result, value productivity shifts will tend to be larger for these groups than for those with higher average productivity. This is illustrated by the larger shift in the distribution for Skill class 2 in Figure 3-2b as demand declines. Relatively low productivity groups will therefore experience exaggerated fluctuations in employment as value productivity shifts occur with short term demand changes. With increases in the minimum wage, employment for those low productivity groups will be increasingly vulnerable to short term employment changes.

At the other end of the spectrum, groups with only small fractions of their members with productivity less than the minimum wage at any phase of the cycle will not be significantly affected. There are, of course, indirect effects as well. An increase in the minimum wage will tend to increase the demand for laborers whose value productivity exceeds the minimum and who are productive substitutes for those with productivity less than the minimum.

Thus, under normal conditions we expect an increase in the legal minimum wage to reduce aggregate employment with the impact falling disproportionately on groups having larger fractions of their members with fairly low productivity. As the productive value of labor varies over the course of the business cycles, we expect increases in the minimum wage to heighten the employment sensitivity to these variations in those groups that are themselves more affected by the minimum wage.

To allow for minimum wages and longer-run trend effects on employment shares the model is estimated according to the form

$$\gamma_{it} = \gamma_{0i} \ (1+r_i)^t \ M_t^{\eta \, pi} \ \text{and}$$

$$\beta_{it} = \beta_{0i} \ (1+r_i)^t \ M_t^{\eta \, \tau i} \ .$$

The basic data are quarterly observations of employment in each of the groups during the period 1954-68 so that the subscripts refer to the ith worker class in

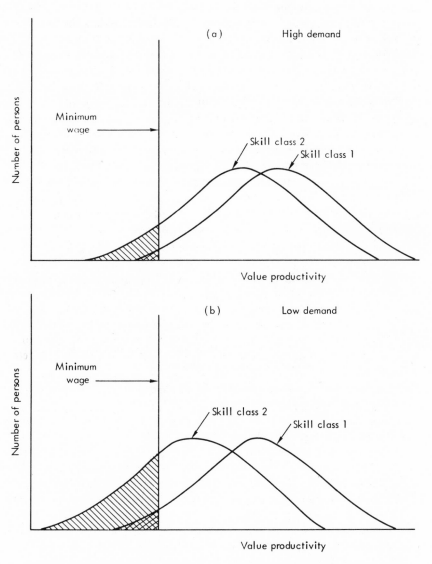

Figure 3-2. Joint effects on employment of a change in labor demand and minimum wage for two hypothetical skill distributions (Skill class 2 is relatively more marginal and has a relatively low value productivity distribution).

the tth quarter, r_i is the quarterly growth rate of employment in this group relative to aggregate employment during the decade 1956-66 (the specific values are given in the Appendix). M_t is the effective minimum wage, and the exponents, η_p and η_T, are elasticities. Specifically, η_p is the elasticity of the share of normal employment with respect to the minimum wage and η_T is the corresponding elasticity for the share of transitional employment. It follows that $\eta_T - \eta_p$ is the elasticity of the marginality coefficient, so that it serves as our measure of how minimum wages affect the cyclical vulnerability of each of the groups.

Operationally, we have defined the minimum wage variable so that it includes coverage as well as level. The minimum wage is normally stated in nominal terms, so that given the upward trend of general increases in labor productivity and increases in the general price level, the effective minimum wage is eroded between legislative adjustments. To capture this effect, we measure the minimum wage relative to average earnings in manufacturing. To adjust for expanding coverage, we have then multiplied this variable by the proportion of aggregate employment covered by minimum wage legislation.[6]

Our estimates of the employment share elasticities appear in Table 3-2. As expected, minimum wages are estimated to have a destabilizing effect upon teenagers and a stabilizing effect on adults. In a sense, minimum wages seem to shift

Table 3-2
Estimated Elasticities of Employment Shares and of Marginality Coefficients with Respect to the Effective Minimum Wage

Employee group	Normal employment, η_p [a]	Transitional employment, η_T	Coefficient of marginality, $\eta_T - \eta_p$
Adults			
White males	.032	−1.44	−1.47
Nonwhite males	−.004[b]	− .47[b]	− .47
White females	.032	−1.00[b]	−1.03
Nonwhite females	−.017[b]	.08[b]	.10
Teenagers			
White males	−.331	2.48	2.81
Nonwhite males	−.356	3.88	4.24
White females	−.241	3.30	3.54
Nonwhite females	−.301	5.31	5.61

[a]Since this is "distributional theory," we have the implicit constraints $\sum_i \gamma_{it} \eta_{pi} = \sum_i \beta_{it} \eta_{Ti}$ = 0. These constraints are not imposed. The estimates are that $\sum_i \overline{\gamma}_i \eta_{pi}$ = .007 and $\sum_i \overline{\beta}_i \eta_{Ti}$ = −.233.

[b]Heuristic "t" statistic less than 2.0. Standard errors are not computed for the difference, $\eta_T - \eta_p$.

Source: The regression results and the estimation procedure are described in the Appendix, pp. 114-117.

much of the burden of variation in aggregate employment from adults to teenagers, from males to females, and from whites to nonwhites; in each case the destabilizing effect is upon those with lower average wages. Consider white adult males as an example. They account for over one-half of normal employment and have the highest wage of any of the groups considered. Our estimate is that an increase in the minimum wage will increase their share of normal employment and reduce the share of transitional to increase employment stability. For the remaining adult classes, the evidence is not as strong but does suggest that minimum wages stabilize employment of white females and nonwhite males but have been mildly destabilizing for nonwhite females. A 1 percent increase in the minimum wage is estimated to reduce the coefficient of marginality for white adult males by 1.5 percent, for white females 1 percent, and for nonwhite males .5 percent. The estimated effect for nonwhite adult females is trivial.

For teenagers, the statistical evidence is more convincing. We estimate that a 1 percent increase in the effective minimum wage will reduce the share in normal employment of white teenage males by .33 percent and would increase their share of transitional employment by 2.5 percent, yielding an increase in the coefficient of marginality of 2.8 percent. Similar results hold for all of the teenage classes: in each case a 1 percent increase in the effective minimum wage results in an increase in the coefficient of marginality of more than 2.75 percent. The effects fall disproportionately upon nonwhites, being 50 to 60 percent greater than for whites.

It appears that minimum wage legislation has been particularly disadvantageous for teenagers, especially nonwhites, in the sense that it has heightened their vulnerability to changes in aggregate employment. It is true that only a 3 to 5 percent increase in marginality coefficients accompanying a 1 percent increase in the effective minimum wage may be unimpressive. For example, at the sample mean a 1 percent increase in the minimum wage would increase the marginality coefficient of nonwhite teenage males by only 0.19 and of nonwhite females by 0.30. Yet, it is important that the increases in the effective minimum wage have been much more than 1 percent. If we compare the average level of the effective minimum wage that existed over the first five years of our sample, 1954-58, to the average for the last five years, 1964-68, we find that it increased by about 32 percent. The implication is that the coefficient of marginality would have been significantly affected for all groups except for nonwhite adult females. In fact, we estimate that a single "jump" in the effective minimum wage, as large as the accumulated increase between the two five-year periods, would reduce the white adult male marginality by one-third, white females marginality by one-fourth, and nonwhite male marginality by one-eighth. At the same time, this change would more than double the coefficients of marginality of all teenage classes. Thus, the evidence is that by the period's end, 1968, increasing minimum wages had made teenagers much more vulnerable to cyclic instability.

Summary and Conclusions

The relative income position of nonwhite families has shown marked improvement over the past decade. One of the most prominent features of the decade in which this improvement occurred is the long period of continuous economic expansion beginning in the early 1960s. Expansionary periods, as reflected in unemployment rates, have previously been accompanied by improvement in nonwhite relative incomes, and conversely, rising unemployment has been accompanied by declines. Thus, part of the recent nonwhite gain in relative income may be cyclical and subject to rapid erosion as economic expansion slows or is reversed.

One of the principal factors influencing income changes is changing employment. If changes in aggregate employment are not shared in equal proportions by whites and nonwhites, relative incomes will be affected. Our estimates show that nonwhites are disproportionately affected by employment changes: of the four nonwhite age-sex classes analyzed, only the employment of adult females moves proportionately with aggregate employment, the other three nonwhite groups share more than proportionately in aggregate changes. For adult males, a short-term change in aggregate employment is estimated to result in a proportionate change in employment for nonwhites almost double that for whites.

The incidence of short-term employment changes rests most heavily on teenagers. Their share in employment changes is estimated to be three and one-half times as large as their proportionate share. Males are more sharply affected than females, and nonwhites are more sharply affected than whites.

Minimum wage legislation has apparently played an important role in increasing the cyclical sensitivity of teenage employment. Increases in the effective minimum wage have increased the vulnerability of teenage employment to short-term changes, and they have decreased teenagers' share of normal employment. Moreover, the employment effects of minimum wages among teenagers are disproportionately concentrated on nonwhites. Thus, as a result of increases in the effective minimum wage, teenagers are able to obtain fewer jobs and their jobs are less secure over the business cycle. A disproportionate share of these unfavorable employment effects accrues to nonwhite teenagers.

Recent gains in relative employment and income achieved by nonwhites were facilitated by a sustained period of economic expansion. Our analysis of the incidence of employment changes indicates that a slackening in the pace of economic growth—or even a leveling off—will adversely affect nonwhites. Teenage employment will also be disproportionately affected, and increases in the effective minimum wage have exacerbated the sensitivity of their employment to short-term changes.

Appendix

The model is estimated one equation at a time without imposing the constraints of internal consistency, $\sum_i \beta_{it} = \sum \gamma_{it} = 1$ and $\sum_i \eta_{pi} \gamma_{it} = \sum \eta_{\tau i} \beta_{it} = 0$. The estimation technique is nonlinear. We simply iterate over values of η_p and η_τ to minimize the residual sum of squares. The typical equation is

$$E_{it} = \gamma_0 Z_{1t} + \beta_0 Z_{2t} + u ,$$

where Z_{1t} and Z_{2t} are constructs of the form,

$$Z_{1t} = (1+r_i)^t M_t^{\hat{\eta}_{pi}} E_{pt} \quad \text{and}$$

$$Z_{2t} = (1+r_i)^t M_t^{\hat{\eta}_{\tau i}} E_{\tau t} .$$

There are 60 observations and 4 parameters, γ_0, β_0, η_{pi}, $\eta_{\tau i}$ are estimated. For particular values of η_p and η_τ, Z_1, and Z_2 are computed and the OLS regression of E_{it} on Z_1 and Z_2 is then calculated, Iterating over η_p and η_τ, that solution is selected to minimize the residual sum of squares.

The standard errors of $\hat{\gamma}_0$ and $\hat{\beta}_0$ are computed as though the regression of E_i on Z_1 and Z_2 were of the standard form except that degrees of freedom are 56 instead of 58. The standard errors of $\hat{\eta}_{pi}$ and $\hat{\eta}_{\tau i}$ are computed heuristically to measure the sensitivity of the residual sum of squares to the constraints $\eta_{pi} = 0$ and $\eta_{\tau i} = 0$. Specifically, to compute the standard error of $\hat{\eta}_p$ we first estimate the equation as described above and then impose the constraint, $\eta_{pi} = 0$ and iterate $\eta_{\tau i}$ to minimize the residual sum of squares. Let Q_0 represent the unconstrained residual sum of squares and let Q_1 represent the constrained sum of squares.
Then compute

$$"F"_{1,56} = \frac{Q_1 - Q_0}{Q_0 / 56}$$

$$"t"_{56} = ("F"_{1,56})^{\frac{1}{2}} , \quad \text{and}$$

$$\hat{0}_{\eta p} = \frac{\hat{\eta}_p}{"t"_{56}}$$

The standard error of η_τ is computed the same way.

The quarterly data are quarterly averages for 1954-1968, computed from seasonally adjusted monthly data reported in U.S. Department of Labor, Bureau of Labor Statistics, *Employment and Earnings and Monthly Report on the Labor Force* 15, No. 8 (February 1969).

The quarterly growth rates in employment for each of the groups are computed from the observed growth rates between averages for the year 1956-III to 1957-II and one decade later, 1966-III to 1967-II. They are

	White males	Nonwhite males	White females	Nonwhite females
Adults	−.0023	−.0003	.0023	.0027
Teenagers	.0077	.0029	.0071	.0063

The estimated equations are summarized in Table 3-3.

The minimum wage and coverage data were obtained from the U.S. Department of Labor and provided to us by Thomas G. Moore, Senior Staff Economist, Council of Economic Advisers. These data are reported in Tables 3-4 and 3-5.

Table 3-3
Least Squares Estimates of Distributional Parameters and Elasticities with Respect to the Minimum Wage for Employment by Age-Color-Sex Classes*

	$\hat{\gamma}$	$\hat{\beta}$	$\hat{\eta}$	$\hat{\eta}_T$	R^2
Adults					
White males	5.53E-01	4.18E-01	.032	−1.44	.947
Nonwhite males	5.97E-02	3.60E-01	−.004	− .47	.979
White females	2.27E-01	5.34E-00	.032	−1.00	.994
Nonwhite females	3.86E-02	2.71E-02	−.017	.08	.990
Teenagers					
White males	7.10E-02	3.59E-05	−.331	2.48	.949
Nonwhite males	1.11E-02	7.53E-08	−.356	3.88	.712
White females	4.26E-02	1.68E-06	−.241	3.30	.925
Nonwhite females	4.96E-03	3.75E-10	−.301	5.31	.744

*Standard errors are not reported. They are reported for the elasticities in Table 3-2; for γ_0 and β_0 all coefficient estimates are more than five times their respective standard errors.

Table 3-4
Estimated Percentage of Aggregate Employment Covered by Federal Minimum Wage Legislation, 1954-1968

	Quarters			
Year	I	II	III	IV
1954	46.3	45.6	46.1	45.7
1955	45.7	45.9	46.6	46.0
1956	45.7	45.5	46.4	45.7
1957	45.3	45.0	45.6	44.6
1958	43.5	43.0	43.9	43.7
1959	43.3	43.8	44.3	43.6
1960	43.4	43.2	43.8	42.7

Table 3-4 (cont.)

1961	41.7	42.1	43.0	51.1
1962	50.8	51.2	51.7	51.3
1963	50.5	51.1	51.4	51.0
1964	50.3	50.5	51.2	50.9
1965	51.0	51.0	51.0	51.0
1966	51.0	51.0	51.0	51.0
1967	60.9	60.7	61.3	60.9
1968	61.7	62.0	62.0	62.0

Source: Thomas G. Moore, Senior Staff Económist, Council of Economic Advisers.

Table 3-5
Federal Legal Minimum Wage, 1954-1968

Year-quarter	Minimum wage
1954-I	$0.75
to	
1956-II	1.00
to	
1961-IV	1.15
to	
1963-IV	1.25
to	
1967-I	1.40
to	
1968-I	1.60

Source: Thomas G. Moore, Senior Staff Economist, Council of Economic Advisers.

Notes

1. See Gary S. Becker, *Human Capital* (New York: National Bureau of Economic Research, 1964), for a discussion of investment in firm-specific human capital.

2. β_i/γ_i is the elasticity of employment in the ith group with respect to the aggregate when changes in the aggregate refer to deviations about the long-term equilibrium path.

3. For example, between 1958 and 1968 the unemployment rate for white adult males dropped from 5.5 to 2.0 percent and for nonwhite adult males from 12.7 to 4.0. Yet white teenage male employment only dropped to 10.1 from 15.7, and nonwhite teenage males dropped from 26.8 to 22.1. U.S. Department of Labor, Bureau of Labor Statistics, *Employment and Earningsand Monthly Report on the Labor Force* 15, no. 8 (February 1969).

4. Although the legislation is couched in terms of what employers pay,

from a profit maximizing perspective, imposition of a legal minimum makes it illegal for covered firms to employ workers whose value productivity is less than the minimum wage.

5. Also, that all firms comply with the legislation.

6. Although it is clear that the effects of an increase in coverage are similar to an increase in the minimum wage, it is not obvious that the relation is as simple as we propose. In this case, to do otherwise would unnecessarily complicate the estimation procedure. The effects can be compared by noting that at a point in time, the number of persons in a group who are working given the existing minimum wage structure is the number who would have otherwise been working times the proportion of the group that is either not covered by the legislation or whose productivity exceeds the minimum. This proportion is one minus the proportion with productivity less than the minimum times the proportion of these persons effectively covered. We have no empirical evidence showing the fractional increase in coverage within specific groups from a one percent increase in aggregate coverage. It would seem that at very low aggregate levels, the effects would be more in the nature of changing the distribution of employment between covered and uncovered firms than of actually reducing employment. But as coverage expands, the effects must eventually be felt.

Our operational definition amounts to the empirical assertion that if a 1 percent increase in aggregate coverage results in, say, a $100a$ percent increase in effective coverage for a particular group, then a 1 percent increase in the minimum wage will also result in a $100a$ percent increase in the fraction of persons affected.

The Economics of Racial Discrimination in Organized Baseball

ANTHONY H. PASCAL
LEONARD A. RAPPING

I. Introduction

Whether it is because we are growing richer as a nation, because urban disorders have frightened us, or simply because of fashion, the problem of inequality of economic opportunity in American society receives increasing attention. Inequality of economic opportunity means, in the simplest terms, that some people start out in life with poorer chances for economic success than others. Disadvantage is caused both by inadequate work preparation and by bias in hiring and promotion, and further, a man's opportunities are importantly affected by the color of his skin.

There have been numerous studies of wage discrimination in the American economy (Becker, 1957; see also Hanoch, 1967; Welch, 1967; Arrow, 1972). Empirical studies have typically failed to overcome a series of problems in definition, measurement, and data retrieval. By way of illustration, it is commonly observed that members of minority groups earn lower incomes than do their counterparts in the majority population. Naturally enough, attempts have been made to explain the observed income differences on the basis of variation between the minority and majority work forces in age and sex composition and in educational attainment. Finally, however, there remains an unexplained difference. Recognizing that it is invalid to attribute this residual difference in earnings entirely to the existence of prejudice in the labor market, analysts have tried to refine their measures further. They take into account that members of disadvantaged minorities typically receive a lower quality of education per year of schooling attained and that their families and neighborhoods may instill in them a set of attitudes and perceptions that are not conducive to conventional economic success. But it is exceedingly difficult to control adequately for such things as attitudes, motivation, and educational quality. This difficulty makes the residual approach to measuring market discrimination extremely treacherous.[1]

If one sets out, then, to study the role of discrimination, it is essential to design experiments in which the true sources of inequality can be separated. Since in the social sciences researchers must analyze data generated in human interactions rather than in laboratories, this separation is exceedingly difficult. Suppose, however, it were possible to find an occupation for which the quality of formal schooling and the general cultural background of an aspirant made relatively little difference in his ability to succeed, an occupation in which abil-

119

ity was clearly apparent to interested observers and in which the link between ability and reward could be observed. Then, differences in earnings for individuals of equal ability but different color would be a relatively unambiguous measure of discrimination in the labor market. The professional athlete follows such an occupation. In this study we explore the impact of race on salary, assignment, and promotion in major league baseball.

Managers and team owners, anxious for success in the pennant race because of its effects at the gate, presumably judge a potential player largely on the basis of his achieved batting, fielding, or pitching ability, and not on where he received his college degree or high school diploma, or even whether he received one. These abilities are clearly indexed and generally available. A player might suffer from the effects of prejudice in the past as indicated, say, by lower levels of health, or less adequate coaching when young; these, however, would be expected to exert an influence on his measured batting, fielding, or pitching performance. We can sum up by stating the major hypotheses we wish to test in this study. They are: (a) salaries paid to baseball players are a function of ability and of alternative earnings but not of the race of the player, and (b) assignment of players to league, team, and position is also independent of race. The chief assumption in testing these hypotheses is that the management of a baseball team acts as if it were managing an ordinary wealth-maximizing firm.

We shall refer to *discrimination* as the discrepancy in treatment between candidates who are identical in all "relevant" characteristics. Among the "irrelevant" characteristics that call forth unequal treatment, the most interesting for our purposes is race. Discrepancies may be manifested in unequal compensation to persons with the same relevant characteristics or through unequal opportunity in entry, promotion, or assignment for people with the same relevant characteristics.[2]

Prejudice, on the other hand, is one of the chief and most interesting causes of discrimination. The market manifestation of prejudice may emanate from any of the following sources: owners or their agents, such as managers; complementary workers such as coaches; customers in the ballpark or TV audience; or white baseball players who are substitutes for black players. A prejudiced person may feel contempt toward those of other races or may merely believe in stereotypes. A stereotype results from the assumption of a correlation between the relevant and irrelevant characteristics of a person, usually to the discredit of the person in question. (The notion that a stereotype may be as much an information-economizing device as a reaction to "differentness" has some interest from a theoretical standpoint but is of little empirical significance in this study.)

In terms of the above discussion, measuring the amount of racial salary or bonus discrimination in organized baseball requires that at any point in time we consider the stock of all baseball players and measure ability (A_i^* for the ith player) and salaries (S_i), and then compare the two variables to determine whether discrimination occurs. Discrimination is indicated when blacks receive lower salaries than whites, ability equal, at each (or some) level of the occupational hierarchy (minor and major leagues) or when it is more difficult for blacks to transit from a lower to a higher league status (salary generally rises as one moves up the hierarchy).

The absence of salary data for minor league players and the difficulty of measuring ability for these players have forced us to concentrate our efforts on major league players only. In particular, we restrict the focus of our study to racial salary discrimination in major league baseball rather than organized baseball in general. Though we do try to derive some implications about the larger industry, in effect, we are defining the relevant occupation for purposes of our study as major league baseball players rather than organized baseball players. Since most occupations are arbitrarily defined anyway, this is not a particularly restrictive point of view.

To estimate the extent of racial discrimination in major league baseball, we examine the problem in four steps. First, we study the relationship among major league salaries, ability, and race in the years 1968 and 1969. Included here is an exploration of major league bonus payments over the period 1950-68. Then, we examine whether there is an entry barrier that makes it more difficult for blacks than whites to transit from the minor to the major leagues. This part of our study covers the year 1968. We conclude with an exploration of the implications of racial assignment practices in major league baseball. In particular, we study the distribution of blacks by league, club, and playing position. Finally, we briefly examine the opportunities for blacks in supervisory positions in baseball (umpires, managers, and coaches).

II. The Baseball Industry

"Organized" baseball refers to the collection of baseball clubs bound together by a complex set of rules and regulations contained in a collection of constitutional documents. In 1968 organized professional baseball consisted of two major leagues of 10 clubs each and a total of 145 minor league clubs in 20 leagues classified into the categories AAA, AA, A, and Rookie. During the regular 1968 playing season these clubs were allowed to maintain on their permanent playing rosters a total of about 3,000 players of whom 500 players were on the major league rosters.

The minor league clubs are either "independent" or "farm" teams of a major league club.[3] The farm club may be owned outright by the major league club or some of its players may be controlled by the major league club by "working agreements." These agreements provide the major league club with access to a specified number of the farm club's players in exchange for financial or other assistance.

Organized baseball rules grant each club an exclusive monopoly to a particular market area. These "territorial rights," coupled with the rules governing the allocation of players among clubs, are the heart of the agreements among organized baseball clubs.

With regard to players, it is useful to follow Rottenberg's distinction among three separate sets of rules governing activities in what is effectively three separate baseball player labor markets (Rottenberg, 1956). Before his first contract, a young high school or college player is a free agent; prior to the winter of 1964 when a free draft was instituted, there was heavy interteam bidding for their services. Bonuses for signing ranged anywhere from a few hundred dollars to over $100,000. Once having signed a "uniform contract" the player is restricted to the club that owns his contract, and he cannot freely solicit offers from other clubs nor can other clubs attempt to negotiate with a player already under contract. This restriction is covered by a contractual arrangement known as the "reserve clause," which permits the club to renew a player's contract for the following year at a price negotiated between the club and the player whose alternative employments are necessarily out of baseball. This clause is enforced by extra-legal sanctions provided for in the rules of organized baseball. Finally, and unlike in other labor markets, the player is an asset owned by the club because of the reserve player clause. This gives rise to a third market in which players' contracts are sold or traded among clubs at prices determined by the clubs participating in the transaction.

This study will be restricted to major league players, defined following the *Baseball Register*, as one who appears on the spring roster. This choice permits us to study a list of players for which considerable data are available in a convenient form.[4] In 1968, 784 major league players were listed on the spring rosters. It appears that this list approximately covers the 40-man reserve lists on the 20 major league teams (*Baseball Roster*, 1968).

In subsequent analyses we separate our sample into "veterans" and "non-veterans," but for purposes of this section we utilize the entire sample of 784 major league players. The distribution of all 784 major league players by age, race, and national origin is shown in Table 4-1. The median age of major league baseball players in 1968 was 25 years. Of the 784 players, 17 were Latin whites, 58 were Latin blacks, 116 were American blacks, and the remaining 593 players were American whites[5] In percentage terms, 2.2 percent were Latin white, 7.3 percent were Latin black, 14.7 percent were American black, and 75.8 percent were American white. Of the comparable age/sex group in the U.S. population as a whole, as of August 1968, approximately 12 percent were nonwhite (U.S. Department of Labor, 1968a: 14).

In regional origin, both white and nonwhite baseball players reflect general demographic patterns; the players appear to have completed about the same number of years of school as the comparable U.S. population in age and sex. In Table 4-2 we give data for three levels of educational attainment for baseball players classified by race and origin. Well over half of the white have attended or graduated from college and slightly over half of the American blacks have had

Table 4-1

Distribution of 784 Major League Baseball Players by Age, Race, and Origin, 1968

Age	U.S. black	U.S. white	Latin black	Latin white	Total
20 and Under	9	25	3	2	39
21-23	23	149	9	2	183
24-26	35	192	11	3	241
27-29	20	113	22	6	161
30-32	10	77	11	1	99
33-35	16	22	2	3	43
36 and Over	3	15	0	0	18
Total	116	593	58	17	784

Source: *Baseball Register*, (St. Louis: *The Sporting News*, 1968).

Table 4-2

Educational Attainment of 784 Major League Baseball Players, 1968 (Percent)

Player's race	Attended or graduated from high school	Attended college	Graduated from college
American black	47	48	5
Latin black	77	21	2
White	39	47	14

Source: *Baseball Register*, 1968.

some college experience. These data suggest that the median years of school completed for American black players was about 12 years and for whites about 13 years. In March of 1967 the median years of school completed by the entire U.S. male population between 18 and 34 years of age was about 12.5 years (U.S. Department of Labor, 1968b: 216).

III. A Model of Salary Determination in Baseball

Clearly, to test for the presence of salary discrimination against black major leaguers it is necessary to control for factors other than race that determine a player's annual salary. Stated differently, we need a theory of annual salary determination in baseball.

Under the reserve clause, each player is required to sell his services to the club that has reserved him unless the club releases, sells, or trades him, or he chooses to retire from organized baseball. This peculiar institutional arrangement generates two questions with which a useful model of salary determination must deal. First, does the resulting allocation of players among clubs tend toward optimality in the sense that players are assigned to those clubs in which their contribution to team revenues is the greatest?[6] Second, how are salaries determined in the absence of competition among buyers that, coupled with the willingness or unwillingness of sellers to change jobs, simultaneously determines the allocation of labor among jobs and salaries in most other industries? With the reserve clause the allocation and salary questions are determined by institutional arrangements peculiar to baseball (and a few other professional sports).[7]

The optimal distribution of players among clubs is constantly changing in response to changing conditions, such as in the tastes of fans, growth of cities, preference of owners, development of technology, and so on. The player draft, player trades, and player purchases serve to reallocate players among clubs in response to these changes. Although the rules governing trading, releases, and sales are complex, they nevertheless guarantee considerable reshuffling of players among clubs, and there are strong economic incentives for clubs to trade in players. At the annual player draft major and minor league clubs are permitted to acquire the contracts of players owned by other clubs. A major league club usually has control of several hundred players who are either owned outright by the major league club or controlled through "working agreements" with minor league clubs. Of all these players, a major league club may protect 40 players—25 of whom play regularly for it and 15 of whom are on option to minor league clubs—from the annual player draft. In November of 1967 (prior to the 1968 season), major league clubs drafted a total of 23 minor league players at the annual player draft. Draft prices are fixed at $25,000 for regulars and $8,000 for first-year picks.

Supplementing the player draft was considerable player movement resulting from trades, sells, and the signing of free agents. The *Baseball Guide* lists a total of 140 players who were traded during the calendar year 1967, 35 players who were purchased, 6 free agents who were signed, and 30 players who were released. Excluding released players, the above list involves 181 players in 1967. Of this total, 90 appeared in the 1968 *Baseball Register*, 17 of whom we had classified as nonveterans and 73 as veterans. Since our total veteran sample was 453 players, the proportion of these veterans who changed clubs between 1967 and 1968 was about 16 percent ($73 \div 453$). This statistic is an estimate of the probability that a major league player chosen at random will move between clubs in any given year.

As a further indication of the amount of player movement among major league clubs, we computed the distribution of players in our 1968 veteran sample (453 players) by number of major league organizations with which the player had been associated. These figures do not imply the number of major league teams for which the players have played since many of the trades, sells, and drafts obtained while the player was a minor leaguer. The distribution is shown below.

Number of organizations	1	2	3	4	5	6	7
Number of players	117	113	74	28	10	8	3

The data suggest quite strongly that the economic incentives for clubs to trade, buy, and sell players are pervasive and do indeed cause substantial movement of players among teams. The results of the free agent draft are thus altered by subsequent transactions. About 16 percent of the 453 veteran players in the sample we describe below changed clubs between 1967 and 1968; the average player had been associated with over 1.7 baseball clubs in his career. All in all, the trading mechanism probably results in a distribution of players among teams not too different from what would obtain in the absence of the reserve clause.[8]

Baseball player salaries are individually negotiated prior to each season.[9] Because of the reserve player clause, the determination of salaries is best thought of as a problem in bargaining theory. We know that for such problems there is no neat, theoretical solution, and so we have opted for a simple but intuitively pleasing approach. As a first approximation we assume that a player's salary for the upcoming season depends on two factors: his expected playing ability in that season and the salary he can earn in some relevant alternative occupation. This formulation assumes that a player's expected ability is proportional to his expected contribution to club revenues because individual ability draws fans and contributes to overall club performance, which also attracts customers. A player's contribution to club revenues is the maximum salary a skillful bargainer could extract from a club. We assume a player's salary will be higher the greater his contribution to club revenues.[10]

The second argument in the salary function is the player's alternative earnings that represent the minimum salary a club owner skilled in bargaining would offer the player. We assume then that the appropriate salary model can be approximated by a linear model of the form

$$S_i = \gamma_0 + \gamma_1 A_i^* + \gamma_2 W_i + \epsilon_i, \tag{1}$$

where S_i = the ith player's salary for the forthcoming season, A_i^* = the ith player's expected ability in the forthcoming season, W_i = the alternative salary that the ith player can earn outside of baseball, and ϵ_i = a random error term assumed to have a mean of zero and constant variance. Among other things, the error term in (1) is assumed to reflect individual differences in bargaining ability.

In predicting ability we assume that both players and club owners process past player experience, including the measurable and nonmeasurable. As a first approximation we assume that the relevant measurable experience for nonpitchers is the past batting performance in the major leagues, and that the most recent experience is weighted more heavily than that of the distant past. This says that the most recent experience is taken as an indication of an upward or downward trend in the projection of past experience. (We later introduce other statistical performance measures, but in the interests of expositional simplicity we temporarily ignore these complications.) Further, we assume that players improve with years of experience and that this improvement is not reflected fully in measured statistical performance. Years of experience, for example, might be expected to increase the certainty with which a past performance measure is projected into the future. Stating these assumptions algebraically we have

$$A_i^* = \beta_0 + \beta_1 \overline{C_i} + \beta_2 B_i + \beta_3 y_i + u_i , \tag{2}$$

where

$\overline{C_i}$ = cumulated batting average of the ith player over his entire major league experience at the time of salary negotiations,

B_i = the ith player's batting average in his major league season immediately prior to salary negotiations,

y_i = years of major league experience for the ith player,

v_i = a random error term with a mean of zero and constant variance.

In (2) if $\beta_2 = 0$ then the same weight is given to all previous experience while if $\beta_2 > 0$ then the most recent past has a greater weight than the more distant past. In the latter event the most recent past is extrapolated, so to speak.

For estimation purposes we replace the years of experience variable with a variable measuring a player's calendar age (Y), which more precisely indexes his overall baseball experience. We also replace the variable, W_i, by several dummy variables indexing country of origin and education. Because Latins have poorer alternatives than North Americans, we express W_i as a zero-one dummy variable (L), where zero is Latin and one is North American. We also assume it to depend on a zero-one high school variable, (E_1), which is zero for having gone beyond high school and one for having only attended or graduated from high school; on a zero-one attended college variable, (E_2), which is one for having attended college but not graduated and zero otherwise; and on a zero-one graduated college variable, (E_3), which is one for having graduated from college and zero otherwise. Mathematically we have

$$W_i = a_0 + a_1 L_i + a_2 E_{1i} + a_3 E_{2i} + a_4 E_{3i} + v_i, \tag{3}$$

where v_i = a random error term assumed to have a mean of zero and constant variance.

If there is prejudice on the part of fans, white coaches, managers, or club owners, black player salaries may be lower than that of white players, other things equal. We test for this possibility by introducing an additive zero-one dummy variable in (1), one for whites and zero for blacks (R). We recognize, however, that a significant finding for this coefficient is subject to either of two interpretations. First, there is the obvious prejudice interpretation. On the other hand, the dummy variable may be viewed as an additional control for alternative earnings, which on the average are poorer for blacks than for whites, in both North America and the Caribbean. Under this interpretation, the effect of race stems from the reserve player clause, which disadvantages those with the poorest opportunities outside of baseball—blacks in general and Latin blacks in particular—because it prevents interclub competition from equalizing salaries by race.

Substituting (2) and (3) into (1) and adding the race variable we have:

$$S_i = (\gamma_0 + \beta_0\gamma_1 + a_0\gamma_2) + \gamma_1 (\beta_1 + \beta_2) \overline{C}_i + (\gamma_1\beta_2) [B_i - \overline{C}_i] + (\gamma_1\beta_3) Y_i$$
$$+ (\gamma_2 a_1) L_i + (\gamma_2 a_2) E_{1i} + (\gamma_2 a_3) E_{2i} + (\gamma_2 a_4) E_{3i}$$
$$+ \gamma_3 R_i + (\gamma_1 u_i + \gamma_2 v_i + \epsilon_i)$$

$$(4)$$

where under our assumptions the error term has an expected value of zero and constant variance.

The explanatory variables in model (4) are not an exhaustive specification of variables affecting interplayer salary variation. Indeed, in models subsequently considered, variables measuring home run producing ability, playing position, fielding percentage, and club standing last season were introduced in addition to the variables in (4). It is of course clear that there also exist characteristics of players—"star quality" and field leadership are examples—that are virtually impossible to measure in quantitative terms.

The Salary Sample

The salary data used in this study were obtained from reported salaries contained in twenty local newspapers and *The Sporting News*. We have reason to believe that the data are fairly accurate and, equally important, there is no a priori reason to think that reporting errors, if any, are systematically related to any of the variables used in our analyses.[11] Our nonrandom sample includes the salaries of 87 players in 1968 and 61 players in 1969. The 1969 figures include 41 players for whom we also had 1968 salary information so that our sample includes a total of 107 nonrepeat salary figures and a total of 148 salary figures including repeats. The mean 1968 salary for our sample of 87 players was $44,400, and the mean 1969 salary for our sample of 61 players was $53,400.

We believe our nonrandom sample is biased toward the upper tail of the entire major league (25-man rosters) salary distribution. The distribution of major league salaries is truncated at a minimum annual salary agreed upon by players and owners; $10,000 in 1968 and $12,000 in 1969. In figures reported for 1966, the mean salary for all major league players was $22,000. Projecting this mean to 1968-69 at a reasonable compound growth rate and comparing it with our sample means indicates that the sample is biased toward the upper tail of the major league salary structure. Our purpose, however, is to estimate the effect of different variables on salary and not to estimate population means. For this, it is important that our salary sample embrace the entire actual salary range, and it does meet this criterion. The salary observations vary from $10,000 to $125,000; 34 of the 148 observations are below $25,000.

Regression Results for Nonpitchers' Salaries

Estimates of the parameters of the nonpitcher model (4) and several variants of this model are shown in Table 4-3. All of the reported regressions are linear in the original variables and relevant dimensions are given at the bottom of the table. The regressions reported in this table were also run in log linear form but this transformation did not appreciably alter any of our conclusions. For ease in interpreting the estimates and not because of any statistical superiority we report the results for arithmetically linear models.[1][2]

In regression 1 the overall goodness of fit is remarkably high. The adjusted R^2 is .68, meaning that 68 percent of the sample variance is explained by the explanatory variables.[13]

The three coefficients for the measures of a player's contribution to club revenues are statistically significant at the one-tail 10 percent test level or better. In particular, the coefficient for lifetime cumulated major league batting average $(\overline{C})$ is highly significant, and the point estimate indicates that a player receives $678 per year for each point added to this average. The estimated coefficient for $(B - \overline{C})$, also significant at the 10 percent test level, suggests that when a player's performance is unusually good it is extrapolated. Thus an untypically good season increases a player's salary by $129 for each batting point in excess of his "normal" performance. The age coefficient (Y) implies that each year of player experience increases his salary by about $2,300. Although we interpret this to be an ability effect, on the assumption that players learn from experience, we cannot rule out the possibility that the coefficient also contains a pure seniority effect, that is, that internal team morale may require that salary increase with age.

Since we measure education in a trichotomous fashion, it was necessary to delete one of the education variables, impounding the effect of the deleted variable into the estimated constant term. The two included variables are zero-one dummies for attended college (E_2) and graduated from college (E_3). The dummy variable for attended or graduated from high school is omitted. Under these circumstances the estimated coefficients for (E_2) and (E_3) are interpreted as estimates of the *marginal* salary contribution for college attendance or college graduation as opposed to attending or graduating from high school. The estimated coefficients for these two variables raise some question as to whether formal years of school completed is a relevant bargaining variable. Although the estimated E_2 coefficient is statistically significant and quantitatively large, the point estimate for E_3 is negative, indicating that college graduates are at a bargaining disadvantage in comparison with high school graduates, a rather peculiar finding.[14] Apparently we have not obtained very sharp statistical control of alternative earnings and in subsequent regressions we abandon the use of education dummies.

The Latin-American dummy variable has a statistically significant negative effect on salaries that is consistent with the view that Latins are at a bargaining disadvantage compared with North Americans because of their poorer earnings alternatives outside of American baseball. The size of the estimated effect of Latin origin, however, is probably overstated in this regression. It is difficult to believe that, other things equal, Latins earn on average $22,000 less per year than North Americans. We suspect this dummy variable is picking up some other unspecified effect.

The time coefficient is statistically significant and the point estimate indicates that between 1968 and 1969 salaries rose by about $7,600. We are not entirely convinced that this estimate reflects the effect of inflation and productivity advance on salaries; in an identical regression, using only nonrepeat salary data, the estimated time coefficient was a small negative number and statistically insignificant.

The main objective of our analysis is to estimate the effect of race on salaries. The estimated race coefficient is statistically insignificant, however. *Apparently, there was no salary discrimination against black baseball players who have achieved major league status.*

In regression (2) we have omitted the unsatisfactory education variables and have replaced them with a home run variable. This variable is measured by total major league home runs divided by an estimate of the number of full seasons played (home runs per 550 times at bat). In broad outline, the estimates in regression (2) are similar to those reported in regression (1). In addition, the home run variable yields a statistically significant and quantitatively important coefficient. The mean number of home runs per season is about 18 for players in our sample. Such players as Killebrew, Robinson, Maris, Mays, McCovey, and Mathews can generate an extra 14 to 22 home runs per season compared with the mean value for players in our sample. Regression (2) tells us that a player who can consistently add 20 home runs to the home run average can also add $7,920 (.396 x 20) to his annual salary.

We added a variable measuring the number of times at bat for each player in the season immediately preceding the salary observation. A player with relatively few appearances who trades off playing with another player or who cannot hit against both left and right handed pitchers would be worth less to clubs than more regular players. We could expect, then, a positive effect from times at bat

Table 4-3
Statistical Explanation of Major League Baseball Players' Salaries: Regression Results, 1968-69

Regression number	Constant	Nonpitchers[a] $\bar{C}$	$B-\bar{C}$	HR	BT	Pitchers[b] $\frac{\bar{G}}{I}$	$\bar{I}$	G	I	s	$P_{\bar{C}-\bar{G}}$	$P_{\bar{I}-\bar{I}}$	Y	L	E_2	E_3	t	R	R^2(adj)
(1)	−221.7 (22.0)**	.678 (.068)***	.129 (.066)*										2.342 (.546)***	22.381 (6.523)***	7.581 (3.983)*	−1.824 (5.301)	7.967 (3.538)*	−2.892 (3.983)	.68
(2)	−195.6 (21.6)***	.600 (.067)***	.147 (.067)*	.396 (.190)									2.149 (.541)***	16.977			8.383 (3.525)***	−2.575 (3.926)	.69
(3)	−188.1 (21.7)***	.540 (.074)***	.151 (.066)***		.016 (.009)**								2.385 (.549)***	14.847 (6.646)**			4.473 (4.004)	−2.914 (3.877)	.69
(4)	−56.8 (27.0)**					2.873 (.660)***					1.419 (.615)**		2.721 (.748)***	−4.403 (10.141)	−4.575 (5.710)	1.691 (10.965)	.424 (5.360)	−10.413 (7.184)*	.49
(5)	−48.5 (27.6)*						.193 (.051)***					.136 (.052)***	2.539 (.743)***	−7.664 (10.287)	−3.294 (5.889)	−.500 (11.151)	.287 (5.490)	−13.019 (7.798)**	.47
(6)	17.4 (8.2)**							.646 (.077)***		−3.420 (1.035)***	.507 (.408)			5.539 (6.654)			5.667 (3.583)*	−7.035 (4.747)*	.77
(7)	27.1 (9.6)***								.036 (.006)***	−2.576 (1.245)**		.072 (.041)**		−.787 (7.780)			5.357 (4.276)	−11.183 (6.004)*	.68

Notes

$\left.\begin{array}{l} * \\ ** \\ *** \end{array}\right\}$ One-tail significance at $\left\{\begin{array}{l} .10 \\ .05 \\ .01 \end{array}\right.$

[a]93 major league players including repeaters.
[b]55 major league players including repeaters.

Table 4-3 (cont)

Key To Variables

Figures in parentheses refer to pitchers' sample, others to nonpitchers' sample.)

	Variable	Mean	Standard Error	Unit
S	Salary	52.5 (41.5)	21.1 (26.1)	$1000
$\overline{C}$	Lifetime batting average	267	32	hits per 1000 times at bat
$B\text{-}\overline{C}$	Difference between last year's and lifetime batting average	−000.5	28.2	
HR	Home runs	17.9	10.6	HR per 550 times at bat
BT	Times at bat last season	463	147	
$\overline{G}$	Major league games won per full season played	(11.2)	(4.1)	
$\overline{I}$	Innings pitched per full major league season	(179.0)	(55.0)	
G	Total major league games won	(62.0)	(48.6)	
I	Total major league innings pitched	(982.0)	(739.0)	
s	Total seasons pitched	(5.5)	(3.4)	
$P_g\text{-}\overline{G}$	Difference between games won last season and $\overline{G}$	(2.0)	(4.5)	
$P_I\text{-}\overline{I}$	Difference between innings pitched last season and $\overline{I}$	(15.0)	(56.2)	
Y	Calendar age	29.6 (28.4)	3.7 (4.0)	years
L	Latinity	.90 (.91)		fraction North American
E_2	Attended college	.34 (.47)		fraction
E_3	Graduated from college	.05 (.07)		fraction
t	Time	.42 (.40)		
R	Race	.59 (.80)		fraction white

last season. The estimated effect on salaries of this variable, regression (3), is positive and statistically significant. The point estimate suggests that an extra 100 times at bat is worth about $1,600.

We have experimented with several additional variables which were separately added to regression (2). The variables were: (a) fielding ability as measured by reported fielding percentages; (b) a zero-one position variable that dichotomized infielders and outfielders; and (c) the team's league standing in the season prior to salary negotiations. None of these variables made a significant contribution to the explanation of salary variation. We also added a multiplicative variable, ($\overline{C}Y$), which was significant but when added did not alter the conclusion with regard to race.

Regression Results for Pitchers' Salaries

For pitchers, we again use the salary model as in model (4) except that we now use performance variables relevant for pitchers. Several different measures were considered. Because of the common practice of ranking pitchers during a season by either earned run average or percent of games won (ratio of games won to total decisions), we experimented with these two variables. We computed the lifetime major league *ERA* and the percent of games won over a player's major league lifetime (*P*) for each of the 55 pitchers in our salary sample. Surprisingly, neither of these variables correlated well with the reported salary variable and they were both statistically insignificant in our multiple regression analyses.[15] We therefore sought alternative pitching performance measures.

Two alternative measures were considered—average games won per major league season ($\overline{G}$) and average innings pitched per major league season ($\overline{I}$). A season is defined as any one year period in which the player appeared in ten or more games. The use of games won per season assumes that owners place considerably more weight on a pitcher's ability to win games than on the number of games he loses. Furthermore, the number of wins reflects the ability of a player to be a consistent starter; it also is related to whether the player is a starter or a reliefer. Starters and particularly consistent starters might be more valuable to clubs than reliefers. The number of total innings pitched per season reflects many of the durability and consistency characteristics of games won per season, as well as reflecting a manager's assessment of durability; and indeed the two variables are highly correlated.

Regression equation (4) in Table 4-3 contains the same variables as regression (1) except that cumulated lifetime batting average is replaced by games won per season and last year's batting average is replaced by games won in the season immediately preceding the one covered by the salary observation (P_g). This regression is based on the augmented sample of 55 players. To aid in interpreting our findings we report in the notes to Table 4-3 the means and standard errors of the variables used in regression (4) and subsequent regressions.

The equation provides a reasonably good explanation of interplayer salary variation with the included variables accounting for 49 percent of the sample variance as evidenced by the adjusted R^2. When compared with our nonpitcher results, the only important difference is the insignificance of the Latin variable, suggesting perhaps that the Latin effect reported for nonpitchers is spurious. We also find a negative race coefficient significant at the 10 percent level indicating that on average blacks receive *higher* salaries than whites. This finding, however, is quite sensitive to the specification of the model utilized. In particular, if the dependent variable is the log of salary, the coefficient on race becomes statistically insignificant at any reasonable test level, but the significance of the other coefficients is not appreciably affected. For interpretive simplicity, we continue to discuss the model in arithmetic terms. The effect of games won per season on salaries is $2,873 per game, at least according to the highly reliable point estimate in regression (4). We find, in addition, that the most recent pitching experience of a player is extrapolated. Thus, a player, who in the preceding season wins two games more than indicated by his lifetime average, can increase his salary by about $2,800 (2 x 1.419) for the upcoming season. Finally, age continues to produce a large and statistically significant effect on salary.

When innings pitched per season is substituted for games won per season—regression (5)—the general qualitative findings are not too different from those reported in regression (4). Based on overall goodness of fit the two variables perform equally well. Regression (5) has an adjusted R^2 of .47, which is only slightly smaller than that of regression (4).

Although the variables games won per season and innings pitched per season work reasonably well in a statistical sense, they were not suggested by anything more than casual speculation. It seems no less reasonable to introduce games won and seasons pitched as separate variables than to introduce them in ratio form. Similar remarks apply to the variable innings pitched per season. When we use the same model as that in regression (4), but introduce cumulated lifetime major league games won (G) and major league seasons played (s) as separate variables, and omit the age variable, because of its obvious high correlation with s, as well as the education variables, which have proven rather uninteresting, we obtain the results shown in regression (6).

First, we note a significant improvement in overall goodness of fit in regression (6) as compared with the games per season model, regression (4), and in this sense one might have greater confidence in the findings based on regression (6) than those based on regression (4). Similar remarks apply to regression model (7), which employs total lifetime innings pitched and seasons pitched as separate variables rather than using these variables in ratio form as was done in regression (5). Because the pattern of estimated coefficient signs and the statistical significance level of these estimates are so similar between regression (6) and (7), we restrict our discussion to the results based on regression (6).

Holding seasons pitched constant, the effect on annual salaries of total games won is positive with the point estimate indicating that each game won is worth $646. The negative effect of the seasons pitched variable should not be surprising. It simply means that the more seasons it takes a pitcher to win a specified number of games the lower his salary. The racial estimate is negative in both (6) and (7), again indicating that whites receive lower salaries than blacks. On the other hand, the Latin estimate is now positive but not statistically significant. The time coefficient indicates that salaries rose by about $5,700 between 1968 and 1969. But for this variable, as well as the race and Latin variables, we do not place much confidence in the estimates, the standard errors being simply too large.[16]

Bonus Payments to Black and
White Players

In the years immediately following World War II, two seemingly unrelated events occurred. First, baseball's racial entry barrier was broken when Branch Rickey of the Brooklyn Dodgers recruited Jackie Robinson in 1947. Second, unbridled free agent bonus competition broke out among clubs mostly because attendance was rising rapidly and the pool of high quality players had been seriously depleted during the war.

By the early 1950s the open payment of large bonuses—some in six figures—for high school and college athletes had become a common practice. Yet owners were reluctant to enter into an arrangement to prohibit bonus competition because of the legal uncertainty surrounding such a move. Indeed, the adoption of the free agent draft in late 1964 followed eight years of extensive Federal lobbying activities on the part of the clubs that eventually succeeded in getting Congress to clarify its willingness to sanction a free agent draft.[17]

To fully appreciate the financial importance of free agent bonus payments, let us consider the year 1958. Although complete bonus data are unavailable, there is some indication that by 1958 the total bonus payments to free agents by major league clubs might have been as high as 5 million dollars or about 80 percent of total compensation of major league players in that year.

Table 4-8 (p. 144) indicates a steady growth in the percent of American blacks who were on the 25-man rosters between 1953 and 1965. (The decline of the black fraction shown after 1965 is probably mostly due to the way team membership is defined.) The Robinson experience undoubtedly demonstrated to other club owners that blacks could be profitably integrated into organized baseball without a player or fan boycott. But a complete explanation of the growth in the percentage of black players requires reference to events other than the unique and insightful decision by Rickey to hire Robinson. In fact, compelling economic factors made it profitable for other clubs to imitate the integrationist policy of the Brooklyn Dodgers. In light of the mounting bonus costs, black players, who were available for modest bonuses or none at all, probably seemed more attractive to club owners than would have been the case in the absence of bonus competition.[18] Large bonus payments were rare for American blacks during the period 1948-58 (see Table 4-4), and clubs that could successfully recruit blacks for small bonuses expected substantial player cost savings. Apparently, there were powerful economic incentives to recruit blacks.

Bonuses are of course an important part of the player compensation package. We shall examine bonus payments by race to further test our hypotheses on salary discrimination in organized baseball. In Table 4-4 we show the percent of major league players in the 1968 *Baseball Register* who received bonuses in excess of $20,000, black and white Latins excluded. The data are cross-classified by year of entry into organized baseball.

Ignoring, for the moment, the time pattern of the white-black differential in the percent of players receiving large bonuses as indicated in Table 4-4, we can interpret the data as supporting the view that prejudice against black athletes on the part of either fans or club owners makes entering blacks less valuable to clubs than whites. This argument is compelling, particularly with respect to large bonuses, which clubs must pay in the search for the baseball hero who can draw fans to the parks.

But the time pattern of the white-black differential adds considerable information and suggests an alternative interpretation of the data. Under combined assumptions of competition, reasonably good information, and no prejudice on the part of club owners or fans, there is no reason to expect bonus payments to differ systematically by race. A club would not continue to pay large bonuses to whites when blacks of equal predicted ability were available for less money. Competition among buyers would equalize bonuses by race even if black athletes had poorer alternatives than white athletes. If, however, we abandon the assumption of perfect information on the part of buyers, bonus payments might indeed differ systematically by race since whites do have better alternatives outside of baseball than blacks. For that subset of players who are scouted by a single club—and the size of this subset is directly related to the amount of information available in the market—bonus payments are determined by a bargaining process between the prospect and the club. Except for the potential competition from activities outside of baseball, clubs that uniquely identify a baseball prospect are free from competitive pressures. Under these circumstances, we would predict that blacks on average would receive smaller bonuses than whites for reasons independent of any prejudice within baseball.

The time pattern of the racial bonus differential is consistent with the view that clubs had some monopoly power. The difference in the percent of whites and the percent of blacks who received large bonuses was substantial and statistically significant prior to 1958.[19] But after that date, the difference began to narrow; and by the period 1965-67, it was almost totally eliminated. This pattern suggests that as clubs developed their black scouting systems, information

Table 4-4
Players Who Received Bonuses in Excess of $20,000 by Year of Entry into Organized Baseball, by Color

Year of entry	Total black	Bonus black	Percent bonus	Total white	Bonus white	Percent bonus
(1)	(2)	(3)	(4)=(3)÷(2)	(5)	(6)	(7)=(6)÷(5)
1958 or earlier	30	0	0	134	26	19.4
1959 - 1961	22	3	13.6	125	43	34.4
1962 - 1964	38	4	10.5	154	31	20.1
1965 - 1967	26	3	11.5	180	23	12.8
	116	10	8.6	593	123	20.7

Source: *Baseball Register*, 1968. (Includes only those players who appeared in the *Register* for 1968.)

spread, and competition among clubs eliminated the racial bonus differential despite the poorer nonbaseball alternatives of blacks. In our sample of 784 players, of which 75 were Latins, not one of the Latins was reported to have received a bonus in excess of $20,000. Latins have unusually poor alternatives outside of organized American baseball.

What, then, can we conclude about direct pecuniary discrimination against American blacks in big league baseball? The evidence we have examined suggests that it does not exist. Black pitchers, black catchers, black infielders, and black outfielders in the major leagues appear to receive compensation commensurate with their demonstrated abilities in the same way that white players do. The original racial differentials in the receipt of bonus payments can reasonably be interpreted as stemming from a combination of information lag and monopolistic practice rather than bigotry, per se. Currently, there is no evidence that even the obviously poorer nonbaseball alternatives of black major leaguers have been sufficient to bring down their relative compensation. Before concluding that baseball is a prejudice-free industry, however, we need to examine entry, promotion, and assignment practices for evidence of systematic racial bias.

*Entry Barriers: The Relative Ability
of Black and White Players*

The purpose of this section is to examine whether it is more difficult for blacks than whites to enter the major leagues. Stated differently, we ask whether a black minor league player must have more baseball-playing ability than a white minor leaguer in order to have an equal chance of being promoted from the minors to the majors. In order to examine the racial entry barrier issue, we compare black and white playing ability among those already in the major leagues. From these comparisons we draw an inference about entry barriers.

To compare the ability of blacks relative to whites, we need to have statistical measures that will constitute an index of ability. For nonpitchers, a wide variety of statistics readily suggest themselves—batting averages, fielding averages, slugging percentages, runs batted in—to name but a few of the more obvious ones.[20] These measures could be combined into an infinite number of overall ability indexes, but we have not attempted to pose the question of what is "the" correct ability measure. We have instead chosen measures that meet two criteria. First, we wanted measures that knowledgeable baseball observers would readily agree are important in relationship to something called "ability." Second, our measures should be highly correlated with an individual player's earning capacity, since it is the playing characteristics that owners and managers deem important.

For nonpitchers, we index ability by the player's lifetime batting average; for pitchers we use games won per season. To compare capabilities we used a sample consisting of 784 major league players listed in the 1968 *Baseball Register*. This sample represents an almost complete enumeration of each club's 40-man protected list. We then divided this sample into two subsamples. Since many of the listed players had no or very limited major league experience, we classified players as either veterans or nonveterans. A veteran nonpitcher was defined as any player who had appeared in 75 or more major league games and a veteran pitcher was defined to include all players who appeared in 25 or more major league games. This definition yielded two subsamples, one consisting of 453 veterans and the other embracing 331 nonveterans.[21] Then, for veterans, we collected statistics for lifetime major league experience. However, for nonveterans, our data covered the latest (usually 1967) minor league season in which as a nonpitcher the player appeared in 25 or more games, or as a pitcher in 4 or more games.

Players were categorized into seven subgroups—pitchers, catchers, first and third basemen, second basemen and shortstops, outfielders, utility infielders, and miscellaneous players.[22]

For each nonpitcher subgroup separately, we have computed the mean difference in black (Latin plus American) and white cumulated major league lifetime batting averages using our sample of veterans only. In this computation, we assume that the basic observation unit is the individual player. Therefore, the figures shown in Table 4-5 are the arithmetic averages of individual lifetime major league batting averages.

Table 4-5
Black and White Individual Cumulated Lifetime Batting Averages, Nonpitcher Veterans, Through 1967

Position	Sample size	Average of batting averages		
		Black	White	Difference
Catcher	N = 35 3 blacks	260	228	32**
First and third	N = 30 10 blacks	272	253	19**
Second and short	N = 44 13 blacks	245	244	1
Outfielders	N = 83 47 blacks	267	255	12**
Other infielders	N = 27 5 blacks	258	252	6
Miscellaneous players	N = 40 12 blacks	255	244	11**

*
** } One-tail significance at { .10
*** .05
.01

Position by position, the arithmetic average of black lifetime batting averages exceeds that of whites. And in four of the six categories the differences are statistically significant at customary test levels.[23] Equally important, the differences are quantitatively interesting and they range from 1 to 32 points. As a basis of comparison, we note that in 1967, the highest team batting average in the American League was 255 (Boston) and the fifth highest team batting average was 238 (California), a difference of 17 points. In the National League, the first (Pittsburgh) and fifth (Cincinnati) place teams in terms of batting performance were separated by 29 points.

Similar calculations for nonveteran nonpitchers are shown in Table 4-6. The data indicate a consistent tendency for black nonveterans to outperform their white counterparts, position by position.

For veterans, we have computed the mean batting average for Latin blacks, American blacks, and all whites separately by position. These figures are shown in Table 4-7. The data indicate that the previously reported black-white differences are not the result of including Latin blacks with American blacks. American blacks were invariably superior to whites; Latin blacks only sometimes.

To measure the ability of pitchers, we have chosen games won per major league season in preference to variables such as major league *ERA* or percent of total major league decisions won (winning percentage).[24] We restrict our discussion to veteran pitchers only. For this sample of pitchers, we computed total games won for the last season in which the player appeared in 10 or more games. In almost all cases this was the 1967 season.

For 19 black pitchers, the mean number of games won was 10.2; for 175 whites it was 7.5 games. This mean difference, 2.7, is significant at the 5 percent

Table 4-6
Black and White Individual Batting Averages, Nonpitcher Nonveterans, Various Years

Position	Sample size	Average of batting averages[a]		
		Black	White	Difference
Catcher	$N = 29$	206	184	22*
First and third	$N = 17$	307	296	11
Second and short	$N = 32$	202	171	31**
Outfield	$N = 49$	201	194	7
Utility infielders	$N = 19$	319	297	22
Miscellaneous players	$N = 24$	233	222	11

[a]All estimates are adjusted for player's age. The adjustment procedure was based on a multiple regression analysis.

$$\left. \begin{array}{l} * \\ ** \\ *** \end{array} \right\} \text{One-tail significance at} \left\{ \begin{array}{l} .10 \\ .05 \\ .01 \end{array} \right.$$

Source: *Baseball Register* (1968).

Table 4-7

Latin Black, North American Black, and White Individual Cumulated Lifetime Batting Averages, Nonpitcher Veterans, Through 1967

Position	Latin black	N. Amer. black	White	Differences	
		Average of individual Lifetime batting averages			
	(1)	(2)	(3)	(2)–(3)	(1)–(3)
Catcher	252	264	228	36	24
First and third	309	268	253	15	56
Second and short	236	278	244	34	-8
Outfield	281	262	255	7	26
Utility infielder	248	273	252	21	-4
Miscellaneous player	255	256	244	12	11

Source: *Baseball Register* (1968).

one-tail test level. On the basis of supplementary tests, we conclude that controlling for age will not account for the mean black-white difference in games won.

What conclusions can be drawn from these data? Under certain assumptions, the results are consistent with the proposition that there is an entry barrier against blacks. This means that on average a black player must be better than a white player if he is to have an equal chance of transiting from the minor leagues to the majors. It is essential to spell out the underlying assumptions that generate this conclusion and then to ask whether these assumptions are plausible.

Assume some distribution of ability for all players in organized baseball. Further, assume that depending on the number of players required by the major league clubs there is some cutoff ability below which players are not promoted. If we assume perfect information about ability (and this argument holds if information is imperfect but there is no systematic error in predicting ability by race), the cutoff value is entirely determined by the required number of players. This is shown in Figure 4-1. In this figure, A_0 is the cutoff ability and all players for which $A \geqslant A_0$ are chosen for the majors. Now if ability is indexed by cumulative lifetime batting average, the mean of the individual lifetime batting average will be the mean for the normalized distribution of ability above A_0. On the other hand, if, because of racial prejudice on the part of fans or owners, blacks were less valuable than whites of equal ability, it would be likely that the cutoff value A_0 would be higher for blacks than whites, $A_0^B > A_0^w$. Under these circumstances, a higher mean ability of blacks than whites, position by position, is evidence consistent with discrimination against blacks. This conclusion, however, requires the prior assumption that the ability distributions of blacks and whites defined over all major and minor league players be the same. If, for any reason, the black distribution had a higher mean than the white ($\mu_B > \mu_w$) or if the black distribution had more variance ($\sigma_B^2 > \sigma_w^2$), then we could not interpret differences in mean major league ability as evidence of racial discrimination.

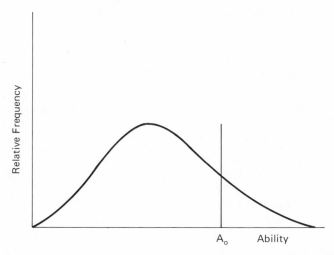

Figure 4–1. Hypothetical Distribution of Baseball Playing Ability.

In general, three arguments might lead one to predict that, on average, the baseball playing ability of blacks within baseball would be greater than that of whites. First, a pervasive man-on-the-street argument holds that blacks have a genetic advantage in athletics. In our view there is neither unambiguous physiological nor anthropological evidence to support this view (Maher, 26 March 1968: 1, 7). In the absence of evidence we choose to be agnostic with regard to this genetic interpretation of our ability findings. We are also skeptical of the second argument, a rather facile assertion that blacks are more highly motivated than whites to acquire athletic abilities. We know of no generally accepted measure of motivation, and this makes the argument even less interesting. Finally, we are somewhat sympathetic to the third argument, that endemic societal wage discrimination in most callings and lesser discrimination in baseball may result in a systematic difference in the ability distributions of black and white baseball players through the process of occupational choice. We consider the problem of occupational choice under the simplifying assumption that there is general societal wage discrimination but an absence of wage discrimination in baseball. Our objective is to determine whether under these circumstances there is reason to suspect that the process of occupational choice will systematically affect the ability distribution of black as compared with white candidates for baseball.

General societal wage discrimination against a minority group will redirect its members into those occupations where discrimination is less prevalent. Although this implies that, other things constant, the *proportion* of blacks will be highest in those occupations where wage discrimination is least prevalent, it does not imply that the average ability of blacks relative to whites will be highest in the nondiscriminatory occupations. The discrimination-free occupations will not only attract a higher percentage of very able blacks but will also attract those that are relatively less able. The net effect on the black ability distribution as compared with the white distribution is unpredictable.

Assume that the present value of the expected income stream from choosing baseball as an occupation is linearly related to actual playing ability.[25] Assume further that although it is undoubtedly difficult for an individual to estimate his future ability, this difficulty is no greater (or less) for blacks than whites. The $f(A)$ function shown in Figure 4-2 is the assumed relationship between the expected present value of baseball income and actual ability. We assume no one below the ability level A' would even consider a career in baseball. Assume further that the ability to play baseball is uncorrelated with some index of ability to perform or learn other tasks in the society. Let the expected present value of wages outside of baseball be w^*, which by the above assumption is independent of baseball playing ability.[26] In the absence of societal wage discrimination, let w^* be given by w_1^* in Figure 4-2. Wealth-miximizing individuals will choose that occupation in which the present value of their expected income streams is greatest. This means that everyone below ability A_1 will enter some occupation other than baseball and everyone above A_1 will enter baseball. Depending on the distribution of A defined above A_1, this will yield some ability distribution of baseball players. If there are no genetic or motivational differences between blacks and whites, then the ability distribution of white and black baseball players should be about the same.

Now, introduce wage discrimination elsewhere in the economy but not in

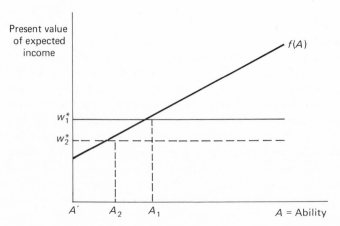

Figure 4-2. Hypothetical Relationship between Ability and Expected Income.

baseball. This is shown in Figure 4-2 as an alternative wage, w_2^*. For blacks, the ability cutoff value into baseball is now A_2, and the result is a *lower* mean ability of black baseball players than in the nondiscriminatory case. Under these assumptions, the principal impact of general wage discrimination is to *reduce* the mean ability of black baseball players relative to whites although it does increase the proportion of black baseball players.

Once we recognize that baseball playing ability may be correlated positively with performance ability elsewhere in the economy, the problem becomes somewhat more complicated.[27] In particular, it depends on how wage discrimination elsewhere in the economy varies with baseball playing ability. Under the assumption that baseball playing and other abilities are perfectly correlated, it can be shown that racial discrimination outside of baseball will augment the proportion of the minority that offers itself to baseball but not the average quality of the candidates relative to the majority population.

Under these rather plausible assumptions, racial wage discrimination outside of baseball will not improve the distribution of ability for blacks relative to whites. But it is clear that one could make assumptions about the occupational choice process that would lead to the conclusion that discrimination outside of baseball increases the proportion of exceptionally able blacks who choose baseball more than it increases the proportion of those who are somewhat less able. Our purpose was not to rule out this logical possibility, but rather to demonstrate that the effect of racial wage discrimination in one sector does not entitle one to predict confidently the effect of this phenomenon on the ability distribution in the nondiscriminating sector. The only unambiguous implication is that it systematically alters the proportion of blacks in the two sectors.

Entry Barriers Over Time, 1953-67

Rosenblatt (1967) reports data on the percent of black American major league players and mean difference in batting performance of American blacks and whites for the 25-man rosters, 1953-65. These data are reproduced in Table 4-8. There is no evidence of a secular decline in racial batting performance differences although over the period there has been a large increase in the percent of black players (see Table 4-8). These appear to be conflicting facts. The stability of batting performance differences is interpreted as evidence that the major league entry barrier is unchanged, and the growing percent of blacks is often interpreted as evidence of a decline in entry restriction. This apparent paradox stems from the assumption that data on the percentage participation by blacks in a particular jurisdiction indicate the degree of racial wage discrimination in that jurisdiction.

Assume that baseball salaries are commensurate with ability within both the minor and major leagues but that all of the discrimination arises from a racial

Table 4-8
**Season Batting Averages of American Blacks and Whites, 1953-65 and 1967, and
Percent American Black Players**

Year	Blacks	Whites	Difference	American black players (%)
1953	288	257	31	5.4
1954	262	244	18	
1955	271	251	20	
1956	270	248	22	
1957	264	252	12	9
1958	274	249	25	
1959	265	246	19	
1960	264	248	16	
1961	264	247	17	14.5
1962	276	250	26	
1963	262	238	24	
1964	255	238	17	
1965	252	234	18	17.2
1967	262	245	17	14.7

Sources: 1953-65: Transcribed from A. Rosenblatt, "Negroes in Baseball: The Failure of Success," *Trans-action* (September 1967). His data are based on 25-man rosters.

1967: Based on veteran sample used in this study (453 players). These data are not entirely comparable to Rosenblatt's. Data not computed for 1966.

barrier between the minor and major leagues. The barrier takes the form of a "discount" on black ability so that for clubs to be indifferent between promoting blacks or whites, blacks must be x percent better than whites. If the discount is independent of the relative number of blacks in the game, then obviously the observed ability difference could remain constant while the fraction of blacks increased if there was a secular increase in the relative supply of black players at every ability level.

This appears to us as rather convincing evidence that a real and important entry barrier prevents equally qualified black players from moving up into the major leagues. If salaries are generally higher in the majors than in the minors, black minor league players are receiving lower salaries than their abilities would warrant. The racial entry barrier to the major leagues, in other words, results in salary discrimination against black professional baseball players as a whole.

IV. Racial Segregation in Baseball

The effects of race prejudice need not be exhibited so blatantly as to violate the equal pay for equal work rule in which Americans profess belief. In an industry where candidates are denied opportunity to enter, to advance, and to choose specialties because of color, then race prejudice is surely generating discrimination, even though no black worker receives lower compensation than whites of identical ability and working at the same level in the hierarchy. Having reviewed evidence on possible racial entry barriers in major league baseball, we now go on to evidence on bias in assignment. Surveying the evidence on assignments by color to team, league, and position in major league baseball permits us to draw some inferences on the existence of racial segregation in the industry. We also present some fragmentary evidence on the existence of nonplaying employment alternatives by race.

Segregation by Team and League

In Table 4-9, we show the distribution of American and Latin blacks among the twenty (1968) major league clubs. The difference in the means for the National and American leagues supports the common observation that there are more blacks on National than American League clubs. On the other hand, there appears to be some within-league variation. These observed differences between and within leagues bear on the problem of segregation but have no necessary implications for the presence or absence of salary discrimination against blacks since there is no observable league effect on salaries.

A χ^2 test of within-league differences failed to uncover any significant intra-league differences at reasonable test levels in the proportion of black players. On the other hand, a proportions test did indicate a significant between-league difference in the proportion of blacks.

It is instructive to explore further the question of why the proportions differ among clubs. We could assume that the percentage of black players on a particular club depends on the attitude of fans, the attitude of white co-players, and the location of the club farm system, because it may prove awkward for a major league club with southern farm teams to hire black players. As an admittedly rough approximation we index each of these factors by: (a) the percent of blacks in the Standard Metropolitan Statistical Area (SMSA) in which the club has its home (X_1); (b) the percent of 1968 white players who were southern born on each club (X_2); and (c) the percent of the club's farm system players who play for minor league clubs located in the South (X_3). Letting p represent the percent of major league blacks on a club, we regress p on X_1, X_2, and X_3 and a zero-one (American League-National League) dummy (X_4). The results are

$$p = 24.5 + .01 \, X_1 - .10 \, X_2 + .09 \, X_3 - 8.9 \, X_4,$$

standard error $\quad$ (31.6) (.32) $\quad$ (.28) $\quad$ (.08) $\quad$ (3.4)**

Table 4-9

Latin and North American Blacks by Baseball Club and League, 784 Players, 1968 (Percent)

National League	Percent black
Atlanta	37
Cincinnati	28
Houston	34
Los Angeles	22
Philadelphia	27
Pittsburgh	30
San Francisco	31
Chicago (Cubs)	14
New York (Mets)	17
St. Louis	29
League percentage	26.9*
American League	
Chicago (White Sox)	20
Baltimore	17
Detroit	12
Kansas City	17
Washington	16
Minnesota	26
Boston	25
Cleveland	22
New York (Yankees)	14
California	6
League Percentage	17.5*

*Arithmetic average of the individual club proportions.

Source: *Baseball Register*, 1968.

where ** indicates one-tail 5 percent significance. Apparently interclub variation is unrelated to every independent variable except the league variable. Therefore, we conclude that for reasons independent of farm club location, percentage of southern white players, and percentage of whites in the SMSA in which the club is located, there is a difference between the two leagues. Perhaps this difference reflects the behavior of club owners or perhaps it simply reflects the fact that the American League was a relative latecomer in acquiring black players.

An alternative explanation of the league-only effect lies in the competitive pressures. Since the clubs in a given league must compete against each other in games, we can surmise that no single club can afford to depart too far from the overall league average in (potential) player ability. Given our tentative identification of a racial entry barrier and the consequent higher average ability of black players, any competitor in the league will find it necessary to hire a fraction of blacks approximately equal to the average proportion in the league. This average proportion may be related to the mean of the prejudice levels, from whatever source, across teams. Since the typical team plays about 160 games against the other members of its league and less than 0.7 games (expected value of number of World Series games for any team) against teams from the other league, the fractions black within a league will be constrained, yet there will be no necessary relationship of the fractions between leagues. Moreover, to the extent that the league rather than the team is the basic decision unit in the baseball business, these conclusions would also be expected (Neale, 1964).

Segregation by Playing Position

In Table 4-10 we show the percentage of blacks by playing position. The conspicuous absence of black pitchers and catchers has often been noted by other writers (Rosenblatt, 1967). One interpretation of this phenomenon is that blacks are purposely excluded from the key positions of pitchers and catchers because they are important decisionmaking positions and blacks are not trusted with this kind of responsibility. It is difficult to verify this hypothesis and of course there are other explanations for the phenomenon. One explanation centers on the fact that pitchers require more coaching and minor league experience than other players, and white coaches and managers may prefer not to interact with blacks. This latter hypothesis seems even more valid when we notice the lower representation of black players in some of the infield positions, where fielding skill is important. Such skills may also require frequent access to coaching and instruc-

Table 4-10
Latin and North American Black Baseball Players by Position, 784 Players, 1968 (Percent)

Position	Percent black
Pitcher	9
Catcher	12
First	40
Second	30
Third	14
Shortstop	26
Outfield	53
Utility infield	19
Not specified (misc.)	33
Total	22

Source: *Baseball Register*, 1968.

tion. Segregation by position will be reinforced as black youngsters concentrate on positions in which black stars are most notable. If our argument is correct, blacks will continue to concentrate in the outfield and at first base, positions in which the primary quality demanded is hitting ability, a more "natural" talent.

We might ask whether our findings with respect to ability differences among black and white players by position are consistent with the evidence on segregation by position. A reasonable view would hold that if the races are distributed equally with respect to innate ability, then in those positions with fewest blacks the greatest black-white ability difference will be found. The interpretation we suggest here is that as the assignment barrier against blacks rises, only the more superior blacks can scale it. Thus, we should find the observed edge for black players relatively highest for pitchers and, descending through catchers and infielders, lowest for outfielders. A comparison of the data for nonpitchers in Tables 4-5, 4-6, and 4-10 does not support this proposition, however.

Nonplayer Opportunities by Race

Because baseball players usually retire as active players in their mid-thirties, post-retirement employment opportunities are of major concern to them. One important employment source for ex-players is within organized baseball itself as managers or coaches. That employment opportunities in these supervisory positions are less available to blacks than whites is readily apparent from the data. At the start of the 1969 season, none of the 24 major league managers were black and only 4 of the 100 major league coaches were black (Luke Easter, Junior Gilliam, Elston Howard, and Satchell Paige). In 1969, only one of the 49 major league umpires were black. Apparently, successful black baseball players are not yet considered qualified for the most important supervisory positions in organized baseball.

Other sources of pecuniary discrimination against black players are quite independent of any decisions made by club owners or managers. Successful black players may find it more difficult than comparable white players to capitalize on their athletic reputation in activities outside of baseball. This includes off season or postretirement employment opportunities, TV and other endorsement opportunities, as well as speaking (luncheon clubs, lodges, and so on) and related opportunities. That these disadvantages are real is indicated by one survey, which alleged that although blacks made up 30 percent of major league baseball players, 26 percent of major league football players, and 44 percent of basketball players, they appeared in only five percent of 351 TV commercials associated with New York sports events in the fall of 1966 (Equal Employment Opportunity Commission, 1968).

V. Conclusions

Let us at this point review our findings with respect to the impact of race on the player market in organized baseball. They include the following:

1. Of all major league baseball players in 1968, 22 percent were black and about 15 percent were North American black. Both black and white players seem representative of the U.S. population in education and regional origin.
2. There is some evidence that teams treat players as economic resources since player performance affects team standing and standing affects attendance by fans.
3. When we estimated the parameters of a model of salary determination in which the independent variables included measures of player performance and experience, of alternative earnings potential, and of race and a trend factor, we succeeded in explaining from one-half to three-fourths of the variation in individual salaries paid pitching and nonpitching players during 1968. Generally, race had no significant impact on salary when considered in conjunction with "objective" measures of player value.
4. Bonus payment differentials by race, though significant in earlier years, seem to have just about vanished. This phenomenon may be attributed either to a decline in prejudice or to an improvement in the quality of information in a monopsonistic industry.
5. Position by position, black players in the big leagues tend to outperform their white counterparts on the basis of objective measurements. This holds for veterans and rookies and at all ages. There is little reason to attribute the observed racial ability differential to the relatively poorer nonbaseball alternatives of blacks.
6. The two major leagues differ significantly in the proportions of black players on their constituent teams; differences among teams within a league are not statistically significant, however, at customary test levels.
7. Blacks are underrepresented as pitchers and catchers and overrepresented as outfielders and first basemen in the major leagues.
8. Very few blacks are found among big league managers, coaches, and umpires; they held only 3 percent of these supervisory slots in 1969.

Ironically, our study indicates that since on average black salaries in major league baseball are higher than white salaries, significant prejudice exists in the industry. The irony stems from the joint occurrence of two phenomena: (a) major league clubs tend to pay players as a function of their demonstrated ability; and (b) baseball appears to restrict major league opportunities to those blacks who are demonstrably superior to their white counterparts. Thus, there seems to be equal pay for equal work but unequal opportunity for equal ability. In addition, we find that once inside major league baseball, players are allocated to positions, including supervisory as well as playing positions, in a manner that is difficult to explain on grounds other than racial bias.

We feel that the findings we derive for baseball are characteristic also of the situation in other parts of the economy. Baseball, after all, is an industry composed of wealth-maximizing firms. It differs merely in being highly public and, since 1948, in being highly prone to praise its own "enlightened" racial attitudes. In fact, taking at face value the public relations rhetoric of baseball spokesmen, if racism is as subtly pervasive as it appears to be on the diamond, it is likely to be exceedingly powerful in the plants, offices, and stores where discriminatory treatment can still be masked by complaints about the absence of qualified applicants.

The ethical tenets of official American culture as well as the difficulties of sustaining patently unjust salary treatment means that in baseball and in other fields racism will be expressed through less obvious forms of discrimination. Our study shows that basing entry, promotion, and assignment on race rather than merit is one important form.[28]

Notes

1. What all of this says is that such factors as age, sex, amount and quality of education, and personal attitudes are expected to affect ability or productivity on the job and will, therefore, have "legitimate" effects on earnings, meaning that an employer who pays a lower wage to a poorly educated, poorly motivated worker may be "maximizing" but is not necessarily discriminating. Research on discrimination has centered on the attempt to separate out the impact of such factors, leaving a residual that could then more confidently be attributed to market prejudice.

2. If occupations are defined narrowly enough, of course, entry barriers become the only expression of discrimination.

3. The farm system of a major league club usually consists of one AAA club, one AA club, two or three A clubs, and a Rookie club.

4. During a playing season anywhere from 30 to 40 players per club may participate in at least one major league game, and there are many players in the minor leagues who have in prior seasons appeared in major league games. Yet, between June 1 and September 1 the club is restricted to a 25-man roster, and the June 1 roster is one obvious definition of a major league player. Each club, however, may protect a total of 40 players from being drafted in the annual player draft, and thus the 40-man protected list is an alternative definition. We have chosen a definition that comes reasonably close to the 40-man definition.

5. A player's color was easily identified by pictures in the Register. Latins were classified by their country of origin—these were mainly Caribbean—and not by their citizenship status. Thus, players born in Puerto Rico were counted as Latin. Except for a few Latin players for whom color was difficult to identify, the classification of players by color is in our view quite accurate in terms of common visual standards.

6. It should be obvious that an individual player's value differs among clubs. For example, a club with one first-rate catcher will generally find a second one less valuable than a club without a good catcher or, to take another common example, a power hitter may be more valuable to one club than another because of differences in playing field dimensions.

7. Basketball, football, and hockey have arrangements similar to those in basketball. See, for example, J.C.H. Jones, "The Economics of the National Hockey League," *Canadian Journal of Economics* (February 1969).

8. Economists and others have often deplored the reserve player clause because they contend that it is a device for collusively lowering the salaries of baseball players (and by the same token increasing the profits of club owners). For these arguments see S. Rottenberg, "The Baseball Players' Labor Market," *Journal of Political Economy* (June), and the brilliant statement by L.M. O'Conner, former President of the Pacific Coast baseball league (U.S. Congress, Senate, Subcommittee on Anti-Trust and Monopoly, *Organized Professional Team Sports*, 85th Cong., 2nd Sess., July, 1958). The owners, on the other hand, have traditionally argued that the reserve clause is essential in helping to equalize team strengths, an objective that is of relevance to the league. But there is compelling reason to believe that the club owners' argument is specious.

The owners argue that without the reserve clause, the richest club will outcompete poorer clubs for talent and, hence, unbalance the league. There are several arguments against this proposition. First, as Rottenberg ("The Baseball Players' Labor Market"), has correctly argued, there are economic forces that place limits on the willingness of the richest club to purchase all or most of the best players. The addition of high quality players will eventually begin to contribute only marginally to club success in winning games, and furthermore, at some point attendance will not increase sufficiently to justify the purchase price of additional high quality talent.

Aside from diminishing returns there is, we think, a far more important consideration. Indeed, there is reason to suspect that with the reserve player clause clubs will be *more* unbalanced than without this clause. Under present arrangements clubs can trade or sell players independently of the player's desire to remain in one location, and economic incentives for players to be reallocated among clubs is not eliminated by the reserve clause, a point emphasized by Rottenberg ("The Baseball Players' Labor Market"). Rather, the reserve clause only shifts the moving decision from the player to the club owner; it does not eliminate the incentive for movement to occur. The reserve player clause is by no means a sufficient condition for preventing the richest club from dominating a league. Between 1946 and 1964 the New York Yankees won 15 of 19 American league pennants.

9. Insofar as our analysis is restricted to player salaries, we are ignoring several fringe benefits, such as World Series and league standing monies as well as the more traditional health and medical insurance, severance pay, life insurance, and most important, pensions.

10. At a subsequent point we will introduce the assumption that expected ability is related to past performance on the playing field. We performed a crude analysis to satisfy ourselves that a player's performance does indeed affect his club's revenue. Aside from the obvious fact that exceptional players can attract fans (and TV viewers) quite independently of their contribution to their team's performance, players also contribute to overall team performance. Team batting average is simply a weighted (by times at bat) average of individual batting averages. Under these circumstances we might reasonably ask what effect team batting average has on gate and TV receipts. Consider a simple, two equation attendance model in which season's attendance or gate (G) measured in thousands of people (with TV receipts assumed to be related to total attendance), is assumed to depend on the percent of total games that the club wins during the season (V) and the size of the ball park (P), measured in thousands. We follow the usual baseball reporting practice of taking the ratio of wins to total games played and then multiplying by 1,000.

Assume further that the percent of games won depends on team batting average (T), on the earned run average of pitchers (ERA), and on team fielding averages (F). We then have:

$$G_j = \gamma_0 + \gamma_1 V_j + \gamma_2 P_j + \epsilon_j, \tag{a}$$

and

$$V_j = \beta_0 + \beta_1 T_j + \beta_2 ERA_j + \beta_3 F_j + v_j, \tag{b}$$

where j = club index and ϵ_j and v_j are error terms.

We have estimated (a) and (b) above separately for the years 1967 and 1968 and for American and National leagues separately. This gives us four sets of estimates of the coefficients in (a) and (b). Least squares point estimates and estimated standard errors of these coefficients are reported below. The asterisk indicates one-tail statistical significance at 5 percent or better.

American League, 1967

$G_j = -730 + 4.2 V_j - 4.3 P_j$, R^2 (adj) = .45
  (881) (1.5)* (6.7)

$V_j = 4754 + 4.6 T_j - 1.5 ERA_j - 4.9 F_j$, R^2 (adj) = .63
  (6813) (1.3)* (.4) - (5.0)

American League, 1968

$G_j = -706 + 5.6 V_j - 19.2 P_j$, R^2 (adj) = .59
  (732) (1.5)* (8.7)*

$V_j = -17276 + 3.2 T_j - .6 ERA_j + 17.6 F_j$, R^2 (adj) = .66
  (5738)* (1.9) (.4) (5.7)*

National League, 1967

$G_j = -1840 + 2.6 V_j + 43.0 P_j$, R^2 (adj) = .80
    (.9)* (7.0)*

$V_j = -7291 + 2.9 T_j - 1.3 ERA_j + 7.7 F_j$, R^2 (adj) = .79
  (6166) (1.0)* (.4)* (6.3)

National League, 1968

$$G_j = -1925 + 2.5\,V_j + 43.2\,P_j \qquad , R^2 \text{ (adj)} = .65$$
$$(1167) \quad (2.1) \quad (10.2)^*$$
$$V_j = 50.7 + 2.1\,T_j - .6\,ERA_j + .1\,F_j \qquad , R^2 \text{ (adj)} = .17$$
$$(90.0) \quad (1.1)^* \quad (.4) \quad (7.2)$$

Given our choice of the dependent variable, two statistical problems arise. First, the error terms cannot be statistically independent and hence the ordinary least squares estimates are inefficient. Second, the error terms cannot be normal and the small sample t test is at best approximate. Despite these difficulties, the point estimates suggest that aggregate player performance as indexed by our batting and pitching measures influences the gate through its influence on percent of games won. The reader should keep in mind, however, that these estimates are reported only to provide some casual numerical support for the proposition that a player's measured performance is linked to club revenues. We recognize that a full analysis of the relationship between attendance and an individual player's performance would require a more careful and comprehensive specification of the relevant equations.

11. This is not only our judgment but is also the judgment of Marvin Miller, head of the Major League Baseball Players' Association, who examined our salary data. Although Miller does not have individual salary data, he does have general knowledge of what baseball players are paid and he was kind enough to point out that several of the figures in our original sample were grossly out of line. These data were deleted from our sample.

12. In estimating coefficients we used two separate data sets. One sample consisted only of the nonrepeat salary observations, of which there were 67 for nonpitchers. The second sample included repeat salary data as well and had 93 observations. When we had data on a player's salary for both 1968 and 1969, we treated the 1969 figure as a new observation. We adjusted the repeat player's age, his cumulated batting average, and so on. Using a player's salary in two separate years as two separate observations raises an important statistical problem. It can no longer be assumed that the error terms are independent since the error terms are assumed to summarize omitted factors such as individual bargaining ability. Although this error dependence leaves our estimates unbiased, the simple least squares estimating procedure is no longer efficient. However, because the qualitative and quantitative conclusions were almost precisely the same regardless of which sample we used, we restrict our presentation and discussion to the augmented sample results only.

13. Experienced analysts will recognize that when the observation unit is an individual and the data cross sectional, an adjusted R^2 of this magnitude is rather rare. But of course our interest centers on individual coefficient estimates, and not on R^2.

14. One reasonable interpretation of this result is that those players who graduate from college may be somewhat inferior in ability to players who are signed while still in college.

15. The simple r ($n = 55$) between salary and lifetime percent of games won was only .38 and between salary and lifetime *ERA* it was small and, curiously, a negative, $-.26$.

16. We added a league standing variable (taking on values of 1 to 10) to the variables in regression (7), but the results indicated that playing for a winning club does not affect individual annual salaries.

17. The Court in 1922 ruled that baseball was not subject to the antitrust laws and this decision was reaffirmed in 1953. But subsequently, the issue of antitrust exemption was clouded by the court's decision in 1955 and again in 1957 that boxing and football were businesses subject to antitrust legislation and the court suggested that Congress should legislate uniform treatment of all sports.

In 1958 a legislative drive for uniform antitrust legislation began. In 1965 the Senate passed a bill subjecting baseball as well as football, basketball, and hockey to the antitrust laws. The bill, however, exempted from antitrust action activities relating to: (a) the equalization of player strengths; (b) the employment, reservation, and selection of players; (c) the right to operate in specific geographic areas; and (d) the "preservation of public confidence in the honesty of sports contests." The Senate bill never passed the House. Prior to the Senate action in 1965, however, a large number of bills with provisions similar to the 1965 Senate bill were introduced in the Congress.

18. Not only were bonus costs high, but many bonus players never successfully became major league players. In 1958 the probability that a player who received a bonus in excess of $25,000 would in fact become a major leaguer was only about one in three.

19. This difference might be overstated to the extent that black players in early years were purchased from independently owned black leagues, the owners of which could have been the recipients of any lump sum payment that might have been made.

20. Fielding average: A fielder's total number of assists and outs divided by his total number of chances, to 3 decimal places.

Slugging percentage: Batter's total bases divided by his times at bat.

21. Since the June 1 to September 1 major league rosters must consist of only 25 players or a total for 20 teams of 500 players, our veteran group apparently covers most of the 25-man rosters.

22. Miscellaneous players were generally those who had played in so many positions during their careers that they were difficult to classify.

23. We performed an additional test in which the performance differences were standardized for age differences between the black and white subsamples on the assumption that age tends to improve performances. This adjustment did not appreciably alter the results by race and position.

24. Earned run average: the total number of earned runs off a pitcher divided by the total number of innings he has pitched.

25. More generally the baseball income stream as well as alternative income streams may contain nonpecuniary as well as pecuniary components—prestige, adventure, arduousness, and so on.

26. Although we could have assumed that for any given baseball playing ability, A, there exists a distribution of w^* with a mean, $\bar{w}^*$, independent of A, this assumption would not alter our conclusions and would only complicate our discussion. Ease of exposition, then, led us to posit a simple deterministic model.

27. The ability to play baseball requires, among other things, physical health, diligence, motivation, concentration, promptness, and dependability, all of which are traits commanding a premium in many occupations. In a recent article (Shafer and Michael, 1968) it was shown that for high school students, participation in organized athletics was positively correlated with academic performance.

28. Just before publishing this study, we saw an unpublished paper by Gerald Scully on salary discrimination in major league baseball. Unlike ourselves (see pp. 128-134, above), Scully reports evidence of direct salary discrimination against black players. Rather than assume that discrimination additively influences salaries with the same absolute effect on all players regardless of ability, Scully assumes that salary discrimination varies with ability. Running separate white and black salary regressions (using our salary data), he finds that the increment in salary with respect to a unit change in ability (measured differently than ours) is smaller for black outfielders than for white outfielders. Although he does not obtain similar results for infielders or pitchers, he nevertheless concludes that, on net, there is salary discrimination against blacks. See G.W. Scully, "The Economics of Discrimination in Professional Sports: The Case of Baseball," *Government and the Sports Business* (Brookings Institution, Washington, D.C.), forthcoming.

References

Arrow, Kenneth J. "Models of Job Discrimination." Chapter 2 of this volume.

The Baseball Guide. St. Louis: The Sporting News, 1969.

The Baseball Guide. St. Louis: The Sporting News, 1968.

The Baseball Register. St. Louis: The Sporting News, 1968.

Becker, Gary S. *The Economics of Discrimination*. Chicago: University of Chicago Press, 1957.

Davenport, D.S. "Collusive Competition in Major League Baseball." *The American Economist* (Fall 1969): 6-30.

Equal Employment Opportunity Commission. *White Collar Employment in New York City Communications Industry*. Mimeographed. (January 1968).

Hanoch, Giora. "An Econometric Analysis of Earnings and Schooling." *Journal of Human Resources* (Summer 1967): 310-29.

Jones, J.C.H. "The Economics of the National Hockey League." *Canadian Journal of Economics* (February 1969): 1-20.

Maher, C. "The Negro Athlete in America." *The Los Angeles Times*, 24, 26, 27, 28, and 29 March 1968, Sports Section, Part 3.

Neale, W.C. "The Peculiar Economics of Professional Sports." *Quarterly Journal of Economics* (February 1964): 1-14.

Olsen, J. "The Black Athlete." *Sports Illustrated* (July 1, 1968): 15-27; (July 8, 1968): 20-31; (July 15, 1968): 30-43; (July 22, 1968): 28-41; (July 29, 1968): 22-35.

Rosenblatt, A. "Negroes in Baseball: The Failure of Success." *Trans-action* (September 1967): 51-53.

Rottenberg, S. "The Baseball Players' Labor Market." *Journal of Political Economy* (June 1956): 242-58.

Schafer, W.E., and J. Michael. "Athletes Are Not Inferior Students." *Trans-action* (November 1956): 21-26, 61, 62.

Sloane, P.J. "The Labor Market in Professional Football." *British Journal of Industrial Relations* (July 1969).

U.S. Congress, Senate, Subcommittee on Anti-Trust and Monopoly. *Professional Sports Anti-Trust Bill*. 89th Cong., 1st sess., February 1965.

U.S. Congress, Senate, Subcommittee on Anti-Trust and Monopoly. *Professional Sports Anti-Trust Bill*. 88th Cong., 2nd sess., February 1964.

U.S. Congress, Senate, Subcommittee on Anti-Trust and Monoploy. *Organized Professional Team Sports*. 86th Cong., 2nd sess., May 1960.

U.S. Congress, Senate, Subcommittee on Anti-Trust and Monopoly. *Organized Professional Team Sports*. 85th Cong., 2nd sess., July 1958.

U.S. Congress, House, Subcommittee on the Study of Monopoly Power. *Organized Baseball* (Series no. 1, Part 6). 82nd Cong., 1st sess., July, August, and October 1951.

U.S. Department of Labor, Bureau of Labor Statistics. *Employment and Earnings and Monthly Report on the Labor Force* (September 1968).

U.S. Department of Labor. *Manpower Report of the President*. Washington, D.C.: U.S. Government Printing Office, 1968.

Welch, F. "Labor Market Discrimination: An Interpretation of Income Differences in the Rural South." *Journal of Political Economy* (June 1967): 225-40.

5 A Process of Residential Segregation: Neighborhood Tipping

Thomas C. Schelling

Tipping is said to occur when some recognizable minority group in a neighborhood reaches a size that motivates the other residents to begin leaving. The term implies that subsequent entrants who take the place of those who leave are predominantly of the minority and that the process ultimately changes the composition of the neighborhood.

The phenomenon was described and illustrated by Morton Grodzins (1957), who said that "for the vast majority of white Americans a tip point exists." He cites 20 percent blacks as a commonly estimated upper limit in some eastern cities. "The tip-point phenomenon is so universal that it constitutes strong evidence in favor of control. Without control there has been a total failure to achieve interracial communities." Once an urban area begins to swing from mainly white to mainly black, he says, the change is rarely reversed.

At the time he wrote, Otis Dudley Duncan and Beverly Duncan (1957:11) published a study of Chicago residential trends in which they found no instance between 1940 and 1952 of a mixed neighborhood—a neighborhood 25 percent to 75 percent nonwhite—in which succession from white to black occupancy was arrested.[1]

Tipping, as described by Grodzins and in common usage, is not merely a phenomenon—a change in neighborhood occupany—but is a mechanism or process that generates, may generate, or is alleged to generate the observable departure of some majority group.

It is not the only mechanism that could account for the generalization that, once an urban area begins to swing from mainly white to mainly black, the change is rarely reversed. Normal turnover combined with a strong local minority demand for housing could account for that. Changes in the character of the neighborhood and its surroundings, changes in opportunities elsewhere, shifts in the location of employment, increases in population density, and a number of other factors could explain dominant trends in the racial composition of neighborhoods that would become noticeable, and seldom reversed, in the course of a decade.

So the question arises, how do we recognize tipping when we see it? How do we know whether or not tipping is the process at work when whites move out and blacks move in? What constitutes evidence for the tipping hypothesis? If we believe in the hypothesis, what pattern of entries and departures should we expect? What are the parameters in a tipping model that might determine the threshold, the speed of evacuation, and the ultimate change in racial composition?

157

There are two main kinds of evidence. One is a direct inquiry into motives and expectations, to the extent that these can be inferred from what people say. The other is quantitative data on who moves in and who moves out or, if only net changes can be observed, on rates of change in the racial composition of neighborhoods, school districts, census tracts, housing projects, or whatever pertinent territories furnish the data.

Evidence of the first kind has been provided by A.J. Mayer (1960) in a vivid case study. Russell Woods was a well-defined neighborhood one-half mile square with about 700 single-family homes, surrounded by racially mixed neighborhoods, close to a boulevard that had recently gone from virtually all white to substantially black. In a brief period in 1955 a few houses in the neighborhood were sold to blacks. "The selling of the third house," Mayer reports, "convinced everyone that the neighborhood was destined to become mixed." During the ensuing year about 40 houses were sold to blacks along two streets. Before the first houses were sold to blacks on any other street, "practically all residents of Russell Woods defined the entire neighborhood as mixed." There was no panic but there was accelerated selling and some increased activity by real estate agents. Opinions still varied in 1956 on whether the neighborhood would become completely black. The author returned in 1958 to find that it was more than 50 percent black and the end result was no longer questioned, although there was still no panic.

Evidence of the second kind was examined by Stinchcombe, McDill, and Walker (1969) in a study oriented precisely to the question, "Is There a Racial Tipping Point in Changing Schools?" Is prejudice, they ask, a threshold or a continuous phenomenon? Like Grodzins, they conclude that *if* there is a tipping point, "one solution to desegregation would be an agreed-upon quota immediately below this tipping point, for at that point a racially mixed unit could be stably maintained." They properly generalize the phenomenon from neighborhoods to apartment buildings, swimming pools, and social clubs. They recognize that there may be alternative mechanisms producing the departure of whites.

Specifically, they say, a threshold notion corresponds to a tipping-point phenomenon, while a continuously increasing abandonment of the school by whites, as the proportion of blacks rises, would correspond to a continuous (or social-distance) notion of prejudice. They continue:

If we find a point or a proportion at which there is an exaggerated increase the following year in the proportion of Negroes, then we will have found a 'tipping point,' or a point of acceleration in the resegregation process. If we find continuous acceleration of the decrease of whites, we will have supported the social-distance notion.

They find no such point. Instead, the more blacks there are in the school, the larger the proportion of whites who leave without being replaced; they conclude that "there is no 'tipping point.' Or rather, the 'tipping point' is zero." If there are no blacks in the school, whites do not leave very fast; once a school is desegregated (in Baltimore), the proportion of blacks is likely to go up steadily. From this they conclude that the setting of quotas for a certain percentage of blacks in desegregated schools would not be an effective policy.

Several characteristics of the underlying mechanism remain ambiguous. Is it that more whites decide to leave, the larger the proportion of blacks in the school, or that whites who leave leave faster, the larger the proportion of blacks? Or is it that whites leave at a normal rate but white entrants become fewer, the larger the proportion of blacks? To what extent do whites leave (or decline to enter) as a result of the observed proportion of blacks, to what extent do they project a trend and react to the anticipated proportion of blacks? Do the whites already know what the authors discovered—that once a few blacks enter a school the percentage of whites decreases at an accelerating rate—and make plans accordingly? Do the rates of departure in years that follow reflect the consummation of plans already made during the first year or two of black entry?

Indeed, if we could identify a tipping point, what would it look like? Would it be, as these authors suggest, the point immediately preceding the sudden acceleration in the rate of white departure? If so, how would that point correspond to the separate tipping points of the individuals involved? Should the white families be expected to have different tipping points, reflecting not only their attitudes toward blacks but differences in attachment to the neighborhood, cost of moving, ease of settling elsewhere, and perhaps their specific locations in the neighborhood, ages and sex of their children, and so forth? And do these different individual tipping points bunch together in a narrow range or spread over a wide set of values? In what order do the tipping whites leave: are the first to go the least tolerant of the minority or the least attached to where they live?

If there were a tipping phenomenon in neighborhoods and schools, would the mechanisms be the same for neighborhoods as for schools? Even if the basic model were the same, some of the parameters would be different. Schools have clearer definitions than neighborhoods. All members of a household live in the same neighborhood; not all the children go to the same school. In a neighborhood everybody has a "next neighbor" or two; in a school, percentages may count more than individual positions. School districts and neighborhoods are not coterminous; schools, furthermore, correspond to fairly large neighborhoods, especially in the higher grades where a neighborhood of corresponding size would contain thousands of families. Finally, whatever the underlying motivation may be, whether prejudice or anything else, it undoubtedly affects people differently according to whether the factors involved are home, family, and neighborhood or school companions and education.

A Model of the Process

Rather than try to infer from empirical data what mechanism may be at work, we can postulate a mechanism and examine what results it would generate. If we can then verify the mechanism by the empirical identification of its components, we can use the model to understand and to predict. Less ambitiously, we can compare the phenomena generated by the mechanism with what we observe, to see whether we can rule the mechanism out or establish its eligibility. Most likely of all, there may be some aspect of the mechanism that alerts us to certain phenomena, or helps to explain bits of what we observe, and sharpens the concepts that guide further research. At the least, an explicit model can help us to check whether or not something like the Grodzins hypothesis of a tipping point is consistent with the kind of aggregate behavior that Stinchcombe and his colleagues have documented.

Suppose, then, that the original residents of some community have limited tolerance for some recognizable minority in their midst. For illustration use Grodzins' figure: something like 20 percent blacks as the point at which the typical white resident will choose to move away. To simplify, suppose that a similar percentage governs the willingness of other whites to move into the area and that the number of whites that might move in within some relevant period of time is small compared with the total number of residents in the community. But since 20 percent is a rough guess, suppose also that for some individuals the tipping point is more like 5 or 10 percent, for others 30 or 40 percent. We have, then, a frequency distribution of the tolerance[2] of the original white residents for the black minority.

We can experiment with different shapes this frequency distribution might take: it could be a bell-shaped distribution with a modal value at 20 percent black; it could be symmetrical or skewed; it could be wide or narrow. A limiting case occurs if everyone has exactly the same tipping point.

Initially assume that the neighborhood is well defined. We can relax this assumption somewhat with no change in our model if we suppose that blacks move into a subneighborhood and that people in adjacent subneighborhoods react to the presence of blacks in the entire neighborhood, but they react less sensitively than if their own subneighborhood were the target area. Thus the shape of our frequency distribution could reflect location within the neighborhood as well as other kinds of sensitivity, if in our model we control the locations at which the in-migrant blacks settle.

We have some choices of interpretation. Does an individual's tipping point mark the percentage black at which he actually moves or the point at which he decides to move at his earliest convenience? Does he begin shopping around for another place to live, the time of his departure depending on how quickly he finds a new place? Does he leave at the end of the school year or when his lease runs out? If he owns his home, does he put it on the market and leave whenever he sells his house? Different interpretations will lead to different quantitative results. I propose that initially we suppose his tipping point reflects his point of decision, not his point of departure, and that there is some average delay of departure, perhaps with acceleration if there is exaggerated entry of blacks after he makes his decision.

A possibly crucial element is being left out at this stage. I am supposing that the individual decides to move when the composition of the neighborhood no longer suits him, not when he predicts that it is going to become unsuitable. The Russell Woods example suggests that anticipation is important: people had expectations; they projected trends. If it was important not to overstay once their tipping points had been reached, people would have been making plans ahead of time, moving out at their earliest convenience once they predicted that the black percentage would shortly exceed their tolerance. It is widely reported that, when home ownership is involved, people expect declining property values and, to avoid losses, put their houses on the market in anticipation not only of an ultimate personal desire to move but of a capital loss if they wait even that long. If in our model we have people move as soon as they expect the neighborhood ultimately to tip, it is not going to be their neighborhood preferences (prejudice) that govern their departure but their expectations. Expectations may be more volatile than preferences, so we shall leave them aside in our initial exploration. Still, if we wish, we can interpret each individual's tipping point as the percentage black at which, projecting the trend and considering his financial and other commitments, he makes his decision to leave. (But in that interpretation his decision must be a function of the percentage of blacks in the neighborhood, not the number of "for sale" signs or other indices that might influence his decision.)

Even before we give quantitative shape to our model we can foresee the possibility of a spiral or domino effect, or unraveling process. There will be some interdependence of decisions. Anyone who moves out reduces, at least slightly, the number of whites remaining, unless his place is taken by another white. Assuming some pressing black demand for housing, perhaps an increasing demand as the number of prospective black neighbors grows, and a diminishing white demand to move into the neighborhood as the black percentage rises, each white who reaches his tipping point and departs brings the remaining whites a little closer to their tipping points.

Once we draw our frequency distribution of individual tipping points, we can study the neighborhood population dynamics as follows. We introduce a few blacks into the neighborhood, calculate the percentage they represent, and ask how many whites would be induced to leave. At some rate over time we remove them, let their places be taken by blacks (or by whites and blacks in proportions that reflect what is already happening to the neighborhood), and examine how many more whites have become discontent through the departure of that first batch. These newly discontent we remove in turn, letting them be replaced by more blacks, calculate the resulting percentage, and ask how many more whites would be induced to move now. If we wish, we can be explicit about the speed of departure; or, neglecting speed, we can just see whether the process is self-limiting or self-aggravating, whether or not there are critical points at which the process becomes irreversible, and what the end result or alternative results may be. For the moment we shall suppose no shortage of blacks to take the place of evacuating whites; later we can consider what happens if the potential black entrants are too few to fill the neighborhood.

**Alternative Frequency
Distributions**

Some alternative frequency distributions are shown in Figure 5-1. The top two distributions, A and B, are smooth, unimodal, and symmetrical. C is skewed; no one can demand more than 100 percent but not everyone has to demand 60 percent. The fourth, D, is bimodal: there is a hump between 10 and 20 percent black for part of the population and, just to illustrate, another hump between 33

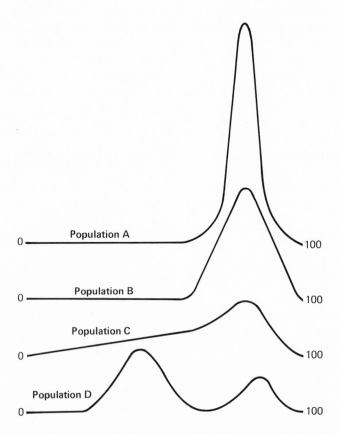

Figure 5-1. Frequency Distributions of Neighborhood Racial Tipping Points = Four Hypothetical White Populations, A, B, C, and D.

and 50 percent reflecting a larger number of whites who are concerned not to be too small a minority but do not insist on majority status.[3]

We could work directly with these frequency distributions, but they can be converted into more usable shape by plotting them cumulatively. In their present form, taking the sum of the frequencies equal to the original white population of the neighborhood, we can read the percentage of residents whose tipping points occur at 15 percent, 20 percent, 25 percent black, and so forth. The corresponding cumulative distributions will let us read directly the percentage of the population that will tolerate *as many as* 15 percent, 20 percent, or 25 percent black. In other words the cumulative distribution will show the percentage of the original population that demands that whites be *at least* 75 percent, 80 percent, 85 percent, or any other specified percentage of the population. The cumulative distribution will rise from 0 on the left to 100 on the right, over the range covered by the initial distribution.

Figure 5-2 shows cumulatively the two symmetrical distributions, A and B; Figure 5-3 is the skewed distribution C, and Figure 5-4 is D, the one with two humps.

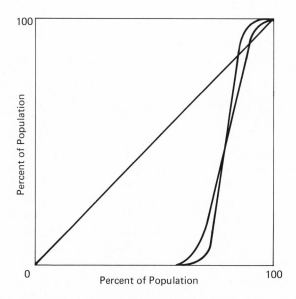

Figure 5-2. Cumulative Frequency Distribution of Neighborhood Racial Tipping Points for White Populations A and B.

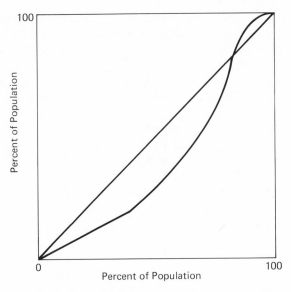

Figure 5–3. Cumulative Frequency Distribution of Neighborhood Racial Tipping Points for White Population C.

Against each of these curves a 45-degree line has been drawn for reference. It has the following significance. If the cumulative distribution falls below the 45-degree diagonal for a given percentage on the horizontal axis, there are not that many whites in the neighborhood population who are content with that many whites in the neighborhood. That is, if at 75 percent on the horizontal axis the cumulative curve reads 65 percent, it indicates that, if the most tolerant 75 percent of the population were all that remained and 25 percent of the population were black, not all those 75 percent would be content to remain. (The diagonal indicates a vertical height equal to the value on the horizontal axis.) If at 75 percent on the horizontal axis the cumulative curve is above the diagonal, say at 80 or 85 percent, it implies that there are 80 or 85 percent of the original whites who would be content with as few as 75 percent white and the rest black. Thus if 25 percent of the whites had left, the more tolerant 75 percent remaining, they would be more than content with their own number and none would leave. (The least tolerant among the remaining 75 percent would be content to comprise the percentage on the horizontal axis corresponding to the 75th percentile

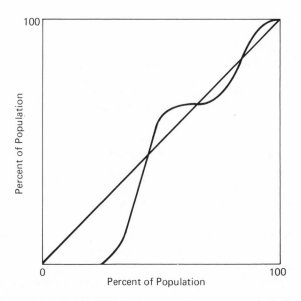

Figure 5-4. Cumulative Frequency Distribution of Neighborhood Racial Tipping Points for White Population D.

on the vertical axis; and if the curve is *above* the diagonal at a horizontal value of 75 percent it is also to the *left* of it at a vertical value of 75 percent.)

For any white-black percentages that we choose, the cumulative curve tells us directly whether or not the whites comprise a "stable" neighborhood population, according to whether the curve at that point is above or below the 45-degree line. *Stable* means that none among the remaining whites is dissatisfied yet, none has reached his individual tipping point, none has made his decision to move; all will stay (subject to normal turnover) unless the black percentage further increases. *Unstable* means that some among the remaining whites are discontent with the percentage that whites comprise; their tipping points have been passed; they have decided to move.

We postulated a well-defined tipping point for each individual. Can we identify an aggregate tipping point, a tipping point for the white population as a whole? Is there a point at which something discontinuous happens—a threshold? If so, what does it correspond to in the frequency distributions? Does it correspond to some abrupt discontinuity in those curves? How does it compare with the modal or median value of individual tipping points? What could we infer about the possible effect of quotas, delayed departures, or inducements to remain?

A Neighborhood Tipping Point

Whether or not we want to call it an aggregate or neighborhood tipping point, the point at which the cumulative curve crosses the diagonal is unique and significant in the dynamics of white response. It is a watershed—a point of black entry prior to which white residency is a self-sustaining condition and beyond which white departure is a self-sustaining process. To the right of that cross-over point, the white population is stable; to the left it is unstable. To the right of it a limit on black numbers could provide a suitable racial mix for the complementary number of whites already resident; to the left of it no quota would hold the complementary number of whites. To the right of that point, white departures would reflect the normal rate of turnover; to the left of it their departure would reflect turnover plus the departure speed we impute to whites whose tipping points have been passed.

If we are to identify *something* as an aggregate tipping point, it probably has to be this critical percentage that divides white residential stability from instability, that is, the point at which black numbers generate a cumulative self-sustaining process of white departure. It is at that point that the white community starts unraveling. No other point on the diagram has any such significance.

This crossover point may not be what people had in mind in speaking of an aggregate or neighborhood tipping point. What they had in mind, though, may not be there. Something else is there, but whether, once they see the implications of the model, they would choose to call it a tipping point, is not entirely clear. As a point, though, it is as interesting as the point they may have imagined, whatever that might have been. It is analytically distinctive and significant. It would have the kind of policy implication we might have imputed to a tipping point, though not the same implications. And it requires some revision of the tipping concept.

Analytically, this point does indeed mark a discontinuity, or threshold. At the same time, the frequency distribution that generates it is perfectly continuous, showing nothing abrupt at the point where the *process* shows a discontinuity. There should be some discontinuity in the rate of departure once that point is passed. (And we might expect some discontinuity in the responses of departing whites to the question, "Why are you leaving?")

At the same time, until we examine the dynamics of departure in more detail we cannot identify just where the maximum rate of white departure would occur. We should not, however, expect it to occur immediately this point has been reached. The number of discontented whites, and the degree of their discontent, just exceed zero to the immediate left of this point and continue to increase over

There are a number of possibilities. Blacks who want to live in mixed neighborhoods, not black neighborhoods, will be concerned about upper as well as lower limits, about the whites' tipping out as well as other blacks' tipping in. They may want enough blacks to be congenial but not enough to cause white evacuation. They, too, may be worried about property values as well as neighbors. But blacks have less choice, and will be motivated by the alternatives available.

Black entrants may define the neighborhood differently from the white residents. If blacks move into a subneighborhood, they may be mainly concerned with the subneighborhood while most whites are concerned with the larger neighborhood. (The relative significance of school and residence will differ for the minority and the majority.)

Furthermore, in the process we are now analyzing, whites are old residents and blacks new. The decision to move out is different from the decision to move in. Tipping out involves *whether* to move, tipping in involves *where*.

Formally, we can examine the tipping-in process by repeating, this time for blacks, what we have done for whites in Figures 5-1 through 5-4. We suppose that for each potential black entrant there is some minimum percentage black that he demands, or else he will not move in. We can again draw a frequency distribution, convert it as we did to cumulative form, and superimpose it on the diagram for whites to obtain a figure depicting both the tipping-in point for blacks and the tipping-out point for whites, if there are such points.

In doing this, we have to keep in mind that the relevant black population may not be equal to the capacity of the neighborhood. We were able to ignore, for simplicity, the potential white entrants and deal with the original residents, who were just enough to fill the place up. But the blacks interested in moving in may be few or many compared with the neighborhood. (The definition of the neighborhood affects this.)

Also, the whites in our diagrams were a fixed population; except for turnover they were the same people from month to month or year to year. The blacks who might move in are less likely to be a specified collection of people. They could be all those blacks living nearby who are dissatisfied where they are and will move in at the earliest opportunity; alternatively, though, they may be blacks currently searching for places—a changing population from year to year. Properly, we should measure the potential entrants not with an absolute number but as some maximum rate of entry per unit of time; but here we are just trying to get acquainted with concepts, and it suits our purpose to suppose a fixed number of interested blacks.

An illustrative distribution of individual black tipping points is in Figure 5-5, together with three corresponding cumulative distributions. They correspond to different sizes of the relevant black population. In one case blacks are assumed to be equal to 50 percent of the capacity of the neighborhood, in the second case 100 percent, and in the third case 200 percent. For the smaller populations there are tipping-in points. To the left of the crossover point there is no potential stable black population; there are not, say, ten blacks satisfied to live in the neighborhood on condition that nine others do, too. To the right of that point the black population is stable and will grow with available vacancies. Whereas white populations were stable only as large majorities of the population, because we assumed individual tipping points with that characteristic, black populations in our model can comprise stable minorities, even rather small ones, because we imputed individual preferences compatible with that result.

With the larger potential black population, the tipping point is at zero; there is at least one black willing to live alone in the neighborhood, another willing to be one of two, at least another willing to be one of three, and so forth.

To put the black and white curves on the same diagram it is useful to invert one or the other. Being more familiar with the location of the white curve, we invert the new one for blacks. We measure blacks in the neighborhood from right to left on the horizontal scale. The cumulative number of blacks willing to live in the neighborhood, at given percentages, will be measured downward from the top on the vertical scale. This has been done (using the middle of the three

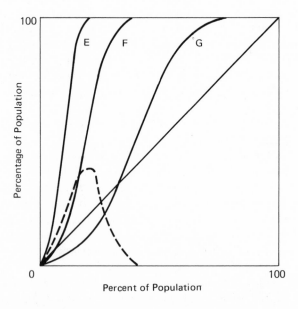

Figure 5-5. Hypothetical Frequency Distributions of Neighborhood Racial Tipping Points: Three Hypothetical Black Populations, E, F, and G.

curves for blacks, Population G, and the curve of Figure 5-3, Population C for whites) in Figure 5-6; the origin of the curve for blacks is at the upper right.

On this diagram, we see the tipping-in point for blacks and the tipping-out point for whites. Furthermore, the blacks tip in at about 10 percent black, the whites tip out at about 18 percent black, and there is a range from 10 to 18 percent black that is stable for both. In this range the whites and blacks satisfied with those percentages are enough to comprise those percentages. (A quota system that guaranteed at least 10 percent black and at least 82 percent white would find whites and blacks consistent with those percentages in sufficient numbers to fill the neighborhood.) This range from 82 to 90 percent white is a kind of *neutral equilibrium*. Neither blacks nor whites are evacuating, but nothing guarantees that the percentages will stay within the range. If in the course of turnover the blacks are not replaced, their numbers may fall below 10 percent; the rest tip out. If in the course of turnover black demand exceeds white for vacancies in the neighborhood, the white percentage will fall to 82 percent and begin to unravel. Within the range from 82 to 90 percent white, the percentages

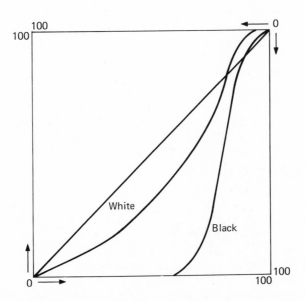

Figure 5-6. Superimposed Cumulative Distributions of Neighborhood Racial Tipping Points for White Population C and Black Population F.

can drift in either direction; at the two tipping points drift stops and exodus begins.

If we experimented with the smallest of the three black populations, we would obtain a curve for blacks crossing the diagonal left of where the white curve crosses. Before the blacks have reached *critical density* for tipping in, they have passed the point at which whites begin to evacuate. There is no stable neighborhood except an all-white or an all-black one. Any self-sustaining black component corresponds to a white component that, though still a substantial majority, is not self-sustaining.

We have to ask, with either of the two smaller black populations, how the number of blacks in the neighborhood might ever achieve sufficient numbers to become self-sustaining. At least two mechanisms come to mind. One is that a few black families, at any given time, are willing to enter irrespective of whether other blacks reside there. Thus we have a very small self-sustaining population of blacks, too small to grow because it has not yet reached critical size for the rest of them. (Technically, the black curve should then cross the diagonal twice, once at a very small figure.) With the passage of time, the number of such blacks may increase until the cumulative total reaches critical mass for the current population of potential entrants. This involves distinguishing the black population potential during some comparatively short period—perhaps a year or two—from the cumulative total over a much longer period. Out of that cumulative total, those few who are willing to be a very small minority remain as a permanent (and growing) part of a population the rest of which continually changes.

A second possibility is that speculation induces entry. Blacks may be willing to bet on an increasing number of like neighbors, enough of them entering to confirm those expectations and reach critical density.

For policy purposes there may be a third important possibility. Black families corresponding in number to a self-sustaining component of the neighborhood make a concerted entry. Evidently if a number that is sufficient to be self-sustaining, once settled, can arrange concerted entry or make convincing arrangements to reach adequate numbers, the problem is reduced to one of transition. There may still be some risk, unless a corporation is formed that negotiates concerted rentals or purchases, but there is less risk than if individuals had to speculate individually.

Before we finish with tipping in, there are more possibilities to notice. An obvious one is that the black tipping-in point is zero. Another is that the number of blacks ready to enter after the tipping-in point is reached is limited; there are not enough blacks in the market to fill the neighborhood.

Literally interpreted, our curves tell us that blacks will enter in sufficient numbers to cause the whites to tip out, and when the whites are all gone the neighborhood will be partly occupied by blacks and partly empty. Empty houses are an unlikely result, over a sustained period. Our model has not allowed for price changes. We can suppose that blacks or whites or both, including some who were not originally looking for homes, would move into the area as rentals and sales prices responsed to the local depression. What we have, therefore, is more complicated than what our pair of curves, for blacks and whites, will display. We are working with an overly restricted model.

Consider what may happen if there are not enough blacks to fill the neighborhood but enough to cause the original whites to tip out: two phenomena are not reflected in the numerical ratio of blacks and whites. If rentals fall, and blacks and whites are attracted who were not originally in the market, the people who end up in the neighborhood will not be the ones for whom we drew our frequency distributions.

If, after a period of vacancies and price reductions, the neighborhood ends up 40 or 60 percent white, 75 or 100 percent of the original whites may have moved out. A large number of whites moved into the newly lower-priced (and probably lower-income) neighborhood. Some of the blacks who might have moved in, perhaps some who actually did move in, are confronted with a neighborhood different from the one in which they were shopping for a home. They may not find entry attractive after all, either because of the blacks or because of the whites that they would be living among. And while lower prices may appeal to them, the prospect of further price declines may deter some of those who intended to purchase.

The same neighborhood may thus tip successively to different groups. Some transient residents may open the neighborhood for others who follow and tip them out.

Speculative Exit and Entry

Recall the case of Russell Woods: when the third black bought a house in a neighborhood of seven hundred houses, white homes began to go up for sale.

The account does not state that immediately adjacent homes went on the market; if that were what had happened, our whole analysis based on neighborhood percentages would have to be discarded in favor of one based on local domino effects. We still have to examine *neighbor* as well as *neighborhood* effects, but for the moment we are dealing with what looks like speculative action at the neighborhood level.

Of course, the presence of three black families may have "spoiled" the neighborhood for some number of whites. If 5 percent of the whites will not stay if there are any blacks at all, 35 families out of 700 would make plans to leave, quite apart from the induced speculative plans of others who anticipated black occupancy of many among those first 35 houses. The author does not tell us how many homes were put on the market, how visible the sales activity was, or what other symptoms there were to nourish speculation. But he does say, perhaps with allowable exaggeration, "The selling of the third house convinced everyone that the neighborhood was destined to become mixed." The fact that the third sale convinced "everyone" of anything is sure evidence that the perceptual basis for speculation was present.

Speculation can reflect alternative degrees of "compounded expectations." A homeowner can believe, rightly or wrongly, that for the kinds of reasons embodied in our cumulative curves, the neighborhood will eventually contain too few whites to suit him, and will make plans to leave. Alternatively, he can believe the neighborhood is basically secure against tipping but sense that other residents lack confidence; by moving out he will cause to happen what they expect to happen. Anticipating the misguided speculation of others of which he would be a victim if he stayed, he joins them in deciding to go. Or, altogether without regard to the underlying proclivities of individuals, there may just be a strong belief that, once a neighborhood becomes 20 percent (or 5 percent or 1 percent) black, an ineluctable process has begun, one that sometimes goes rapidly, so that the wise thing to do is to move at one's earliest convenience if not sooner. If capital losses are involved, the whole process can be aggravated by the attempt to get rid of one's house a little sooner than everyone else.

This is less like speculation in stocks than like speculation on the solvency of one's bank. Rumors and scares or the misreading of a downtrend can cause a company's stock to fall drastically. Sooner or later, if the company's earnings are really all right, the market can readjust. But if depositors believe their bank is insolvent (or just believe others may think so and act accordingly) and withdraw their funds to be on the safe side, the bank can go broke and when it does it will stay broke.[5] Neighborhood change, if home ownership is involved, is not usually reversible.

The Speculative Costs of Delay

It is important, though, to recognize an ingredient that has to be present for this speculative mechanism to work. There must be some cost or risk in delaying action, once neighborhood change is expected.

If the cost of moving does not change over time; if there is no drop in the value of owned houses and no penalty on mistakenly staying around; if there is no harm in somewhat overstaying as the neighborhood becomes unattractive or if one can move out at a moment's notice; if there is consequently no need to plan in advance, then everyone can wait to see whether the percentage black rises above the percentage that he himself can tolerate. The true distribution of tipping points (that is, the distribution that reflects the tolerance of individual residents and does not incorporate the residents' guesses about the reactions of their neighbors) will then determine what happens.

The speculative reaction requires that people find it advantageous to anticipate, to plan now an action that may become appropriate soon, to avoid the penalty of delay. If one has to sign a year's lease and believes that in a month or two the neighborhood will become uncomfortable, instead of waiting a month or two to see what happens he may forego the lease and move away. If he owns a home and believes that it will take time to sell it, he may immediately put on the market the house that he would otherwise have held—to wait and see—if houses could be disposed of instantaneously.

We expect, then, that the speculative acceleration of tipping, or the speculative reinforcement of it, would be related to any penalty on delay and any lack of penalty on premature or mistaken departure. If the neighborhood is a hard one to get back into, if people are attached to their homes, or if the alternative places to live are substantially less attractive or less convenient, to move too early can be a mistake entailing permanent loss, while to delay departure, unless financial loss occurs, subjects one at the worst to a limited period of dissatisfaction prior to departure.

Speculative tipping, then, to cause permanent change, requires: (1) the asymmetry on penalties—heavier on delay than on premature departure—and (2) an incapacity for corrective reversal. For physical reversal the two often go together: easy, prompt, and costless exit is usually associated with easy, prompt, and costless re-entry. A man can easily return to his favorite hotel or restaurant if it didn't tip after all, but if only a night's reservation or a luncheon date is involved he needn't act in advance of the event anyway. It is when the speculative departure passes the real underlying tipping point that irreversibility is more than the costliness of a return move; the old tipping-out point is now a tipping-in point for re-entry, and those who left are as far short of tipping in as they are beyond tipping out.

Home ownership should be expected to aggravate speculative departure because it makes shifting of residence more cumbersome and costly. Long leases work in the same direction. An expected shortage of places to go might aggravate speculative departure. And if the homeowner is more concerned about capital loss than his own prolonged stay in a neighborhood that becomes progressively less suitable, the important speculative action is not moving but selling. The two often go together, but we ought to distinguish them. Rented homes and apartments involve decisions by two different people: an owner's decision to sell before values become depressed and a tenant's decision to move before the neighborhood ceases to please.

Neighborhoods and Boundaries

Our formal analysis was abstract and, among other things, assumed a well-defined neighborhood. What defines a neighborhood?

Russell Woods was well defined. In literature and in daily life one does come across neighborhoods that are well defined, but one also comes across neighborhoods that are not. Some are divided into subneighborhoods; some have definitions that depend on just where within them one happens to live. Neighborhoods can be defined differently by people who live in them, people who live adjacent to them, and people newly arrived in search of a place to settle. Neighborhoods will be differently defined by families with and without children, by people who work in them and people who commute, by transients and longer-term residents, and by people sensitive to particular ethnic groups and income or social classes.

An important characteristic of a homogeneous neighborhood may be that its residents have a common appreciation of its boundaries and of what makes it homogeneous. Heterogeneous neighborhoods can be diversified not only in the people who live in them but in their definitions of boundaries and of what, if anything, makes them neighborhoods.

For the analysis of tipping, neighborhood need not have its ordinary definition. Or, to put it differently, a resident can be conscious of different neighborhoods in which he lives, the definitions corresponding to work, play, school, travel, social activities, civic and cultural identity, sentimental attachment, and (especially for homeowners) financial interest.

And, of course, definitions of neighborhood may vary with racial sensitivity— or for sensitivity to any social, cultural, linguistic, or ethnic intrusions that impinge on a resident's environment, his taxes, or the value of his house. His definition for this purpose will depend not only on whom he likes to live with or send his children to school with, but on his beliefs of what people do to his environment and on his theories of neighborhood dynamics. He may have beliefs about who comes next and how fast, once a minority enters, on how his own neighbors will react, on domino effects and the contagion of real estate values, and indeed on the very phenomenon of tipping that we are analyzing in these pages.

If tipping occurs primarily because people believe that it does, the relevant definition of neighborhood will be the one they give it in their hypotheses about tipping.

Still, neighborhoods are somewhat consensual and, though often arbitrary, are not arbitrary with the individual. Natural barriers and boundaries help to define them. Wide boulevards, railroad tracks, parks, vacant land, rivers, and other characteristics of terrain have a natural or traditional quality that appeals to the need for definition. Neighborhoods are partly defined by the equality of housing and the characteristics of people. Racial boundaries that merely exist for some time may acquire the status of neighborhood boundaries. Definitions can change; a neighborhood can be cut in half by a turnpike, fragmented by public buildings or shopping centers, or squeezed by encroachment at its boundaries.

The definition will be pertinent both to tipping in and to tipping out. The definition not only affects whether a black is in the neighborhood or out but affects the denominator in his percentage. Ten families in a subneighborhood of fifty look like 20 percent. If nobody perceives the subneighborhood as an entity, the ten blacks will be 5 percent or 1 percent of a larger neighborhood; or on the other hand, they may look like 50 percent of a one-street neighborhood of twenty families.

The pattern of entry can itself redefine neighborhoods. Ten blacks who buy houses on the same street may establish a subneighborhood; the same ten families dispersed in a larger area will leave the original definition intact. (If the school is the relevant neighborhood, exact residential locations may not matter.)

Suppose there are no neighborhoods: all terrain is homogeneous and any graduations of housing, status, or ethnic density are smooth. If a certain area is black and the remainder white, and a few blacks move into the white area, it will be hard to say just what area has acquired these few blacks. There will be no percentage because there is no denominator. One can perceive movement or expansion, but not on a neighborhood basis.

This leads to the possibility of gradual, continuous tipping, rather than discrete tipping by finite neighborhoods. It raises issues of closeness, adjacency, and distance rather than inclusion and exclusion. Schools and swimming pools are discrete; spatial relations like residence almost always have some quality of adjacency and distance.

If a neighborhood is well defined, with a distinct boundary, particularly one that separates it physically or by convention from surrounding areas, the residents may be almost equally within the neighborhood. Physically some will be more toward the center and some more toward the periphery, but those on the frontier may not feel like frontiersmen and those who live in the center may not feel themselves buried in the heartland. If blacks move in they move into one person's neighborhood as much as another's. But in the absence of discrete, commonly defined, traditional, and physically separate neighborhoods, one person will be closer to blacks than another when blacks move in. Tipping then needs to be analyzed at least somewhat in terms of closeness or adjacency, but this will not be done here.[6]

Convergent Forces on Neighborhood Tipping

It should not be surprising that tipping, if it occurs, occurs widely. The more it occurs the more it will be expected, and the more it is expected the more it will occur. Furthermore, if tipping is anticipated the reactions of real estate brokers and others will facilitate it. A neighborhood that signals that it is a prospective tipper is likely to attract disproportionate interest from real estate agents and others who not only facilitate tipping but aggravate it by their actions (and in some cases conspire to reinforce it).

Most important, in most metropolitan areas we begin with a bottled-up demand for housing by blacks. It is not merely that blacks live in some places and whites in others, and once in a while a white or black moves into the other's territory. A large portion of black demand gets *channeled*, for it is excluded or intimidated in so many areas that when one area opens, black demand is focused on it. Whether or not there is a shortage of leaders to venture in, followers will be ready to move in after them.

If neighborhoods tip rapidly they may appear to tip in succession, so that there is at any moment an obvious next neighborhood ready to tip. If the process is drawn out there may be a number of neighborhoods with a few blacks each, some of which are expected to tip and some not. There may not be enough blacks to tip them all, and the whole process will be damped. But if blacks tend to follow the leader into one neighborhood after another, filling up each before venturing into the next, an unconcerted process of divide and conquer can bring about successive tipping of one neighborhood after another. Expectations make the process self-reinforcing.

Well-defined neighborhoods may therefore invite successive entry on a more nearly all-or-none basis, while ill-defined neighborhoods might be more conducive to dispersal.

Third Parties in the
Tipping Process

In addition to those who move out and those who move in there are others. People concerned with lending and real estate will be involved, and whatever their prejudices or preferences it is not their own homes that are involved. They have an interest, but not as residents; they may be formally or informally constrained by the prejudices of others; and they are in competition with each other. There are at least four different levels at which brokers and agents can contribute to the process, and several degrees of organization or collusion that can be involved.

First, bankers and real estate brokers may be inhibited from facilitating a black's purchase of a home in a white neighborhood. The inhibition can be a personal prejudice, a belief that it is good for real estate, a loyalty to convention, or some fear of penalty. Penalties can be resentment by potential customers of one's complicity in "spoiling" a neighborhood, accusations by one's competitors that one has broken a tacit or explicit agreement to abstain from that kind of business, or general opprobrium from the business or social community, which in turn could lead to financial disadvantage. The resulting inhibitions can be potent even though informal, unorganized, and inexplicit.

Once a neighborhood has already been entered by a few blacks, these inhibitions may rapidly dissolve. A recent study of discrimination in Cleveland turned up a universal compunction about the first loan to the first black in any neighborhood (Kovachy, 1968). The unwritten rule applied only to the first. When the inhibition dissolved it did so on a neighborhood basis. (The study did not make clear just how bankers defined neighborhood.) It was not that blacks could get loans more readily once a first black had penetrated some white neighborhood, but that blacks could get loans for *that particular neighborhood*. Thus the very inhibition that kept blacks from dispersing normally, and that contributed to pent-up demand for homes on the part of blacks, channeled blacks into one neighborhood once the first had secured entry. This contributes to the concentration of blacks and to the identification of a particular neighborhood target.

Second, even if they have no direct causal role in tipping, lenders and realtors are attracted by the business. They will allocate time and advertising to a neighborhood believed about to tip or in process of tipping, and will thus contribute to the tipping.

Third, there is evidence that real estate agents, if not lenders, sometimes knowingly contribute to the process by helping to generate expectation that the neighborhood will go black. Among the signals that the former residents will be alert to are "for sale" signs, blacks being shown houses, and direct inquiries by agents whether one's house is up for sale. This activity may appear unethical but probably cannot be made effectively illegal. It happens, with or without feigned innocence.

Fourth, a widely deplored activity, *blockbusting*, involves dramatizing the unattractiveness of the new entrants and the risks and discomforts of remaining in the neighborhood or of keeping one's home off the market. In fictional treatments the first blacks are planted and instructed to make noise, to see that their children are dirty, to keep a broken-down truck parked in front of the house, to act in a manner that threatens the comfort if not the peace of the neighborhood, and even to attract the attention of the police. The object is to create the reality corresponding to the worst prejudice, and to do it visibly and unmistakenly.

This is a polite form of racketeering. Somebody could threaten to beat up one's children, splash paint on one's house, throw tear gas in one's living room, or set off firecrackers all day Sunday, demanding cash to abstain. Instead, he gets members of some minority group "innocently" to create an obnoxious environment, forcing an owner to abandon his property at a financial loss, of which some part will accrue to him.

Both the motives and the consequences of these third-party actions are hard to judge. At the first level, that of inhibitions, moral and ethical sensitivity may do as much harm as good, causing people to respect (or giving them an excuse to respect) the wishes, opinions, or prejudices of the community. It is not easy to decide which is more unattractive: piously declining a loan to the black who wants to buy the first house in a white neighborhood, or eagerly doing business with the second and asking him if he doesn't have a friend who would like a loan.

The mere focus of realtors' attention is a natural commercial response. They are not much more to be blamed than the residential whites or the blacks who are making personal choices in their own interests. The deliberate attempt to stir up business by zealous and anticipatory salesmanship is hard to censure in comparison with ordinary commercial activity. Furthermore, a realtor may believe, and quite correctly, that the neighborhood is going to tip and that he does nobody a disservice by persuading him to put his house quickly on the market.

In addition, although the tipping phenomenon is deplored by people interested in integration, its local effect can be to increase housing opportunities for blacks. Its wider effect may be to constrict it by augmenting inhibitions, generating barriers and organized resistance, and making the "first black" unpopular wherever he appears. The process may also make it too easy for blacks to cluster when they might otherwise have dispersed among several neighborhoods. Nevertheless, the white realtor who tries to persuade potential customers that they should offer their houses for sale before the "invasion" reaches flood level, is not behaving all that differently from the black realtor who is engaged in a similar part of the process; both of them can argue, correctly from a narrow point of view, that they are helping blacks both to acquire houses and, perhaps, to move into white neighborhoods.

Another neighborhood or some of its residents could also have a third-party interest in a *forward defense* if their neighborhood is second or third domino down the line. (Or, like people who live near a river that may overflow its banks, they may have an interest in cutting the dike downstream if they think they are next but the flood can be diverted.) The forward defense strategy is undoubtedly an expressive one for the prejudiced, and is probably behind some of the demonstrations against blacks that occur on a supraneighborhood basis.

Large-Area Tipping

Tipping is usually hypothesized as a neighborhood phenomenon, and that is the way it has been treated here. We should ask, though, whether it happens on a larger scale. Can an entire city or metropolitan area tip?

If *city* is defined by municipal boundaries, not including suburbs, a city can apparently become fully or almost fully occupied through a process of successive tipping. Neighborhood after neighborhood or area after area may tip until the entire city has been occupied by the former minority.

There is a sense in which this is the tipping of a whole city. The process, neighborhood by neighborhood, might work so visibly and dramatically that the tipping of each neighborhood in succession accelerated the tipping of the next. This would be the racial-residential equivalent of the domino process.

It is a different question whether an entire metropolitan area might tip through intercity migration. Can the process be potent enough to cause whites to evacuate a metropolitan area in large numbers, moving not just locally but to other cities? Can the tipping in of blacks work through intercity migration? Can a metropolitan area become recognized as black to the extent of being a dominant influence on intercity residential decisions and on business location, which in turn can influence migration patterns?

There probably is a process akin to tipping in, which works through the differential attraction on intercity migrants of the size or density of black populations in different metropolitan areas. If blacks are attracted to places where blacks are, either because numbers attract them or because personal relations and communications lead blacks to settle in cities where they have contacts, the result may be disproportionate growth. But whether this can lead to genuine tipping we do not know for sure. We are only on the threshold of some city governments' becoming significantly black, and we do not know how publicity—about racial strife or about the comparative calm of a city with a black government—will eventually affect intercity migration.

What is awesome is the irreversibility of such a process. Within a city, tipping can be locally irreversible without making the city more segregated; it can expand the area occupied by blacks without changing the degree of segregation. Furthermore, within a city one can hope for an impact on residential movement in the future, bringing more dispersion at a later time. It would be much harder to influence intercity residential decisions in decades to come, once whole metropolitan areas have tipped.

A near analogy may be the evacuation by Europeans of former colonial areas, such as Algeria. The evacuation of former residents was on the order of a million and accounted for an actual majority of them. This was not mainly residential; perhaps large-area tipping is not primarily residential. It has to do with political discrimination, job favoritism, loss of institutionalized status and privileges, growing hostility, and personal danger, or, at least, an expectation of them.

If integration should finally prove infeasible and separateness provides a viable coexistence, large-area tipping through intercity migration could be a significant part of the process. Its probable irreversibility would make it a risky social experiment. And if it turned out that, after it happened, blacks did not like it, it might prove to be a large-scale analogy of the vacated and underpopulated neighborhood we observed in one version of our model.

Nonneighborhood Tipping

Schools and swimming pools have been mentioned. Where else can the process occur? Apartments and hotels differ from single-occupancy neighborhoods. Restaurants and night clubs can tip. A dramatic difference between a night club and a neighborhood is that for the former the number of potential occupants is large compared with the capacity, and actions are almost instantaneous with decisions. A few whites seeking cultural integration can "spoil" a black night spot or gathering place with remarkable speed. (And, when they do, they may lose interest and leave a depressed area that is beyond recovery.)

In instances other than residence, tipping in may be even more important than tipping out. Schools, occupations, and professions may be forbidding to a minority until some critical number or density is reached. The effective numbers may be not merely company and congeniality but acculturation of the whites as well. Tipping in can be a process in which both races participate. But there may be tipping out.

Third parties may be important here. If blacks come to dominate an occupation, whites may decline to enter or begin to evacuate. More effectively, personnel managers may act like real estate brokers, even inadvertently, in advertising and recruiting among blacks and in supposing that whites will no longer be interested.

Among the relevant parameters in occupations, an important one may be "nextness" or adjacency, which we noticed was probably effective in connection with residence. White and black taxi drivers do not drive in permanent formations; no one is next to another. In some occupations one is "next" to another man, but many job relations are not as continuous and unbroken as spatial relations in a neighborhood. An integrated police force can send out segregated patrol cars.[7]

Just as the definition of a neighborhood and its boundary is important in residence, the definitions of occupations and their boundaries would be significant for tipping. So would be the definitions of establishments.

Professional sports was a possibility. In the major leagues the tipping-in point, if it existed, has long since been passed. Tipping out, if any, has been moderate. Managers and owners, as well as players, are evidently involved. Maybe there is a serious tipping-out point for whites, but it has not been reached. Very likely the tipping point can shift with time, and if black entry is gradual the white tipping-out point recedes as custom changes and expectations change. Concerted action, of course, is more feasible among major-league sports teams than among residential neighborhoods.[8]

An important nonresidential possibility would be one of the military services; most likely the Army or some part of it. A tipping-out process could be a serious possibility if there were no organized means of control. The military services are a good example of where quotas can be used (and may have been used) effectively to achieve stable mixes.

The Generalized Tipping Phenomenon

Not only is tipping not confined to residence, it is not confined to race. There can be tipping by age, sex, language, income, and social class. Tipping in may be as important as tipping out. The technique of formerly male colleges for getting past the women students' tipping-in point has recently been concerted entry by affiliation of whole colleges. Where this solution is unavailable, women students often appear not to have reached critical mass. Business schools have sometimes estimated that a larger number of women would be self-sustaining over the years; but until the initial large number is achieved, women are inhibited from applying.

Tipping by age group is a common phenomenon at ice cream parlors and other gathering spots where teenagers can suddenly supplant lady shoppers. Families with noisy small children can tip out quieter and more elderly residents of an apartment building. Examples can be found in animal ecology.[9]

Thus the mechanism that underlies the phenomenon is scientifically respectable and nearly ubiquitous. Evidence for how it works, even whether it works, in connection with the racial mixture of residential areas in American cities, is still hard to interpret. This is one of those many instances in which the collective or mass phenomenon does not reflect in any simple way the individual behavior that underlies it. The system is not merely individual behavior numerically magnified. People may tip and neighborhoods may tip, but there is no simple translation from the behavior of the individual to the behavior of the system.

Notes

1. The Duncans found succession rarely reversed once it reached 10 percent black.

2. Tolerance here is a comparative concept: the "more tolerant" white is either more tolerant of blacks or less tolerant of moving. As far as the model is concerned we could as well call it "immobility." It is a tolerance/mobility ratio.

3. Bimodal distributions can often be divided into two components of the population. In this case they might be families with and without children, people who own and people who rent their homes, distinct ethnic or religious populations, or any other dichotomous groupings that had significantly different tolerances for blacks but considered each other residentially acceptable.

4. The cumulative curve rises by one-third its vertical distance from the top of the diagram. Alternatively, if chosen from around the median tolerance level (demanding 60 to 75 percent white company), fewer than one-fourth need to be so induced to shift the bottom two-thirds of the curve leftward to cross the diagonal again, stabilizing the white population at 60 to 65 percent white and immunizing it against further instability.

5. Deposit insurance has been a potent means for damping those destructive expectations and may be suggestive of programs that could forestall neighborhood panic.

6. See T.C. Schelling, "Dynamic Models of Segregation," *Journal of Mathematical Sociology*, 1 (1971): 149-66, for some results of a simulation model in which individuals are distributed over a plane surface and define their own neighborhoods as the areas within a given distance from themselves.

7. See Kenneth J. Arrow, "Models of Job Discrimination," Chapter 2 of this volume, on the general theme of the impact of race on occupational and industrial patterns.

8. See Anthony H. Pascal and Leonard A. Rapping, "The Economics of Racial Discrimination in Organized Baseball," Chapter 4 of this volume, for a discussion of racial segregation in major league baseball.

9. In the case of noisy children, tipping out may depend on absolute numbers, not percentages, of the offending population; tipping in may be even more dependent on absolute numbers. The diagrammatic analysis can usually be interpreted in terms of numbers as well as percentages.

References

Arrow, Kenneth J. "Models of Job Discrimination." Chapter 2 of this volume.

Duncan, Otis Dudley, and Beverly Duncan. *The Negro Population of Chicago.* Chicago: University of Chicago Press, 1957, Chapter 6.

Grodzins, Morton. "Metropolitan Segregation." *Scientific American* (October 1957): 24, 33-41.

Kovachy, Edward M. "The Causes of Negro Residential Segregation in Cleveland, Ohio." Unpublished senior honors thesis, Department of Economics, Harvard University, 1968.

Mayer, A.J. "Russell Woods: Change Without Conflict." In Nathan Glazer and David McEntire, eds., *Studies in Housing and Minority Groups.* Berkeley: University of California Press, 1960.

Pascal, Anthony, H., and Leonard A. Rapping. "The Economics of Racial Discrimination in Organized Baseball." Chapter 4 of this volume.

Schelling, Thomas C. "Dynamic Models of Segregation." *Journal of Mathematical Sociology*, 1 (1971): 143-86.

Stinchcombe, Arthur L., Mary McDill, and Dollie Walker. "Is There a Racial Tipping Point in Changing Schools." *The Journal of Social Issues* 25 (January 1969): 127-36.

Part Two
Mathematical Analyses of Racial Discrimination

Some Mathematical Models of Race Discrimination in the Labor Market

KENNETH J. ARROW

A

For a starkly dramatic model to bring out some broad tendencies, assume all firms have identical utility functions and identical production functions. There is only one commodity, other than labor, and white and black labor are perfect substitutes in production. The supplies of the two kinds of labor are both perfectly inelastic. Finally, start with a short-run analysis in which the supply of capital to each firm is given, so that output is a function of the labor employed. Let W and N be the amounts of white and black labor hired by a representative firm; then output is given by $f(W + N)$, where the function f is strictly concave and increasing. The profits of the firm are given by

$$\pi = f(W + N) - w_W W - w_N N, \tag{1}$$

where w_W and w_N are the wages of white and black workers, respectively. The aim of the firm is to maximize,

$$U(\pi, W, N), \text{ where } U_W \geqslant 0, U_N \leqslant 0. \tag{2}$$

One of the two inequalities must be strict if there is in fact discrimination.

This model is a straightforward generalization of that in Becker.[1]

Since all firms are identical and all utility and production functions have the appropriate convexity properties, the choice of W and N will be the same for all firms at any given set of wage rates. Since total supplies of W and N are given, it follows that at equilibrium each firm will demand W and N equal to the respective total supplies divided by the number of firms; assume these values for W and N in what follows. The maximization of (2) with respect to W and N, with due account being taken of (1), implies

$$U_\pi (f' - w_W) + U_W = 0, \quad U_\pi (f' - w_N) + U_N = 0,$$

or

$$f' = w_W + d_W = w_N + d_N, \tag{3}$$

where $d_W = -U_W/U_\pi$, $d_N = -U_N/U_\pi$; these are Becker's *discrimination* coefficients against white and Negro labor, respectively. From the inequalities in (2), $d_W \leqslant 0$ (Becker uses the term, *nepotism coefficient*, for $-d_W$,) $d_N \geqslant 0$, so that,

$$w_W \geqslant f' \geqslant w_N, \tag{4}$$

so that, as is obvious, this model does imply higher wages for whites than for Negroes of identical productivity.

It should be remarked that in this model production is thoroughly efficient. Efficient production requires only that each firm get an equal amount of labor. It may be noticed that this conclusion is not completely robust under relaxation of the assumption of identical production functions. From (3) it is clear that the general condition for efficiency is that d_W and d_N be the same for all firms (more strictly, for all firms that in fact employ both kinds of labor). This condition need only hold at equilibrium; however, a sufficient condition is that d_W and d_N be constants, independent of π, W, and N, and, of course, be the same constants for all. This condition is equivalent to stating that the utility function can be linear in π, W, and N, which is the particular form of the model set forth by Becker.

If allocation is efficient, then the presence of discrimination has a purely redistributive effect. Since f' is the same as it would have been in the absence of discrimination, white workers gain only if there is positive preference for them, not merely a distaste on the employer's part for Negroes. The effect on employers' profits can be seen by substituting (3) into (1):

$$\pi = f(W+N) - f'(W+N)(W+N) + d_W W + d_N N.$$

If π_O is the volume of profits in the absence of discrimination,

$$\pi_O = f - f'(W+N)(W+N),$$

so that,

$$\pi - \pi_O = d_W W + d_N N. \tag{5}$$

The right-hand side has the following simple interpretation: it is the amount of profits needed to compensate the employer for a unit increase in his labor force that preserves its racial proportions.

One possible hypothesis is that the employers' satisfactions are governed by the *proportion* of Negro workers, that is, an increase in labor force scale that preserves racial proportions leaves him indifferent. In that case, (5) tells us that employers do not profit by discrimination, the net effect of which is a transfer from black to white workers. On the other hand, if the primary motivation of the employer is a distaste for black workers, and this is little offset by increased numbers of white workers, then d_W is small in absolute value, d_N is large, and the effect of discrimination is primarily a pecuniary transfer from black workers to employers. In any case, however, it is elementary that the white community (employers plus white workers) gains in pecuniary terms precisely the gap between marginal product and wage for black workers. This simple but important point has been brought out by Thurow.[2]

It is important to emphasize the incidence of racial discrimination, in particular, the possibility that employers may actually gain in pecuniary terms by their discrimination. This point seems not always to be grasped; of course, any individual employer would gain by a reduction in discrimination, but it is at least plausible that employers collectively gain by discrimination.[3]

B

Becker has shown that if there is a third factor of production (for example, another type of labor such as management) that discriminates against black workers and is complementary to or imperfectly substitutable for them, it will follow that Negro wages will fall below those of perfectly substitutable whites.[4] Similarly, Welch has suggested that the possibility of observed discrimination may arise because white and black workers are not perfect substitutes for each other, but, because of different educational levels, are also complementary.[5] Complementarity creates a motive for the employer to integrate, which offsets the other tendencies to segregation and therefore can lead to wage differentials.

The following model elaborates Becker's and seeks to catch the spirit of Welch's ideas. Assume now that there are two types of labor. White and black workers are perfect substitutes in type 1 labor (which might be thought of as unskilled). There is a complementary type of labor, however, type 2 (perhaps foremen), who prefer to work with whites rather than blacks. We assume that,

$$w_2 = w_2(L_{1W}/L_1) \tag{1}$$

where L_{1W}, L_{1N}, L_1, and L_2 are the respective amounts of type 1 white workers, type 1 black workers, all type 1 workers, and type 2 workers hired by the firm. Profits are given by

$$\pi = f(L_1, L_2) - w_{1W} L_{1W} - w_{1N} L_{1N} - w_2 L_2, \tag{2}$$

where w_{1W} and w_{1N} are the wages of type 1 white and type 1 black workers, respectively, and $f(L_{1W} + L_{1N}, L_2)$ is output. Maximization of (2) with respect to the three types of labor yields,

$$f_1 = w_{1W} + (\partial w_2/\partial L_{1W}) L_2, \tag{3a}$$

$$f_1 = w_{1N} + (\partial w_2/\partial L_{1N})\, L_2, \tag{3b}$$

$$f_2 = w_2. \tag{3c}$$

Since $\partial w_2/\partial L_{1W} < 0$, $\partial w_2/\partial L_{1N} > 0$, it immediately follows from (3a-b) that $w_{1W} > w_{1N}$. Since w_2 is homogeneous of degree 0 in L_{1W} and L_{1N},

$$(\partial w_2/\partial L_{1W})\, L_{1W} + (\partial w_2/\partial L_{1N})\, L_{1N} = 0.$$

If we multiply (3a) by L_{1W} and (3b) by L_{1N}, we find,

$$f_1\,(L_{1W} + L_{1N}) = w_{1W} L_{1W} + w_{1N} L_{1N}.$$

It then follows from (3c) and (2) that the profits of the firm are exactly what they would be with no discrimination, if the firm had the same quantities of the two types of labor in the two situations.

If, for given w_{1W}, w_{2W}, and schedule $w_2(L_{1W}/L_1)$, each firm had a unique optimum, then, under the assumptions made, all firms would have the same amounts of L_{1W}, L_{1N}, and L_2, which would be the same as in the absence of discrimination. Hence, allocation would be efficient; profits would be the same in the two situations; from (3c), the wages of type 2 labor would be the same, and the net effect would be a transfer of income from Negro to white type 1 workers, even though any discriminatory feelings the latter might have are irrelevant to the final equilibrium.

It is possible, however, that the shape of the function $w_2(L_{1W}/L_1)$ is such that there can be multiple optima for the firm. The equal allocation might not even satisfy the second-order conditions for an optimum. It is therefore possible that at equilibrium there will be a number of different niches for firms. Each niche is characterized by a different value of L_{1W}/L_1 and therefore a different value of w_2. This possibility requires further investigation.

Some insight can also be obtained into the determinants of the magnitude of racial wage differences in type 1 labor. If (3b) is subtracted from (3a), we deduce,

$$w_{1W} - w_{1N} = [(\partial w_2/\partial L_{1N}) - (\partial w_2/\partial L_{1W})]\, L_2.$$

On the other hand, by setting $L_1 = L_{1W} + L_{1N}$ in (1) and then finding the partial derivatives with respect to L_{1W} and L_{1N}, it is easy to see that,

$$\frac{\partial w_2}{\partial L_{1N}} - \frac{\partial w_2}{\partial L_{1W}} = -\,\frac{w'_2}{L_1},$$

where prime denotes differentiation with respect to $L_1 _W/L_1$. Thus,

$$w_1 _W - w_1 _N = - w_2' \quad L_2/L_1 .$$

Since f_1, the marginal productivity of type 1 labor, is the wage in the absence of racial discrimination, the relative racial wage differential is

$$\frac{(w_1 _W - w_1 _N)}{f_1} = - \frac{(w_2'}{w_2)} \frac{w_2 L_2}{f_1 L_1} = - \frac{w_2'}{w_2} \frac{(S_2}{S_1} ,$$

where S_1 and S_2 are total payments to type 1 labor and to type 2 labor, respectively. Thus, the more important type 2 labor is as an input, the greater the discrimination in the payment to type 1 labor.

C

The analysis of Technical Note A is strictly short run, but so long as the assumptions of the model are literally adhered to, the extension to long-run equilibrium offers no difficulty. Assume that firms have access to capital on perfect markets. Some long-run equilibrium rate of interest prevails at which firms can borrow freely. Then for given W and N, assume that the firms borrow optimally. Hence, we need only reinterpret the production function $f(W + N)$ as representing output after optimal acquisition of capital; the rate of interest then enters the production function as a parameter, but this point does not affect any conclusions previously arrived at. If the production function displays constant returns to capital and labor, then the derived function, f, now displays constant returns to labor. Then f' is a constant, independent of W and N, though in general dependent on the rate of interest. All previous conclusions hold.

However, if the condition of the model that states that utility functions are identical is relaxed, the model may have some implications that are not acceptable factually. Specifically, except under improbable conditions, we would expect that the less discriminatory firms should drive out the more discriminatory, so that discrimination should have been eliminated or reduced over time. Let us spell this argument out a bit. Assume that all firms have identical production functions and operate under constant returns to scale in the long run. Then, in (3) of Note A, f' is a given constant. It is no longer necessary, however, that each firm employ both types of labor; corner maxima are possible, so that (3) must be replaced by

$$f' < w_W + d_W \text{ with equality if } W > 0, \tag{1a}$$

$$f' < w_N + d_N \text{ with equality if } N > 0. \tag{1b}$$

Relations (1a) and (1b) hold for each firm; since utility functions vary over firms, W, N, and the discrimination coefficients d_W and d_N vary from firm to firm. Since equilibrium implies full employment of both types of labor, the equality must hold in (1a) for at least one firm and similarly for (1b). Hence, all whites are employed in those firms for which d_W is the algebraic minimum, and similarly all blacks in those firms for which d_N is a minimum.

First, suppose there are some firms that do not discriminate against blacks, that is, $d_N = 0$. Then $d_N = 0$ for all firms for which $N > 0$. The only way, then, that there can be any black-white wage differential is for $d_W < 0$, for example, nepotism. But it is reasonable to postulate that any preference a firm might have for the hiring of whites per se arises as an offset to the presence of disliked blacks. That is, for a firm that has no black employees, $d_W = 0$. On the other hand, for a firm that does not discriminate against blacks, there will also be no reason to pay anything extra for white employees. That is, we assume,

$$\text{if either } N = 0 \text{ or } d_N = 0, \text{ then } d_W = 0. \tag{2}$$

Since it has been shown that either $d_N = 0$ or $N = 0$ for all firms, $d_W = 0$ for all firms. Therefore $w_W = f' = w_N$, and there is no observed discrimination (there may, however, be some segregated white firms).

> If (2) holds and there are some firms that do not discrimi-
> nate against blacks, then there is no market discrimination
> against blacks in the long run. (3)

This conclusion suggests some limits of the employer discrimination model. It predicts the absence of the phenomenon it was designed to explain.

It may be worthwhile to generalize the analysis of the long-run case a bit before drawing even tentative conclusions. Suppose then we drop the assumption that there is any firm that fails to discriminate. At equilibrium the minimum value of d_N among all firms is now positive. Let N be the set of firms that hire some blacks; then d_N is at its minimum value for all firms in N. Let SW be the set of firms that hire no blacks (segregated white). From (2), $d_W = 0$ for such firms. If $d_W < 0$ for any firm, then, it must be for a firm in N. Then it would follow that no white workers are in SW firms, that is, we would have the remarkable conclusion that there are no segregated white firms, though now market discrimination would exist.

If we insist that both market discrimination and the existence of segregated white firms are empirical facts that must be explained by any model, we are forced then to agree that $d_N > 0$ and $d_W = 0$ for all firms. This implies that a firm that discriminates against blacks nevertheless derives no satisfaction from "diluting" the black labor force with white employees. The explanation of segregation in this model is, however, a little weak; the allocation of the white labor force between segregated and integrated firms is in neutral equilibrium; it would be consistent with all equilibrium conditions for all whites to work for integrated firms.

D

It is a straightforward and intellectually appealing hypothesis that discrimination against blacks arises from the dislike of white employees for working alongside them.[6] This hypothesis may be considered either as an alternative or as a supplement to that of employer discrimination. But, as Becker has shown, it is difficult to set forth a model in which employee discrimination can induce market discrimination through ordinary economic channels, though it is easy to explain segregation. This argument will now be reviewed; Technical Note E will show that it needs modification if we recognize that there are costs associated with replacing white workers by blacks in response to wage differentials.

To begin with, assume, as in Becker, that white workers have an indifference map between wages, w_W, and the proportion, W/L, of white workers in the firm. For any fixed level of satisfaction, w_W is a decreasing function of W/L. The cost to any given firm of hiring W white and N black workers is, then,

$$C(W, N) = w_W (W/L) W + w_N N, \text{ where } L = W + N, \tag{1}$$

which is homogeneous of degree one. For fixed L, the cost of an all-white labor force is $C(L,0) = w_W(1)L$ and that of an all-black labor force is $C(0,L) = w_N L$. Since $w_W(1) < w_W(W/L)$ for $W < L$, it is obvious that an integrated labor force is more expensive than the cheaper of the two possible segregated labor forces.

Suppose as before that whites and blacks are perfect substitutes in production, but now assume that firms do not have discriminatory tastes. Then clearly any firm will maximize profits by complete segregation. Those firms that have only white employees will pay a wage rate, $w_W(1)$, while those with only black employees will pay w_N. Then it must be that $w_W(1) = w_N$, for otherwise it would pay a firm segregated in one way to switch to the opposite. Hence, as far as the argument has gone, employee discrimination produces segregation but not discrimination in observed wage rates.

Welch has proposed a somewhat different mechanism, however, that has the same implications. Suppose that when white and black workers are in the same plant, there is sufficient dissatisfaction and loss of morale that production is adversely affected. Together with the assumption of equal ability of white and Negro workers, it is implied that, for given L, output is the same when $W = 0$ as when $N = 0$ but is less if both W and N are positive. Then clearly if $w_W(1) = w_N$, each firm will segregate completely in the cheaper type of labor, a condition not compatible with equilibrium. Then $w_W(1) = w_N$; each firm will find it profitable to segregate, though it will be indifferent in which type of labor to specialize. Hence again equilibrium implies segregation but equal wages.

E

The argument of Technical Note D hinges strongly on a complete flexibility of the firm with regard to its labor force; it must be prepared to fire its entire labor force and replace it by one of the opposite color if this act will lower its costs. Suppose we assume instead that there is a capital cost associated with the addition of a worker to the labor force. (The capital costs may be hiring costs, training, or more subtle kinds of organizational adjustment.) Then replacement of white by black workers involves a sacrifice of this capital and may therefore be avoided.

A full analysis of this possibility in a dynamic context where both production functions and the supplies of the two kinds of labor are changing is rather complex. To indicate the possible implications for the analysis of racial discrimination, I consider here only a very simple situation in which initially there are no blacks in the labor force. Then some enter, and, at the same time, there is an additional entry of whites, and a new equilibrium emerges. As before, firms are assumed to have identical production functions; it is also assumed that no new firms enter in response to the increased labor force.

In accordance with the previous remarks, we now assume that a return, r, must be earned on each additional worker hired. Thus is a firm now hires N black workers, it will have to incur a flow cost of rN. There is no corresponding gain by releasing workers.

Finally, with regard to the function, $C(W, N)$, which gives wages costs as a function of W and N, we make a stronger assumption that hitherto; we assume that

$$C(W,N) \text{ is a concave function of } W \text{ for fixed } L = W + N. \tag{1}$$

Assumption (1) has the following interpretation: if we add any linear function of W and N, say $aW + bN$, to $C(W,N)$, then as W and N change, L remaining constant, the total, $C(W,N) + aW + bN$, is either monotone increasing or monotone decreasing or rises to a maximum and then decreases. This is stronger than the previously observed property that minimum cost is always found at one of the two segregated extremes.

Before the introduction of black labor into the market, each firm has an equal number, L_O, of white workers. Consider a firm that, after the change, has decided to have a labor force of W white and N Negro workers. If $W \geqslant L_O$, then the firm is adding $N + (W - L_O)$ and thereby incurring a training cost of $r[N + (W - L_O)]$. If, however, $W < L_O$, then the firm is adding N workers for a training cost of rN (there is no rebate for the $L_O - W$ white workers released). Therefore the total costs are

$$C(W, N) + rL - rL_O \text{ if } W \geqslant L_O,$$

$$C(W, N) + rN \text{ if } W < L_O, \tag{2}$$

where $L = W + N$. Now for any fixed L the firm will certainly seek to minimize its costs. If in fact $W \geqslant L_O$, then (2) tells us that costs will be minimized at one of the extreme values for W, that is, either $W = L_O$ (and therefore $N = L - L_O$) or $W = L$ (and $N = 0$). If $W < L_O$, then costs are minimized for either $W = L_O$ or $W = 0$ ($N = L$). Thus any firm will be in one of the three situations:

(SN) $\quad W = 0, N = L$;

(I) $\quad W = L_O, N = L - L_O$;

(SW) $\quad W = L, N = 0.$

Let $v(W/L)$ be the difference between white and black wages if the proportion of whites in the labor force is W/L, that is, $v(W/L) = w_W(W/L) - w_N$. Then the costs for each of the above situations can be written, from (1) of Technical Note D and (2) of this Note,

(SN) $\quad (w_N + r) L$;

(I) $\quad w_W(L_O/L) L_O + (w_N + r) (L - L_O)$
$\quad = (w_N + r) L + [v(L_O/L) - r] L_O$;

(SW) $\quad w_W(1) L + r(L - L_O) = [w_W(1) + r] L - rL_O. \tag{3}$

The profits for a given total labor force in each situation are then given by

(SN) $\quad \pi_{SN}(L) = f(L) - (w_N + r)L,$

(I) $\quad \pi_I(L) = f(L) - (w_N + r) L - [v(L_O/L) - r] L_O,$

(SW) $\quad \pi_{SW}(L) = f(L) - [w_W(1) + r] L + rL_O. \tag{4}$

If a firm is in situation SN, it will choose L so as to maximize $\pi_{SN}(L)$; call this value L_{SN}. Similarly, let L_I and L_{SW} be the values of L that maximize $\pi_I(L)$ and $\pi_{SW}(L)$, respectively. Note that

$$\pi'_{SN}(L) = f'(L) - (w_N + r),$$
$$\pi'_I(L) = f'(L) - (w_N + r) - L_O \, \partial v(L_O/L)/\partial L,$$
$$\pi'_{SW}(L) = f'(L) - [w_W(1) + r].$$

The magnitudes L_{SN}, L_I, and W_{SW} are obtained by setting these three derivatives respectively equal to zero. Hence, by subtraction,

$$f'(L_I) - f'(L_{SN}) = L_O \; \partial v(L_O/L)/\partial L \; \Big|_{L = L_I},$$

$$f'(L_{SW}) - f'(L_{SN}) = v(1).$$

Since $v(L_O/L)$ differs from $w_W(L_O/L)$ only by w_N, a constant from the viewpoint of the firm, and $w_W(L_O/L)$ is a decreasing function of L_O/L and therefore an increasing function of L, it follows that,

$$\partial v(L_O/L)/\partial L > 0,$$

and therefore $f'(L_I) - f'(L_{SN}) > 0$. Since f' is decreasing this means that

$$L_I < L_{SN}. \tag{5}$$

Similarly,

$$L_{SW} < L_{SN} \text{ if } v(1) > 0. \tag{6}$$

Under the assumptions made here, only a firm in the SW situation is hiring more whites than before while only those in the SN or I situations are hiring blacks. But the general equilibrium of the labor market requires that more whites be hired than before and that blacks be hired. Hence, some firms must be in situation SW while others are in situation SN or I. This requires that the firms in the SW situation be as profitable as the more profitable of those in the SN or I situations. There are then two possibilities: $(SW \; \& \; SN)$; SW and SN firms are equally profitable while I firms are no more profitable while SN firms; $(SW \; \& \; I)$ SW and I firms are equally profitable while SN firms are not more profitable than I firms.

$(SW \; \& \; SN)$: It must certainly be true that if $L = L_{SN}$, a firm following policy I cannot have lower costs of operation than an SN firm. From (3), a comparison of the costs of SN and I firms shows that this condition can be written,

$$v(L_O/L_{SN}) \geqslant r. \tag{7}$$

Since $\pi_{SW}(L_{SW}) = \pi_{SN}(L_{SN})$, we have, from (4),

$$f(L_{SN}) - (w_N + r) \, L_{SN} = \pi_{SW}(L_{SW}).$$

By definition,

$$f(L_{SN}) - [w_W(1) + r] L_{SN} = \pi_{SW}(L_{SN}) - rL_O.$$

Therefore subtraction of the last equation from the previous yields

$$v(1) L_{SN} = \pi_{SW}(L_{SW}) - \pi_{SW}(L_{SN}) + rL_O. \tag{8}$$

Since L_{SW} was the value of L that maximized $\pi_{SW}(L)$, we know that $\pi_{SW}(L_{SW})$ $\geqslant \pi_{SW}(L_{SN})$. Hence, $v(1) L_{SN} \geqslant rL_O > 0$, so that $v(1) > 0$, that is, $w_W(1) > w_N$.

We thus conclude it is indeed possible to have total segregation and wage discrimination simultaneously.

Some idea of the conditions under which the general equilibrium has the configuration (SW & SN) can be derived. If we use the definition of $v(W/L)$, we can write $v(L_O/L_{SN}) = w_W(L_O/L_{SN}) - w_N$, $v(1) = w_W(1) - w_N$. Then (7) can be interpreted as an inequality in w_N, (8) as an equation. In combination, we have,

$$w_W(L_O/L_{SN}) - r \geqslant w_N = w_W(1) - r(L_O/L_{SN}) - [\pi_{SW}(L_{SW}) - \pi_{SW}(L_{SN})]/L_{SN}.$$

Add $r - w_W(1)$ to the extreme terms, and divide by $1 - (L_O/L_{SN})$.

$$\frac{w_W(L_O/L_{SN}) - w_W(1)}{1 - (L_O/L_{SN})} \geqslant r - \frac{\pi_{SW}(L_{SW}) - \pi_{SW}(L_{SN})}{L_{SN} - L_O}$$

The left-hand side is a measure of employee discrimination; it is the rate of change of wages demanded by white workers with respect to the proportion of white workers in the labor force. The case (SW & SN) will then arise when employee discrimination exceeds an adjusted version of the capital cost per new worker.

(SW & I): Now it must be true that if $L = L_I$, a firm following policy SN cannot have lower costs than an I firm. Again, from (3), we have the condition,

$$v(L_O/L_I) \leqslant r. \tag{9}$$

Since $\pi_I(L_I) = \pi_{SW}(L_{SW})$, we have, from (4),

$$f(L_I) - (w_N + r) L_I - [v(L_O/L_I) - r] L_O = \pi_{SW} (L_{SW}).$$

By definition,

$$f(L_I) - [w_W(1) + r] L_I + rL_O = \pi_{SW}(L_I).$$

Subtract this last equation from the previous one, and then add $v(L_O/L_I) L_O$ to both sides.

$$v(1) L_I = v(L_O/L_I) L_O + [\pi_{SW}(L_{SW}) - \pi_{SW}(L_I)] . \tag{10}$$

As before, the expression in brackets is non-negative since L_{SW} maximizes π_{SW}.

$$v(1)L_I \geqslant v(L_O/L_I)L_O. \tag{11}$$

Since all blacks are being absorbed into the I firms, these must be doing some net hiring, so that $L_I > L_O$. Since $w_W(W/L)$ is a decreasing function, $w_W(1) < w_W(L_O/L_I)$, and therefore $v(1) < v(L_O/L_I)$. From (11),

$$v(L_O/L_I) L_I > v(L_O/L_I) L_O.$$

With $L_I > L_O$, it must be that $v(L_O/L_I) > 0$, and, from (11), $v(1) > 0$.

Thus, in this case, some firms are integrated and some are segregated white. Wages of white workers are higher in integrated firms than in segregated white firms, and the latter are, in turn, higher than black wages.

As in the previous case, we can get some idea of the conditions under which the $(SW \& I)$ case will occur. Equation (9) can be used to derive a lower bound on w_N, while we can solve for w_N in (10).

$$\frac{w_W(1) L_I - w_W(L_O/L_I) L_O - [\pi_{SW}(L_{SW}) - \pi_{SW}(L_I)]}{L_I - L_O} = w_N$$

$$\geqslant w_W(L_O/L_I) - r .$$

Add

$$r - \frac{w_W(1) L_I - w_W(L_O/L_I) L_O}{L_I - L_O}$$

to the first and third expressions

$$r - \frac{[\pi_{SW}(L_{SW}) - \pi_{SW}(L_I)]}{L_I - L_O} \geqslant \frac{w_W(L_O/L_I) \, \phi \, w_W(1)}{1 - (L_O/L_I)}$$

Thus the case where blacks are hired in integrated firms is that for which the rate of employee discrimination does not exceed an adjusted version of the capital cost per new worker.

The crudity of the foregoing model needs no emphasis; in particular, the existence of normal turnover in the labor force means that the opportunity cost of introducing black labor may be less than suggested here. But the model puts in evidence the strong possibility that, because of costs of addition to the labor force, discriminatory attitudes of white employees can result in wage differentials as well as some degree of segregation.

F

Suppose there are two types of labor, 1 and 2. Type 1 labor is unskilled. Type 2 labor, however, is created only if both the employer and the worker invest some human capital. A worker who has made his investment is said to be *qualified*. An employer cannot know whether or not a worker is qualified, but he holds subjective beliefs about the respective probabilities, to be denoted by p_W and p_N, that white and black workers, respectively, are qualified.

As in Technical Note E, let r be the return per worker that the employer must earn on his human capital investment. Assume further that the employer is risk-neutral. Then, in the notation previously used, the equilibrium condition for hiring of both white and black workers is

$$r = (f_2 - w_{2W}) p_W = (f_2 - w_{2N}) p_N, \tag{1}$$

where w_{2W} and w_{2N} are white and black wages for type 2 labor, respectively. It follows that

$$w_{2W} = q\, w_{2N} + (1-q) f_2, \tag{2}$$

where $q = p_N/p_W$. Then if $p_N < p_W$, we find discrimination in wages in type 2 labor.

If for reasons of social pressure or administrative convenience, it is not easy to maintain an adequate differential between w_{2W} and w_{2N}, blacks will be excluded from occupation 2.

It can be argued within the model that, if one considers the factors governing the supply of human capital by the workers, the realized equilibrium is very likely to result in market discrimination. Suppose now that employers do not misperceive, that p_W and p_N are indeed the actual proportions of "qualified" whites and blacks in the relevant population. Since the employer cannot directly observe the possession of qualifications by workers, the relevant population in each case is the totality of workers. Finally, suppose that the acquisition of human capital (qualification) by workers is costly and that they face imperfect capital markets in any effort to finance this acquisition. Then p_W will be an increasing function of $w_{2W} - w_1$ and p_N of $w_{2N} - w_1$ since these determine the returns to the investment in qualifications. If we assume no difference in the basic structure of motivation between whites and blacks, the two functional relations will be the same.

Let L_1 and L_2 be the numbers of workers of types 1 and 2, respectively; in the absence of employer misperception,

$$L_1 = (1 - p_W) W + (1 - p_N) N, \quad L_2 = p_W W + p_N N,$$

where W and N are the total supplies of white and Negro labor, respectively. Then f and therefore f_2 are functions of p_W and p_N, respectively. With w_{2W} and w_{2N} functions of p_W and p_N, (1) constitutes a pair of equations in p_W and p_N for given w_1.

Under all these hypotheses, the equations are symmetric in the two variables, and therefore they have a solution for which $p_W = p_N$. It might appear then that in long-run equilibrium, the absence of misperceptions would imply the absence of discrimination.

But the nondiscriminatory equilibrium may well not be stable. Intuitively, a possible sequence of events might be described as follows. If p_W is, for some reason, slightly greater than p_N, then, from (2), w_{2W} will slightly exceed w_{2N}. In response to this differential there may be some incentive for p_W to rise relative to p_N, thereby reinforcing the original discrepancy. At the same time, the rise in p_W will have a negative effect on w_{2N} since it means increased competition from whites and thereby also serves to discourage an increase in Negro attempts at qualification.

The verbal account of instability is, of course, by no means conclusive or even very convincing. To develop a formal model, let us suppose that the labor markets and the determination of wage levels are short-run phenomena, which come into equilibrium quickly relative to changes in the supplies of the two kinds of labor between the two races. Assume then that p_W increases or decreases as the desired supply of type 2 labor among whites is above or below the actual. That is, we postulate an increasing function $\varphi(w_{2W} - w_1)$, the desired supply of type 2 labor, and a dynamic adjustment relation,

$$\dot{p}_W = k \left[\phi \left(w_{2W} - w_1 \right) - p_W \right] ; \tag{3}$$

similarly,

$$\dot{p}_N = k \left[\phi (w_{2N} - w_1) - p_N \right] . \tag{4}$$

Since it is assumed that white and Negro workers have the same motivation, the adjustment coefficients k and the supply functions ϕ are assumed the same for both races.

Write the marginal productivity relations (1) together with that for type 1 labor as,

$$w_1 = f_1, \quad w_{2W} = f_2 - (r/p_W), \quad w_{2N} = f_2 - (r/p_N),$$

so that,

$$w_{2W} - w_1 = (f_2 - f_1) - (r/p_W), \quad w_{2N} - w_1 = (f_2 - f_1) - (r/p_N). \tag{5}$$

For a fixed total labor force, $L = W + N$, let

$$F(L_2) = f(L - L_2, L_2),$$

the output obtained by allocating L_2 laborers to type 2 labor and the rest to type 1 labor. Then F is a strictly concave function if f is, so that

$$F'' < 0,$$
$$F' = f_2 - f_1,$$

and,

$$\partial F'/\partial p_W = F''(\partial L_2/\partial p_W) = F''W, \quad \partial F'/\partial p_N = F''N.$$

From (5) and these remarks,

$$\partial(w_{2W} - w_1)/\partial p_W = (\partial F'/\partial p_W) + (r/p_W{}^2) = F''W + (r/p_W{}^2),$$
$$\partial(w_{2W} - w_1)/\partial p_N = F''N. \tag{6}$$

Interchanging W and N in these expressions yields

$$\partial(w_{2N} - w_1)/\partial p_W = F''W, \quad \partial(w_{2N} - w_1)/\partial p_N = F''N + (r/p_N{}^2). \tag{7}$$

We use (6) and (7) in the analysis of the stability of the system (3) and (4). Since the adjustment coefficient, k, is the same for both differential equations, it plays no role in the stability analysis and can be set equal to 1 without loss of generality. Form the matrix whose elements are $\partial \dot{p}_i/\partial p_j$, where i, j range over W, N. The condition for stability is that the characteristic roots of this matrix are both negative (or they are complex-conjugate with negative real parts), when the matrix is evaluated at equilibrium. We are here considering the nondiscriminatory equilibrium. If we define

$$a_W = \phi'F''W, \quad a_N = \phi'F''N, \quad b = \phi'(r/p^2) - 1,$$
$$c = \phi'[F''L + (r/p^2)] - 1 = a_W + a_N + b,$$

where all functions are evaluated at the nondiscriminatory equilibrium values and p is the common value of p_W and p_N there, then the matrix is

$$\begin{pmatrix} a_W + b & a_N \\ a_W & a_N + b \end{pmatrix}$$

The sum of the characteristic roots is the trace (sum of diagonal elements) of this matrix, which is $(a_W + b) + (a_N + b) = (a_W + a_N + b) + b = c + b$; the product of the characteristic roots is the determinant, which is $(a_W + b)(a_N + b)$

$- a_W a_N = b(a_W + a_N) + b^2 = b(a_W + a_N + b) = bc$. Since the sum of the roots is $b + c$ and their product is bc, the roots must be the real numbers b and c. Stability requires that both be negative. But since

$$c = b + \phi' F'' L ,$$

and $\phi' > 0$, $F'' < 0$, $L > 0$, we must have $c < b$; hence, the condition $b < 0$ is necessary and sufficient for stability, that is, the nondiscriminatory equilibrium is stable if and only if,

$$\phi' r < p^2 . \tag{8}$$

Whether or not this condition is apt to be met in practice obviously depends on the three magnitudes involved, which are ϕ', the supply responsiveness, r, the cost of the employer's investment, and p. Thus, if type 2 labor is relatively rarely used, so that p is small, we would expect ϕ' to be correspondingly small, but p^2 to be much smaller yet, so that (8) might well be violated. Again, a large r, for example, a large investment by the employer in his potential employees, makes for instability.

A rewriting of (8) may help understand the condition. Let E be the elasticity of supply of type 2 labor; under our assumptions, this must be taken as an elasticity with respect to the *differences* of wages between type 2 and type 1 labor,

$$E = (w_2 - w_1) \phi' / \phi. \tag{9}$$

Since $p = \phi(w_2 - w_1)$, we can divide through in (8) by p^2 and obtain, $E[(r/p)/(w_2 - w_1)] < 1$ which is necessary and sufficient for stability. Note here that r/p is the amount the firm must recover on its human investment per type 2 laborer finally employed, that is, the equilibrium gap between marginal productivity and wages for type 2 labor. Thus, the second factor in (9) is the ratio between the extent to which type 2 wages fall short of marginal productivity and the extent to which they exceed type 1 wages.

As a clarifying remark, it might be noted that the two characteristic roots correspond to two kinds of movements. The root b, which is dominant, corresponds to the motions of the difference $p_W - p_N$ between the proportions of qualified workers in the two races. In what follows, let asterisks refer to equilibrium values; the symbol $\approx$ means "equivalent up to linear approximations."

$$d(p_W - p_N)/dt = k[\phi(w_2{}_W - w_1) - \phi(w_2{}_N - w_1) - (p_W - p_N)]$$
$$\approx k[\phi'(w_2{}_W - w_2{}_N) - (p_W - p_N)] .$$

But from (5),

$$w_{2W} - w_{2N} = (r/p_N) - (r/p_W) \approx (r/p^{*2})(p_W - p^*) - (r/p^{*2})(p_N - p^*)$$
$$= (r/p^{*2})(p_W - p_N),$$

so that

$$d(p_W - p_N)/dt \approx k[\phi'(r/p^{*2})(p_W - p_N) - (p_W - p_N)] = kb(p_W - p_N),$$

and within linear approximations, the convergence of the discriminatory elements of the system to 0 depends on b. The characteristic root c governs rather the movement of the total proportion of qualified workers. For if we now define

$$p = (Wp_W + Np_N)/L,$$

it can easily be calculated that, to a first-order approximation,

$$\dot{p} = k c(p - p^*),$$

for which the stability condition, $c < 0$, is less stringent. This is also the stability condition for a corresponding model in which there is in fact only one kind of worker.

Notes

1. Gary S. Becker, *The Economics of Discrimination* (Chicago: University Chicago Press, 1957).

2. Lester Thurow, *Poverty and Discrimination* (Washington, D.C., The Brookings Institution, 1969), pp. 113-15.

3. See A.O. Krueger, "The Economics of Discrimination," *Journal of Political Economy* 71 (1963): 481-86, for a related argument.

4. Becker, *The Economics of Discrimination*, pp. 51-53.

5. Finis Welch, "Labor Market Discrimination: An Interpretation of Income Differences in the Rural South," *Journal of Political Economy* 75 (1967): 225-40.

6. Becker, *The Economics of Discrimination*, Chapter 4; Welch, "Labor Market Discrimination."

7

The Simple Mathematics of Information, Job Search, and Prejudice

JOHN J. MCCALL

I. Introduction

Even a cursory study of poverty in the United States reveals the special economic problems confronting nonwhites. The proportion of poor who are nonwhite far exceeds the proportion of nonwhites in the total population. Indeed, if attention is restricted to the chronically poor or the "stayers" in poverty (those who remain in poverty year after year regardless of such exogenous factors as economic growth), it has been estimated that nonwhites constitute 40 percent of this group (Miller 1966). If attention is further restricted to the 1962-65 time period,[1] approximately one-third of the prime working age (25-54) males who were covered by Social Security and earned less than $3,000 per year for each of these four years were nonwhite (McCall 1969). This chapter is an attempt to explain this poor performance of nonwhites in the job market.

It is clear that ever since Negroes[2] were brought to the United States, they have incurred a variety of injustices ranging from slavery to racial discrimination. The effects of these injustices have been cumulative and difficult to disentangle. It does seem, however, that the current economic plight of the Negro is a combination of past injustices and present day discrimination. Discrimination appears in a variety of ways and in several distinct fields. The primary fields in which discrimination occurs are education and training (Thurow 1967), housing (Pascal, 1967), and occupation. The economic analysis described herein could be applied to any one of these fields. It could also be applied to other groups who are subject to discriminatory practices, such as women and the aged. For specificity, this chapter will present an economic analysis of discrimination as it occurs in the job market for nonwhites. Most of the economic models of job discrimination and empirical results are not novel (Arrow 1972; Becker 1957; Gilman 1965; Hanoch 1967; and Thurow 1968). A novel feature of this study is the introduction of a model of racial discrimination that incorporates uncertainty and explicitly considers both the cost of searching for employment by potential employees and the cost of searching for productive employees by employers. (The economics of job search has received much attention in the recent literature. See Dufty 1969; McCall 1965, 1970b; Alchian, Holt, Mortenson, and Phelps in Phelps 1969; Reder 1969; and Stigler 1962.)

In the literature on job market discrimination, a question that frequently arises is the economic value of discrimination accruing to the discriminator (in the case to be discussed here, the employer). Is it positive or negative? If positive would it pay the minority group to engage in retaliatory discrimination? The answers to such questions have usually been obtained by applying a static economic model. Different answers are given depending on which static model is used. The answer to this question is quite important from a policy perspective. If discrimination does not pay economically, then one can estimate the cost of indulging this taste. Employers may then decide that the cost is too high and reduce discrimination without altering their attitudes toward nonwhites. If discrimination does pay economically, then different policies may be required to reduce it. It will be argued here that in the presence of uncertainty, discrimination may be economically justified for both the white employer and the nonwhite employee.

The employer discriminates on the basis of color if, when presented with two individuals, one nonwhite and one white, who are otherwise equally qualified (on the basis of such variables as education, experience, age, sex, and so on) for a single job occupancy, he does not flip a fair coin and choose the nonwhite if a head appears and the white if tails (or vice versa). If the probability of a head is less than one-half, he discriminates against nonwhites; if this probability exceeds one-half, he discriminates against whites. Employees discriminate if they do not search for employment with the same intensity in firms and industries that are similar with respect to such variables as distance from home, wage rates, and so on and only differ in the proportions of nonwhites in their labor forces.

It may pay employers to discriminate because information concerning the productivity of a potential employee is quite costly. He may, therefore, use color as a cheap screening device, in the same way that he uses a high school diploma. He does this because he believes that the probability that an employee will be productive given that he is nonwhite is less than the corresponding conditional probability for whites. In the same way, assuming similar jobs across firms, it may pay nonwhites to restrict their job searching activities to firms that have a relatively high proportion of nonwhite employees, the belief being that this proportion is a good measure of employer discrimination.[3]

Nevertheless, although the value of discrimination tends to be positive, the theory presented here assumes the value is a function of the business cycle. A changing economic environment is assumed to induce employers to engage in experiments, for example, hire nonwhites in periods of tight labor markets. The outcomes of these experiments may alter whatever incorrect attitudes they might have toward nonwhites, and in this way discrimination could decline in a very natural way. Similarly, with nonwhite employees, their beliefs regarding the intensity of discrimination in certain industries would never be altered unless they or someone in their information network were employed by these industries. (For a discussion of Negro job searching behavior, see Sheppard and Belitsky 1966; Liebow 1967; and Lurie and Rayack 1968.) Again in periods of tight labor markets, employees are also assumed to be experimenting with new industries and revising their beliefs concerning discrimination intensities.

The main point in both of these illustrations is that discrimination by both employers and employees is explicable on purely economic grounds when uncertainty is explicitly considered and, furthermore, changes in the economic environment may cause both employers and employees to alter the beliefs that give rise to discriminatory practices.

Section II summarizes the results of several empirical studies concerning the presence of discrimination in the job market. Section III presents three static models of racial discrimination. The first is a simple trade model, the second is a model developed by Becker (1957), and the third is an elementary production function model. The main question addressed by all three is the economic value of discrimination to the discriminator. In Section IV uncertainty is introduced and the employee-seeking behavior of a discriminating employer is modeled. Section V switches emphasis from the employee-seeking employer to the job-searching employee. Uncertainty continues to be present and the searching employee has definite expectations regarding the discriminating behavior of various employers. The concluding section contains some suggestions for future research.

II. Some Empirical Results on Racial Discrimination in the Job Market

This section presents a brief summary of the empirical findings of several studies that have addressed the problem of racial discrimination in the job market. None of the measures of racial discrimination is ideal in that each is consistent with hypotheses other than racial discrimination.[4] Nevertheless, all three measures discussed here, unemployment, returns to education, and persistent poverty and nonpoverty, suggest that racial discrimination is present in the job market and that further research is necessary both to assess its actual extent and importance and to devise policies for its elimination.(See Arrow 1972, for a more complete plete discussion.)

The first measure of discrimination is the difference in the persistence of poverty and nonpoverty among whites and nonwhites. In a period of sustained growth (1962-65) the probabilities of remaining in poverty ($3,000 poverty line) for the entire period were .20 and .05 for nonwhite and white males, respectively, in the 25-34 age group. Almost identical probabilities were obtained for nonwhite and white males in the 35-44 and 45-54 age groups. The probabilities of remaining in poverty the entire four-year period were remarkably similar for nonwhite males and white females (see Table 7-1). On the other hand, the probabilities of remaining in nonpoverty ($3,000 poverty line) for the entire four-year period were .60 and .29, for white and nonwhite males, respectively, in the 25-34 age group. Similar results were obtained for the 35-44 and 45-54 age groups (see Table 7-2). (See McCall 1969, for a more complete discussion of

Table 7-1

Probability of Remaining in Poverty for the Period 1962-65 ($3,000 poverty line) by Sex, Age, and Color

Age group	White females	White males	Nonwhite males
25-34	.16	.05	.20
35-44	.21	.05	.19
45-54	.25	.06	.21

Source: McCall 1969.

Table 7-2

Probability of Remaining in Nonpoverty for the Period 1962-65 ($3,000 poverty line), Males by Color and Age

Age group	White males	Nonwhite males
25-34	.60	.29
35-44	.65	.36
45-54	.63	.35

Source: McCall 1969.

these results.) Some portion of these differences could probably be explained by job market discrimination. It is very likely, however, that a large fraction of the differences could be explained by differences in education and training.[5]

Another more refined measure of racial discrimination in the job market is the difference in unemployment rates between whites and nonwhites. Gilman (1965), was able to adjust for differences in age, education, occupation, industry, and region. After making these adjustments he discovered that nonwhite unemployment rates were still 50 percent higher than white rates. This suggests that employers have a preference for white employees.

The final indicator of job market discrimination is the difference in annual income as a function of years of education and years of experience. Estimates of these differences were made by Thurow (1967) and are presented in Table 7-3.

Table 7-3

Differences in Annual Income, between Whites and Nonwhites by Education and Experience, 1960

Education (20 years of experience)		Experience (10.5 years of education)	
Years of education	White-nonwhite income	Years of experience	White-nonwhite income
0	$ 624	0	−$ 700
8	1446	5	1351
12	2356	15	1724
16	5477	35	2626

Source: Thurow 1967.

(Also see Arrow 1972; Hanoch 1967; and Miller 1966; for alternative measures.)

III. Static Models of Racial Discrimination

In this section three elementary models of racial discrimination are presented. All are static and assume perfect information. The first is a simple trade model; the second is a model of a discriminating employer; and the third is a model in which the employer does not discriminate, but instead is confronted by a production function that reflects the discriminating attitudes of white employees against nonwhite employees. (See Arrow 1972, for a deft analysis of more sophisticated static models.)

A Simple Trade Model of Discrimination

Assume there are two individuals, W and B, and two goods, X and Y. The utility functions of W and B are, respectively, $U_W(X,Y)$ and $U_B(X,Y)$. The marginal rates of substitution of X for Y by W and B are, respectively, m_1 and m_2.[6] Let m_1 be greater than m_2. (This situation is represented by point A in the Edgeworth box diagram of Figure 7-1.) Then under normal conditions trade would take place. Since X is more valuable to W than it is to B, B will give up some X to get more Y and W will give up some Y to get more X. Both will be better off and improvements will persist until the contract curve ($O_W O_B$ in Figure 7-1) is reached, that is, until the marginal rates of substitution are equal, say, to m (point C in Figure 7-1). Discrimination certainly exists if before trade commences, W is made aware of the color of B and for that reason refuses to trade. A lower bound on the intensity of W's discriminations can be measured by the utility that W would derive in moving from m_1 to m. This is the pecuniary cost of indulging in discrimination.

The question immediately arises as to who benefits from this discrimination. Obviously, in purely pecuniary terms both W and B are losers since both remain at m_1 and m_2, respectively.[7] When the taste for discrimination is included in W's utility function, then W gains and B loses.[8]

Employer Model of Racial Discrimination

Consider now a production function in which there are two inputs, black bricklayers, B, and white carpenters, W, and a single output, houses, q,

$$q = f(B,W)$$

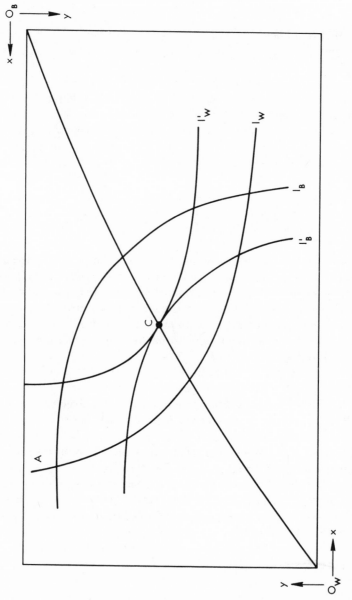

Figure 7-1. Edgeworth Box Diagram Illustrating the Gains from Trade Between Two Economic Entities and the Impact of Discrimination on the Final Outcome.

As usual assume that the employer (contractor) wishes to minimize the cost of producing a given number of houses.[9] Let p_B and p_W be the wage rates for blacks and whites, respectively, and mp_B and mp_W their respective marginal products. The marginal rate of technical substitution, $MRTS$, is the slope of the isoquant, $q_0 q_0$, in Figure 7-2. Symbolically,

$$MRTS_{BW} = \frac{mp_B}{mp_W}$$

If the contractor initially spends C dollars then his budget line is given by:

$$P_W \, W + p_B \, B = C.$$

This is the line in Figure 7-2 with end points $(C/p_W, C/p_B)$. In the absence of discrimination the employer will operate at the point A where

$$MRTS = p_B/p_W,$$

hire B_0 black bricklayers and W_0 white carpenters and achieve the required output q_0. Now suppose the contractor discriminates against blacks. The discrimination manifests itself in the following way. Instead of observing the true market wage for blacks, p_B, he observes $p_B + d$, $d > 0$, where d is a measure of the intensity of his discrimination. This being the case he now operates at the point where

$$MRTS = \frac{p_B + d}{p_W}.$$

The slope of his budget line increases. He still desires to produce q_0. Hence, he moves from point A to point D. The actual cost of producing q_0 is the cost, C', associated with the line, $l'l'$, that passes through D and is parallel to the line with slope p_B/p_W. The cost C' exceeds C, so once again discrimination does not pay on purely economic grounds. The difference $C'-C$ is the monetary loss incurred by the contractor when he discriminates with intensity d. This monetary loss is an increasing function of d. If this model were applicable to the real world, employers might alter their discriminatory practices when made aware of their real monetary costs.

Jack Hirshleifer has proposed an alternative model in which resources (instead of wages) are held constant. In this circumstance, the labor supply curves are vertical at B_0 and W_0 for the representative firm of Figure 7-2. With the introduction of discrimination, the equilibrium must remain at A. This can occur only if the black wage rate, p_B, declines by exactly the amount of the discrimination coefficient, d. Thus, discrimination affects wages rather than employ-

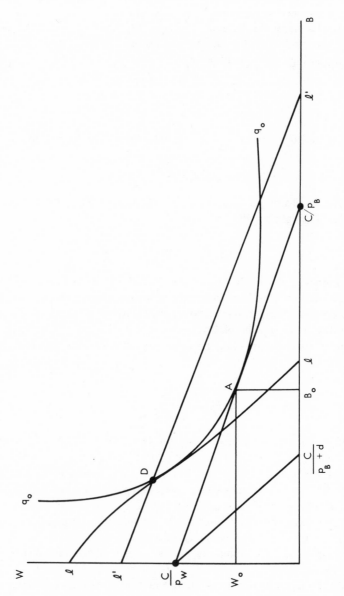

Figure 7-2. Isoquant-Isocost Diagram Illustrating the Determination of Factor Inputs and the Effect of Discrimination on Factor Purchases and Production Costs.

ment. The "correct" model in this context is probably some combination of the Becker and Hirshleifer models.

Employee Model of Discrimination

In this model the employer practices racial discrimination because of the tastes and preferences of his white employees. The presence of such tastes and preferences results in lower production when white employees work with blacks. Assume that there are three factors of production, capital, K, black labor, B, and white labor, W. For simplicity assume further that capital is fixed and labor is the only variable factor. The production function is given by:

$$q = a_1 KW + a_2 KB - a_3 W^2 - a_4 B^2 - a_5 K^2 - \delta B, \quad W > 0,$$

where all the coefficients are positive and δ measures the discrimination intensity of white employees. The marginal products of white and black labor are, respectively,

$$mp_W = a_1 K - 2a_3 W$$
$$mp_B = a_2 K - 2a_4 B - \delta.$$

The marginal rate of technical substitution of blacks for whites is therefore

$$MRTS_{BW} = \frac{a_2 K - 2a_4 B - \delta}{a_1 K - 2a_3 W}.$$

The number of whites that can substitute for one black and keep output constant is a decreasing function of δ. The greater the employees' discrimination intensity, the smaller the number of blacks that will be employed (for fixed amounts of capital).

IV. Racial Discrimination and Uncertainty: The Employer Search Process

In the models of the previous section, it was assumed that employers had perfect information about prices, marginal products, and all other relevant economic variables. Such information is, of course, not actually possessed by employers who produce in an environment that is characterized by uncertainty and costly information. For example, the prior assessment of potential employees' marginal products could be very costly. Hence, when searching for productive employees, the employer will attempt to utilize relatively costless information devices. Cheap information sources such as age, race, sex, and education credentials will very probably be used as screening devices. This is especially true in surplus labor markets.

Considering only racial discrimination within this context, the employer will hire white employees rather than nonwhites with the same apparent abilities. This choice will be based on the prior assessment that the employer has regarding the relative productivity of whites and nonwhites, namely that the probability of a success given that the employee is white is greater than the probability of a success given that the employee is nonwhite.

The employer also has prior evaluations of the discrimination intensities of his white work force and their effect on total production.

Both sets of prior assessments will remain unaltered until the employer begins hiring nonwhites. This will increase in tight labor markets when the apparent quality differentials between whites and nonwhites outweighs the information provided by the nonwhite filter. More specifically, the prior assessment of the quality of the white unemployed labor pool will be revised downward as samples from this pool contain more individuals who have failed to make it in other firms. At some point then experiments with nonwhite employees will commence and employers may revise their prior assessments. If their experience with nonwhites is favorable, then presumably the use of color as a screening device will diminish when the labor market becomes less tight.

As an illustration, suppose there are two possible states of nature:

S_1: Nonwhites inferior (in production) to whites with comparable (easily observed) characteristics.

S_2: Nonwhites as productive as their white counterparts.

Suppose also that the employer's prior probability distributions over these two states of nature are

$$P'(S_1) = .9$$

and

$$P'(S_2) = .1$$

The employer hires a nonwhite and observes one of two outcomes:

Z_1: Nonwhite is inferior (in production)

or

Z_2: Nonwhite is as productive as white.

Let the probability of observing each of these outcomes given S_1 and S_2 be given by:[10]

$$f(Z_1/S_1) = .8 \qquad f(Z_1/S_2) = .2$$
$$f(Z_2/S_1) = .2 \qquad f(Z_2/S_2) = .8$$

If a Z_2 is observed, the employer's posterior assessments of S_1 and S_2 are by Bayes' rule:

$$P''(S_1/Z_2) = .7$$

and

$$P''(S_2/Z_2) = .3$$

If employers' prior distributions are adjusted in this way and nonwhites are at least as productive as their white counterparts, then racial discrimination should diminish over time.

To provide a more theoretical framework for analyzing employer searching behavior, several alternative models will be discussed. The first is a sample adaptive model that assumes that the employer is uncertain about the marginal productivities of both white and nonwhite potential employees. An employee is successful if his marginal product exceeds some critical value; otherwise he fails and is discharged. The employer is assumed to have prior distributions over the proportion of nonwhites who will be successful and the proportion of whites who will be successful. He will hire a white or a nonwhite depending on the relative expected gain. Each white (nonwhite) observation provides the employer with an opportunity to revise his white (nonwhite) prior distribution. Several variations of this model will be presented. The second model is also adaptive with the employer's goal of profit maximization being explicitly assumed. Once again the employer is uncertain about production function parameters, but gains information over time.

A Simple Adaptive Model

In this formulation it is assumed that an employee is successful if his marginal product exceeds some critical value, m^*; otherwise he fails and is discharged. The employer has prior probability distributions over the two unknown parameters, p_1 and p_2, where p_1 is the proportion of prospective white employees whose marginal product exceed m^* and p_2 is a similar measure for nonwhites. These prior probability distributions are based on both the past experience of the employer and his subjective assessments. Obviously, his subjective assessments will tend to dominate his nonwhite prior distribution if he has had only limited experience with nonwhite employees.

The employer is also assumed to have estimates of the costs of determining whether white and nonwhite marginal products exceed m^*. Let these costs be denoted by c_1 and c_2, respectively. They include the cost of search and the costs incurred while a decision is being made with respect to the employee's productivity. Clearly, c_1 and c_2 are also random variables and presumably the employer will also be revising his estimates of them in the same way as for p_1 and p_2. For simplicity, it will be assumed that these revisions are occurring, but the adaptive method will not be spelled out. These costs should therefore be interpreted as expected costs given all previously relevant information, and for this reason, will be denoted by $\bar{c}_1$ and $\bar{c}_2$.

The employer is assumed to minimize the cost per success.[11] For example, if he hires n individuals, he wants the ratio of total expected cost to expected number of successes, $\frac{nc}{np}$, to be as small as possible.[12] That is, he will hire whites or nonwhites so as to

$$\frac{\text{MIN}}{1,2} \left(\frac{\bar{c}_1}{p_1}, \quad \frac{\bar{c}_2}{p_2} \right)$$

For analytical simplicity, it is assumed that the prior distributions over p_1 and p_2 are both beta with parameters (r_1, n_1) and (r_2, n_2) respectively.[13] The density functions for p_1 and p_2 are given by

$$\phi_i(p_i) = k_i p^{r_i - 1} (1-p)^{n_i - r_i - 1}, \quad i = 1,2$$

where k_i is a normalizing constant.

The employer's adaptive decision rule is simply:

Sample from labor market 1(2) if

$$\frac{\bar{c}_1}{\int_0^1 p_1 \phi_1(p_1) dp_1} \underset{(>)}{<} \frac{\bar{c}_2}{\int_0^1 p_2 \phi_2(p_2) dp_2},$$

where ϕ_1 and ϕ_2 are the updated posterior success distributions for whites and nonwhites, respectively.

Presumably, in periods of tight labor markets ϕ_1 will shift to the left, that is, the number of qualified whites who are currently searching for employment diminishes as the white unemployed labor pool becomes dominated by those who have tried and failed. Under these conditions, it will no longer be economical to use simple screening devices like race and employers will begin sampling from the nonwhite distribution.[14] A simple model like this is another, possibly partial explanation of the empirical results presented in Wohlstetter and Coleman (1972), Kosters and Welch (1972), and McCall (1970a, 1969). Wohlstetter and Coleman found that during periods of growth (recession) the gains (losses) in nonwhite income relative to white have been greatest at the lower end of the income distribution. In their analysis, Kosters and Welch discovered that the nonwhite employment rate increases (decreases) more rapidly during periods of growth (recession) than the white employment rate. A recent analysis of Social Security data showed that in a period of sustained growth (1962-65), the nonwhite group who hovered around a given poverty line made greater progress than the corresponding white group. A full test of the discrimination hypothesis presented here would require an analysis of white and nonwhite earnings over several business cycles. One could then attempt to measure the changes in employer attitudes caused by cycle-induced experimentation. In this way, the discrimination hypothesis could perhaps be distinguished from other equally plausible hypotheses. Clearly, this is an important topic for future research.

Another version of this model assumes that the employer is aware of the nonstationarity of the hiring process over the business cycle and adjusts his prior distributions accordingly. In the previous model, information about employees was the only factor influencing the employer's prior distributions. Adjustments to shifting productivity parameters would be more rapid if the employer knew the nature of the shifting process.

For simplicity, assume that only the white productivity parameter changes with the business cycle. Furthermore, assume that the employer adjusts to this phenomenon in the following manner. If the economy is growing, his prior distribution on p_1 is ϕ_1'; if the economy is declining his prior distribution is ϕ_1''. In a growing economy new information is fed into ϕ' in order to calculate the posterior distribution; in a declining economy, the posterior distribution is calculated by incorporating new information into ϕ_1''. As before, all of this is done in Bayesian fashion, with prior and posterior distributions members of the beta family. The same switching rule is used as before except that now the employer's behavior is directly influenced by the business cycle.

This remains a simple model of adaptation, but could be easily generalized to accommodate more complex physical phenomena. For example, both white and nonwhite productivity parameters could be changing and in a much more complicated manner than the zero-one process discussed here. At this point, however, further generalizations of this model do not seem necessary.

An Adaptive Model of Profit
Maximization

Let the employer's production function by given by:

$$q = f(X_1, X_2; Y)$$

where X_1 and X_2 are the number of white and nonwhite workers, respectively, and Y denotes all other factors of production assumed to be fixed. Assuming a normal production function but without specifying its exact form, let $a = (a_1, a_2, \ldots a_n)$ be the random vector of coefficients of the production function.

The employer wishes to maximize profits where profits are given by:

$$\pi = pq - W_1 X_1 - W_2 X_2 - b$$

where p is the constant per unit price of q, W_1 and W_2 are the competitive wage rates of X_1 and X_2 and b denotes the fixed costs of the other factors. Differentiating π with respect to X_1 and X_2, and solving for the optimal values of X_1 and X_2, say X_1^* and X_2^*, gives the optimal profit, π^*,

$$\pi^* = pf(X_1^*, X_2^*, y) - W_1 X_1^* - W_2 X_2^* - b$$

where

$$X_1^* = g_1(p, W_1, W_2, a)$$

and

$$X_2^* = g_2(p, W_1, W_2, a)$$

Finally, assume that p, W_1, and W_2 are known constants, but that a is a random variable with a joint normal prior distribution, F. Each period provides information on a and these are assumed to be generated by a normal process. The prior normal distribution is updated as these new observations occur and a posterior normal distribution is calculated. For example, suppose $a = (a_1, a_2)$ and that a_1 and a_2 are independent and normally distributed with means $\bar{a}_1$ and $\bar{a}_2$ and known variances. Then the employer chooses X_1^* and X_2^* to maximize

$$E\pi = \iint \pi^* f(a_1, a_2) da_1 da_2 .$$

As $F(a_1, a_2)$ changes over time, the relative employment of whites and nonwhites also changes.[15]

V. Racial Discrimination and Uncertainty: Employee Search Process

The searching activities of individuals for job vacancies is very similar to the employer's search process. One of the costs of search incurred by nonwhites is the probability that they will be rejected because of their color. These probabilities vary from industry to industry and among firms. If this probability is above a critical level for a particular firm or industry, then not applying for a job is the best policy for nonwhites.

More specifically let

    c = cost per period of search

    x = a random variable denoting the job offer, $x \geq 0$

    $\phi(x)$ = the probability density function of x

    $f(x)$ = maximum return obtainable when a job offer x has just been ob-
        served.

The cost, c, is incurred simultaneously with the offer, x. Costs of search include purely economic components such as transportation costs and the value of for-gone alternatives as well as psychic components such as the frustration accompanying rejection and the discrimination (by race, age, and sex) present in many employment markets. Here the focus will be on the racial discrimination component of this cost. When the random variable, x, takes on a value of zero, this means that the firm did not make a job offer. The cost of search is an increasing function of the probability that $x = 0$, that is, the higher this probability the greater the chance of rejection.

If search terminates, that is, employment commences after N job offers, then the return, f is simply the value of the Nth offer, x_N, less the cost of search, c, times the number of job offers:

$$f = x_N - cN.$$

If an x is observed at the first period and the process continues in optimal fashion thereafter, the return is given by

$$E[f(x)] = -c + E\left\{\max\left\{x, E[f(x)]\right\}\right\}.$$

Letting $\epsilon = E[f(x)]$, it is clear from this equation that the optimal policy has the following form:

    continue searching if $x < \epsilon$

    accept employment if $x \geq \epsilon$,

where ϵ satisfies the following equations

$$c = \int_\epsilon^\infty (x-\epsilon)\,\phi(x)\,dx = H(\epsilon).[16]$$

Let ϵ_0 denote the expected return from remaining unemployed. Note first that since $H(\epsilon)$ is a decreasing function of ϵ,[17] large values of c are associated with small values of ϵ. This in turn implies that, if other things are equal, as c increases, the length of search decreases. Similarly, small values of c are associated with larger values of ϵ and longer periods of search. Consider an individual whose expected returns from remaining unemployed are ϵ_O. If this individual is confronted with search costs in excess of c_O, not searching at all is his best strategy. The value of ϵ associated with any value of c greater than c_O is less than ϵ_O, the expected return from remaining unemployed. This is another way of saying that the optimal policy for such an individual is to drop out or join the ranks of the discouraged workers. Alternatively, if the costs of search are less than c_O, the individual will continue to seek employment until he receives an offer exceeding the corresponding value of ϵ. The time until such an offer is forthcoming is a period of frictional unemployment. A description of the structure of the optimal policy is a convenient device for summarizing the preceding discussion. The optimal policy for choosing between dropping out and frictional unemployment has the following form:

if $c \geqslant c_O$, do not search (drop out)

if $c < c_O$, search (choose frictional unemployment).

The cost of search tends to be larger for nonwhites because of racial discrimination. In addition, the wage distribution, $\phi(x)$, for nonwhites tends to be inferior to that of whites because of discrimination. Such factors could account for the disproportionate number of nonwhite dropouts.

In the tight labor markets that accompany sustained economic growth employers should discriminate less.[18] The cost of search should decline and $\phi(x)$, the wage distribution should shift to the right with less mass being concentrated at zero.[19] Consequently, more nonwhites will be employed. More precisely, the number of nonwhite dropouts will decline, that is, it will now pay them to search for employment. One would also expect that nonwhites would enter new industries and occupations. This, however, is an empirical question in that non-discriminating industries may benefit more from economic growth. Nonwhites, however, would probably begin to search in industries where search was previously uneconomical.[20]

VI. Conclusion

The primary purpose of this study was to present elementary models of racial discrimination in job markets where the presence of uncertainty was explicitly considered. Models of both employer and employee behavior were developed.

These models are preliminary and have not been empirically tested. Nevertheless, they do provide new insights into the discrimination phenomenon and suggest the kind of empirical research that should be undertaken. Three types of empirical data were discussed. The first were used to construct crude measures of racial discrimination. Although these measures were suggestive, none was adequate. Indeed, their most important function was to demonstrate the difficulty of measuring racial discrimination. Development of adequate measures is an important task for future research in racial discrimination. The second set of data were used to construct three different measures of the influence of economic growth on the economic welfare of nonwhites. The measures were considerably different, but all implied that the effects of economic growth and the attendant tight labor markets were strong and positive. This has definite implications for monetary and fiscal policy. Additional research on this important topic is clearly necessary. The final set of data concerned the behavior of the economic welfare of nonwhites over a series of business cycles. Such data could be used to test the discrimination models presented here. Empirical analysis of such data should be a significant component of any future research on racial discrimination.

The interaction between the employer and employee searching activities was not investigated. Similarly, the process by which information is transmitted and disseminated was not studied. These are important topics for future theoretical research.

Notes

1. Money GNP grew by approximately 20 percent during this period, with a relatively constant price level. The male unemployment rate dropped from 5.2 percent in 1962 to 4.0 percent in 1965. By 1966 it had decreased to 3.3 percent.

2. Approximately 90 percent of nonwhites are Negro.

3. Actually, employer discrimination may be measured by much cruder variables such as the number of friends and relatives that have been hired or are employed by a particular firm.

4. Indeed, the inadequacies associated with these measures are so great that any interpretation of them must proceed with extreme caution. They do, however, clearly illustrate the modifications needed to achieve a true measure of racial discrimination, that is, one that adjusts for all differences in qualifications. Unfortunately such an empirical measure is very difficult to obtain.

5. One could claim that these differences simply indicate the natural inferiority of nonwhites in regard to whites. Unfortunately, this hypothesis cannot be refuted by any of the empirical findings reported here.

6. The marginal rate of substitution, MRS_{xy}, is the amount of Y the individual is willing to give up to get one more unit of X. More precisely, it is the first derivative of the indifference function relating X and Y (see Figure 7-1).

7. Actually, W will look for someone with a utility function like B's, but of the right color. Presumably B will do likewise. The cost of this added search would represent the true pecuniary loss.

8. Becker presents a more elaborate trade model in which a white country possessing excess capital considers trade with a nonwhite country possessing excess labor. Becker 1957. For a discussion of this model see Arrow, "Models of

Job Discrimination," Chapter 2 of this volume; Krueger, 1963: 481-86; and Albert Wohlstetter and Sinclair Coleman, "Race Differences in Income," Chapter 1 of this volume.

9. The exact number of houses produced is, of course, determined in order to maximize contractor profits. Here it is assumed that the market for houses is perfectly competitive, that is, the contractor has no control over product prices.

10. This assumes that the experiments do not yield perfect information.

11. The desired number of successes will again be dictated by the profit maximizing criterion.

12. In terms of the profit maximizing criterion, successes will have some explicit value to the firm, say $V(np)$. Then, the appropriate criterion is to sample from that distribution so as to maximize $V(np) - n\bar{c}$.

13. When this is the case the posterior distribution of p given sample information is also beta.

14. A model could also be devised in which an employer is considering the possibility of hiring a fixed number of nonwhites. This experiment will provide him with sample information about nonwhite productivities. Such an experiment will be performed when the expected value of sample information exceeds its cost. See Pratt et al. 1965.

15. As before if the employer knows more about the relationship between a_1, a_2 and the business cycle, this information can also be incorporated into his decision process.

16. For a derivation of this result and a more general description of this model, see McCall 1970b.

17. The derivative of $H(\epsilon)$ is equal to minus the probability that the wage offer, x, will exceed ϵ.

18. See preceding section.

19. For an analysis of search behavior when the searcher is uncertain about $\phi(x)$, see McCall 1970b.

20. The effect of a minimum wage can also be interpreted within this model. In many ways it has the same implications as racial discrimination. For example, with respect to $\phi(x)$, higher minimum wages will cause more mass to be concentrated at zero. See McCall 1970b.

References

Arrow, Kenneth J. "Models of Job Discrimination," and "Some Mathematical Models of Race Discrimination in the Labor Market," Chapters 2 and 6 in this volume.

Becker, Gary S. *The Economics of Discrimination*. Chicago: University of Chicago Press, 1957.

Dufty, Norman F. "A Model of Choice in an Australian Labor Market." *Journal of Human Resources* (Summer 1969): 328-42.

Gilman, H.J. "Economic Discrimination and Unemployment." *American Economic Review* (December 1965): 1077-95.

Hanoch, G. "An Economic Analysis of Earnings and Schooling." *Journal of Human Resources* (Winter 1967): 130-329.

Kosters, M. and F. Welch. *The Effects of Minimum Wages on the Distribution of Changes in Aggregate Employment*, RM-6273-OEO. Santa Monica, Calif.: The Rand Corporation, September 1970. Also, "The Effects of Minimum Wages by Race, Age, and Sex," Chapter 3 in this volume.

Krueger, Anne O. "The Economics of Discrimination." *Journal of Political Economy* 71 (October 1963): 481-86.

Liebow, Eliot. *Tally's Corner*. Boston: Little, Brown and Company, 1967.

Lurie, Melvin and Elton Rayack. "Racial Differences in Migration and Job Search: A Case Study." *Southern Economic Journal* (July 1966); reprinted in *Negroes and Jobs*, edited by Ferman, Kornbluh and Miller, Ann Arbor: University of Michigan Press, 1968.

McCall, John J. "The Economics of Information and Optimal Stopping Rules." *Journal of Business* 38 (July 1965): 300-17.

McCall, John J. *An Analysis of Poverty: Some Preliminary Empirical Findings*, RM-6133-OEO. Santa Monica, Calif.: The Rand Corporation, December 1969.

McCall, John J. "An Analysis of Poverty: A Suggested Methodology." *Journal of Business* (January 1970). (a)

McCall, John J. "Economics of Information and Job Search." *Quarterly Journal of Economics* 84 (February 1970). (b)

Miller, Herman P. "Poverty and the Negro." In Leo Fishman, ed., *Poverty Amid Affluence*. New Haven, Conn.: Yale University Press, 1966.

Miller, Herman P. *Rich Man, Poor Man*. New York: Crowell, 1964.

Pascal, Anthony H. *The Economics of Housing Segregation*, RM-5510-RC. Santa Monica, Calif.: The Rand Corporation, November 1967.

Phelps, E. S., ed. *Microeconomic Foundations of Employment and Inflation Theory*. New York: W.W. Norton, 1969.

Pratt, John W., Howard Raiffa, and Robert Schlaifer. *Introduction to Statistical Decision Theory*. New York: McGraw-Hill, 1965.

Reder, M.W. "The Theory of Frictional Unemployment." *Economica* (February 1969): 1-28.

Sheppard, Harold L. and A. Harvey Belitsky. *The Job Hunt*. Baltimore: Johns Hopkins Press, 1966.

Stigler, G.J. "Information in the Labor Market." *Journal of Political Economy, Supplement* 70 (October 1962): 94-105.

Thurow, Lester. "Occupational Distribution of Returns to Education and Experience for Whites and Negroes." *Proceedings, American Statistical Association* 62 (1967): 233-43.

Thurow, Lester. *The Economics of Poverty and Discrimination*. Washington, D.C.: Brookings Institution, 1968.

Wohlstetter, Albert and Sinclair Coleman. *Race Differences in Income*, R-578-OEO. Santa Monica, Calif.: The Rand Corporation, October 1970. Also published as Chapter 1 in this volume.

Wohlstetter, Albert and Roberta Wohlstetter. "Third Worlds Abroad and at Home." *The Public Interest* 14 (Winter, 1969): 88-107.

Index

Ability, 45–46; among baseball players, 125–126, 137–143, 148
Alchian, A., et al., 205
Age, as related to income, 40–42; of baseball players, 122–123
Algeria, 181
American Indians, income of, 69
American League, 139, 145, 146, 152–153
Anticipations, in residential location decisions, 161, 174
Archibald, K., 18
Arrow, K. J., 71, 119, 184, 205, 207, 209
Assignment, in baseball, 120
Attitudes, of blacks toward business firms, 206

Baron, H. M., 93, 98
Barriers to entry, general, 63; in baseball, 120, 137–145
Baseball, characteristics of the industry, 121–123; salaries in, 123–134, 137–142
Baseball Guide, 124
Baseball players: ability, 125–126, 137–143, 148; age, 122–123; education, 122; ethnic breakdown, 123, 142; nonplaying opportunities, 148; performance, 138–140, 144; bonuses to, 134–137, 139
Baseball Register, 122, 124, 135, 138
Batchelder, A., 5, 73
Becker, G., 30, 39, 46, 72, 73, 86, 119, 205, 207
Belitsky, A. H., 206
Bernoulli, D., 72
Blacks: see under separate subjects, e.g., Employment, Discrimination, Income, Segregation, Unemployment, etc.
Blau, P., 46, 54, 55
Blockbusting, 179
Blummer, H., 14
Bonus payments (to baseball players), 134–137, 139
Boston Red Sox, 139
Brady, D., 24
Brooklyn Dodgers, 134
Business cycle: effects on black income, 19–25, 32; as related to propensity to discriminate, 206, 216, 217; and unemployment by race, age, and sex, 104–107, 110–112

Cain, G., 47, 69, 100
Cairnes, J. E., 84

California Angels, 139
Caplan, N. S., 10
Carmichael, S., 4
Catchers, 147, 149
Cincinnati Red Legs, 139
Cognitive dissonance, theory of, 97
Coleman, S., 216
Coleman, J., 44
Coleman Report, 63
Competition, as related to discrimination, 91, 92, 191–193
Consumer Purchases Study of 1935-36, 30
Consumption function, 24
Convexities, in economic theory, 93, 94, 187
Cramer, G., 72
Crow, J. F., 46
Current Population Survey, 7, 8, 27, 29, 33, 34, 56, 74
Customers, as source of discrimination, 88, 120, 145–146
Cycle, see Business cycle

Discouraged worker, 220
Discrimination: definition of, 120; by employees, 87, 92, 94, 189–191, 197, 213–124, 218–220; by employers, 86–87, 90–92, 187–189, 191–193, 200–206, 209–213, 213–218; equilibrium conditions for, 98; gains from, 88, 188–189, 205–206, 209; past and present, 43–44
Doeringer, P., 98
Duberman, M., 4
Duncan, B., 54, 157, 183
Duncan, O. D., 44, 46, 54, 55, 85, 157, 183
Duesenberry, J., 24
Dufty, N. F., 205

Earnings: see Income, Wages
Earnings differentials between blacks and whites, 84, 205, 207
Easter, L., 148
Eckland, B. K., 46
Economic Report of the President, 1970, 84
Edgeworth, F. Y., 86
Education, differentials between blacks and whites: advantages in, 43; attainment, 13, 84; rates of return to, 53–60, 62, 86–88, 208–209
Education, graduate, 65, 68
Education, formal and informal, 44, 64
Employees, see under Discrimination

225

Employers, see under Discrimination
Employment, normal and transitional, 104–107, 114–116
Endorsement opportunities (for baseball players), 148
Entry barriers: see Barriers to entry
Equal Employment Opportunities Commission, 148
Equality of opportunity, 15, 16
Exploitation: see Group interests

Fair employment practices laws, 64
Fair Labor Standards Act, 19
Faltermayer, E., 4
Family composition, comparison of blacks and whites, 18
Fans: see Customers
Farrell, M. J., 93
Fein, R., 5, 44, 71
Feldman, P. H., 98
Females: see Women
First basemen, 149
Festinger, L., 97
Fielding ability, 132
Foremen: see Supervisors
Friedman, M., 24, 45, 76, 85
Future, attitudes toward, 85

Genetics, role in racial disparities of, 43, 44, 47, 141
Gillian, J., 148
Gilman, H., 21, 46, 71, 208
Gordon, D. M., 98
Grodzins, M., 157, 158, 160
Group interests, as related to discrimination, 89, 98, 100
Guthrie, H., 4

Hamilton, C. V., 4
Hanech, G., 54, 55, 65, 76, 119, 205, 209
Hare, N., 54
Hicks, J. R., 90
Hill, H., 72
Hirshleifer, J., 211
Hodge, C., 48
Hodge, R. W., and P. Hodge, 47, 100
Howard, E., 148
Hyner, B., 93, 98
Hiestand, D. L., 46
Human capital, differentials between blacks and whites, 97–98, 103–104

Income: of American Indians, 69; of Orientals, 69
Income changes over time for blacks and whites, 10, 19–20, 24, 26, 29, 66
Income comparisons, black to white:

averages, 9–10; entire distributions, 10–14, 29–32, 33–34; ratios-at-quantiles, 14–20, 26–34, 37, 42, 50–52, 59, 62; relative differences (as compared to absolute dollar differences), 25–29, 29–32, 32–35, 39–40; stability in, 19–21, 23
Income differentials between blacks and whites: to families, 9, 12, 20, 24, 27, 34; to men, 17–19, 32, 48–50, 58–60; by region, 19–20; by residence (farm and non-farm), 19–20; to persons 12, 66, 205; to women, 17–19, 32, 50–52, 60–62
Infielders, 137
Information costs: of employees, 218–220; of employers, 96, 199, 216; see also Stereotypes

Jensen, A., 44, 46, 75
Job qualifications, 97, 98, 199
Jones, J. C. H., 151

Kain, J., 5
Kaun, D., 71
Killebrew, H., 129
Kosters, M., 71, 216
Kovachy, E. M., 178
Kuznets, S., 45

Labor force participation rates, 24
Labor markets, tightness of: see Business cycles
Labor turnover, 94
Labor unions, 87
Landes, D., 91
Latin Americans (in baseball), 122, 127, 135–139, 145
Lederberg, J., 46
Lewis, W. A., 65
Liebow, E., 206
Lipset, S. M., 18
Lurie, M., 206

Major League Baseball Players' Association, 153
Males: see Men
Marginal productivity, theory of, 88
Marginality, of various groups of workers in employment, 106–108, 109–113
Maris, R., 129
Marris, R., 90, 94
Marshall, A., 90
Marx, K., 93
Matthews, E., 129
Mayer, A. J., 158
Mays, W., 129
McCall, J. J., 25, 71, 205, 207, 216
McCovey, W., 129

McDill, M., 158
McGraw-Hill Special Report No. 2005, 5
Men: see under separate subjects, e.g., Income, Occupation, Unemployment, etc.
Michael, J., 155
Michaelson, S., 71, 72
Migration, effects on income, 36–38
Miller, H. P., 54, 55, 86, 205, 209, 223
Miller, M., 153
Mincer, J., 54, 55, 75
Minimum wages: characteristics of, 116–117; effects on various groups of workers, 108–113
Monopoly power, 91
Mood, A., 63
Moore, G. H., 69
Mortgages, 178
Motivation, 85, 141
Moynihan, D. P., 4, 44

National Advisory Commission on Civil Disorders, 4
National League, 139, 145, 146, 152, 153
National Planning Association, 48
Neale, W. C., 147
Neighborhoods: definition of, 175–177; tipping points in, 157, 166, 167; see also Tipping
Newhouse, J. P., 24
Newman, D. K., 38
New York Yankees, 152
Nonwhites, as compared to blacks, 69, 122
Northrup, H., 48

Occupation, as related to income, 39
Occupational distributions by race: for men, 48; for women, 50
Occupational dissimilarity index, 47
Occupational status of blacks and whites, 39, 46
Occupational tipping, 182
O'Conner, L. M., 151
On-the-job training, 42, 54
Orientals, income of, 69
Outfielders, 137, 149

Pacific Coast Baseball League, 151
Paige, J. M., 10
Paige, S., 148
Pascal, A. H., 74, 85, 184, 205
Penrose, E., 94
Personal income: see Income to persons
Personnel costs, 95–97, 193–194
Phelps, E. S., 205
Piore, M., 98
Pitchers, 132–134, 137–139, 147–149

Pittsburgh Pirates, 139
Poverty line, 35, 207–208
Prejudice: definition of, 120; see also Discrimination
Price theory, applicability to racial discrimination, 83
Productivity differences between blacks and whites, 84–85, 96, 217
Professions, discrimination against blacks in, 13, 15, 48, 63–66
Promotion, difficulties for blacks in, 13, 15, 63–66, 87–88, 120, 144, 148
Proximity, as related to discrimination, 89

Racial segregation: in baseball, 144–148; of business firms, 93, 95, 192–198; in housing, 87 (see also Tipping); of jobs, 87
Rapping, L. A., 74, 184
Rayack, E., 72, 73, 206
Real estate agents and brokers, 179
Reder, M. W., 205
Reich, M., 98
Relative deprivation, theory of, 69
Reserve clause (in baseball), 123, 151–152
Rickey, B., 134
Robinson, J., 129, 134
Rosenblatt, A., 143, 147
Ross, A., 5–6, 71–72
Rottenberg, S., 122, 151, 152
Rowan, R. L., 48
Russel Woods, 158, 161, 173–175
Rustin, B., 4

Savings propensities, 85
Schafer, W. E., 155
Schelling, T. C., 183
Schooling: see Education
Schultz, T. P., 69
Screening devices: see Stereotypes
Scully, G. W., 155
Segregation: by race, see Racial segregation; by sex, age, and class, 182–183
Sex discrimination, 17–19
Sheppard, H. L., 206
Shiskin, J., 71
Siegel, P. M., 14, 54
Simon, H., 90
Smith, Adam, 93
Social Security Administration's Continuous Work History Sample, 207–208, 217
Speculation, in residential location decisions, 173–175
Sporting News, 127
Stereotypes, racial, 25, 96, 199–203, 206, 214; see also Information costs of employers

Stigler, G. W., 205
Stinchcombe, A. L., 158, 160
Subneighborhoods, 169, 176
Supervisors: as objects of discrimination, 88, 189–191; as sources of discrimination, 87–88
Supervisory positions (in baseball), 148
Survey of Economic Opportunity, 7

Taeuber, A. F. and K. F. Taeuber, 47, 64, 85, 100–101
Tastes, as related to discrimination in hiring, 86–89, 91–99, 188–189; effect of variance in, 92, 191
Teenage workers: unemployment among, 107–108; effects of minimum wage on, 108–113
Thurow, L., 5, 44, 74, 205, 208
Tipping: aggregate tipping point, 166; bankers' role in, 178–180; community tipping point, 167; critical density for, 172; as a general phenomenon, 157, 182–183; neighborhood, 157–180; non-neighborhood, 180–182; real estate agents in, 178–180; speculation as it effects, 161, 173–175; subneighborhood, 175–177; successive, 178; "tipping-in," 168–173, 176
Tobin, J., 5, 24, 71
Trading (of baseball players), 124–125
Transportation costs, in job seeking, 219
Training: see Human capital, On-the-job training

U. S. Department of Labor, 123
Uncertainty, 96–97, 199, 213, 215
Unemployment: cyclical, see Business cycles; frictional, 220
Unemployment rate differentials between blacks and whites, 21, 84, 107–108, 108–113, 208
Utility function, 187, 209
Utility, theories of, 88–90

Wage differentials between blacks and whites, 29–31, 84, 87, 89–90, 95–96, 98
Wages: as compared to earnings and income, 8; as determined by training, 84–85, 104
Waldman, E., 18
Walker, D., 158
Walras, L., 84
Welch, F., 71, 119, 216
Williamson, O., 90
Wohlstetter, A., 216
Women: education of, 60; income to, 17–19, 32; labor force participation by, 24; effects of minimum wage on, 108–113; occupational status of, 50; unemployment among, 104–108
World Series, 147, 152

Young, W., 4

Zeman, M., 54

About the Contributors

Kenneth J. Arrow, Professor of Economics, Harvard University, is past President of the American Economic Association and the author of *Social Choice and Individual Values*.

Sinclair Coleman, Rand staff member, received his B.A. from Hampton Institute and is currently a Ph.D. candidate at the Rand Graduate Institute.

Marvin Kosters, a former Rand staff member, is currently Director of Planning and Analysis, Cost of Living Council, Executive Office of the President.

John J. McCall, Professor of Economics, University of California at Los Angeles, is a regular consultant to Rand and the author of several articles in mathematical economics and the economics of poverty.

Anthony H. Pascal, Director of Rand's Human Resources Research Program (currently on leave at the Department of Economics, UCLA) is the editor of *Thinking About Cities*.

Leonard A. Rapping, Professor of Economics, Graduate School of Industrial Administration at Carnegie-Mellon University, is the author of numerous articles in labor economics.

Thomas C. Schelling, Professor of Economics, Harvard University, is the author of *The Strategy of Conflict, Arms and Influence*, and other books and articles.

Finis Welch, Chairman of the Department of Economics, Graduate Center, City University of New York, has written extensively in the field of human resource economics.

Albert Wohlstetter, University Professor at the University of Chicago and a regular consultant to Rand, is the author of studies in the fields of strategic theory and of race relations.

SELECTED RAND BOOKS

Arrow, Kenneth J. and Marvin Hoffenberg, *A TIME SERIES ANALYSIS OF INTERINDUSTRY DEMANDS*, Amsterdam, North-Holland Publishing Company, 1959.

Averch, Harvey A., John E. Koehler, and Frank H. Denton, *THE MATRIX OF POLICY IN THE PHILIPPINES*, Princeton, Princeton University Press, 1971.

Bagdikian, Ben, *THE INFORMATION MACHINES: Their Impact on Men and the Media*, New York, Harper and Row, 1971.

Clawson, Marion et al., *THE AGRICULTURAL POTENTIAL OF THE MIDDLE EAST*, New York, American Elsevier Publishing Company, 1971.

Cooper, Charles A. and Sidney S. Alexander, *ECONOMIC DEVELOPMENT AND POPULATION GROWTH IN THE MIDDLE EAST*, New York, American Elsevier Publishing Company, 1972.

Davies, Merton and Bruce Murray, *THE VIEW FROM SPACE: PHOTOGRAPHIC EXPLORATION OF THE PLANETS*, New York, Columbia University Press, 1971.

Downs, Anthony, *INSIDE BUREAUCRACY*, Boston, Little, Brown and Company, 1967.

Fisher, Gene H., *COST CONSIDERATIONS IN SYSTEMS ANALYSIS*, New York, American Elsevier Publishing Company, 1971.

Goldhamer, Herbert and Andrew W. Marshall, *PSYCHOSIS AND CIVILIZATION*. Glencoe, Illinois, The Free Press, 1953.

Haggart, Sue A. (ed.) et al., *PROGRAM BUDGETING FOR SCHOOL DISTRICT PLANNING*. Englewood Cliffs, Educational Technology Publications, 1972.

Harman, Alvin, *THE INTERNATIONAL COMPUTER INDUSTRY: Innovation and Comparative Advantage*, Cambridge, Harvard University Press, 1971.

Hearle, Edward F. R. and Raymond J. Mason, *A DATA PROCESSING SYSTEM FOR STATE AND LOCAL GOVERNMENTS*, Englewood Cliffs, Prentice-Hall, Inc., 1963.

Hirshleifer, Jack, James C. DeHaven, and Jerome W. Milliman, *WATER SUPPLY: ECONOMICS TECHNOLOGY, AND POLICY*, Chicago, The University of Chicago Press, 1960.

Hitch, Charles J. and Roland McKean, *THE ECONOMICS OF DEFENSE IN THE NUCLEAR AGE*, Cambridge, Harvard University Press, 1960.

Johnson, William A., *THE STEEL INDUSTRY OF INDIA*, Cambridge, Harvard University Press, 1966.

Jorgenson, D. W., J. J. McCall, and R. Radner, *OPTIMAL REPLACEMENT POLICY*, Amsterdam, North-Holland Publishing Company and Chicago, Rand McNally Publishing Company, 1967.

Kecskemeti, Paul, *STRATEGIC SURRENDER: THE POLITICS OF VICTORY AND DEFEAT*, Stanford, Stanford University Press, 1958.

Kecskemeti, Paul, *THE UNEXPECTED REVOLUTION*, Stanford, Stanford University Press, 1961.

Kershaw, Joseph A. and Roland N. McKean, *TEACHER SHORTAGES AND SALARY SCHEDULES*, New York, McGraw-Hill Book Company, Inc., 1962.

Leites, Nathan, *ON THE GAME OF POLITICS IN FRANCE*. Stanford, Stanford University Press, 1959.

Leites, Nathan and C. Wolf, Jr., *REBELLION AND AUTHORITY*, Chicago, Markham Publishing Company, 1970.

Marschak, Thomas A., Thomas K. Glennan, Jr., and Robert Summers, *STRATEGY FOR R & D*, New York, Springer-Verlag N.Y., 1967.

Melnik, Constantin and Nathan Leites, *THE HOUSE WITHOUT WINDOWS: FRANCE SELECTS A PRESIDENT*, Evanston, Row, Peterson and Company, 1958.

Meyer, John R., Martin Wohl, and John F. Kain, *THE URBAN TRANSPORTATION PROBLEM*, Cambridge, Harvard University Press, 1965.

McKean, Roland N., *EFFICIENCY IN GOVERNMENT THROUGH SYSTEMS ANALYSIS: WITH EMPHASIS ON WATER RESOURCE DEVELOPMENT*, New York, John Wiley & Sons, Inc., 1958.

McKinsey, J. C. C., *INTRODUCTION TO THE THEORY OF GAMES*, New York, McGraw-Hill Book Company, Inc., 1952.

Nelson, Richard R., Merton J. Peck, and Edward D. Kalachek, *TECHNOLOGY ECONOMIC GROWTH AND PUBLIC POLICY*, Washington, The Brookings Institution, 1967.

Nelson, Richard R., T. Paul Schultz, and Robert L. Slighton, *STRUCTURAL CHANGE IN A DEVELOPING ECONOMY: COLOMBIA'S PROBLEMS AND PROSPECTS*, Princeton, Princeton University Press, 1971.

Novick, David (ed.), *PROGRAM BUDGETING: PROGRAM ANALYSIS AND THE FEDERAL BUDGET*, Cambridge, Harvard University Press, 1965.

Pascal, Anthony, *THINKING ABOUT CITIES: NEW PERSPECTIVES ON URBAN PROBLEMS*, Belmont, California, Dickenson Publishing Company, 1970.

Phillips, Almarin, *TECHNOLOGY AND MARKET STRUCTURE: A STUDY OF THE AIRCRAFT INDUSTRY*, Lexington, Massachusetts, D. C. Heath and Company, 1971.

Pincus, John A., *ECONOMIC AID AND INTERNATIONAL COST SHARING*, Baltimore, The Johns Hopkins Press, 1965.

Quade, Edward S. and Wayne I. Boucher, *SYSTEMS ANALYSIS AND POLICY PLANNING: APPLICATIONS IN DEFENSE*. New York, American Elsevier Publishing Company, 1968.

Rosen, George, *DEMOCRACY AND ECONOMIC CHANGE IN INDIA*, Berkeley and Los Angeles, University of California Press, 1966.

Schurr, Sam H. and Paul T. Homan, *MIDDLE EASTERN OIL AND THE WESTERN WORLD: Prospects and Problems*, New York, American Elsevier Publishing Company, 1971.

Sharpe, William F., *THE ECONOMICS OF COMPUTERS*, New York, Columbia University Press, 1969.

Williams, J. D., *THE COMPLEAT STRATEGYST: BEING A PRIMER ON THE THEORY OF GAMES OF STRATEGY*, New York, McGraw-Hill Book Company, Inc., 1954.

Wolf, Charles Jr., *FOREIGN AID: THEORY AND PRACTICE IN SOUTHERN ASIA*, Princeton, Princeton University Press, 1960.